Midnight Meditations

A Journey Through Cancer, and the Lessons Learned Along the Way

Roger and Debbie Bennett

Midnight Meditations House, LLC
Thompsons Station, TN

Printed in Smyrna, TN, by Courier Printing.

Cover Design by Chelsea Bennett
Edited by Debbie Bennett and Chelsea Bennett

For additional information, or to purchase other products, visit www.rogerbennettdirect.com or write to:
> Roger Bennett Direct
> P.O. Box 681075
> Franklin, TN 37068-1075

To access the online journal, visit http://rogerbennett.typepad.com.

16. Therefore we do not lose heart. Though outwardly we are wasting away, yet inwardly we are being renewed day by day.
17. For our light and momentary troubles are achieving for us an eternal glory that far outweighs them all.
18. So we fix our eyes not on what is seen, but on what is unseen. For what is seen is temporary, but what is unseen is eternal.

II Corinthians 4:16 – 18 (NIV)

Written by Dr. Michael J. Keating

Roger Bennett died at 48 years of age. He was a patient at the University of Texas M.D. Anderson Cancer Center in Houston, Texas for 12 years. During the entire time, I knew him as a patient; I was the physician looking after his initial diagnosis of chronic lymphocytic leukemia and subsequent diagnosis of acute myelogenous leukemia. For me twelve years was not enough. Not long enough for Roger and not long enough for me to understand the breadth and depth of this man. I got to know him as a patient, a friend, a lover of a wife and family, and a person of great personal faith. Roger's musicianship is known to many and I had a mere glimpse into his accomplishments. Many of my patients were Roger's fans and would always ask about his well-being when they came to visit me. He generated such a level of "connectedness" with people at all levels. I got to know part of him by observing his beautiful relationship with his wife, Debbie, and for a lesser time his children. My limited view of Roger did not enable me to experience the complete person, as described in Debbie's book.

It is tough enough for a young person to be diagnosed with a slow-moving disease like chronic lymphocytic leukemia but when, after having experienced long remissions of this disease, he then developed acute myelogenous leukemia it was almost too much. While searching for a potential stem cell donor, he received the surprising gift that his father was a match for him for a transplant. Transplants are not easy. They are frightening and questions continue to whirl around creating uncertainty as to the future. The first transplant worked for a time and then a relapse occurred. Subsequent relapses continued to challenge the inner heart of the man. He knew and felt depths of sadness and hopelessness.

1

The mark of a person is the ability to function with "grace under pressure." Roger epitomized this concept and never surrendered his sense of optimism and faith that eventually the outcome that God had intended for him would be acceptable to his family, friends, and him. If God has a checklist of who gets into heaven and verifies as to whether someone fulfilled His wishes as a man, husband, father, and professional and more importantly, if he had a generous spirit, all of these boxes would be checked. I know that Roger is still looking after all of us, as I know he leaves a hole in the hearts of all who knew him. The world is stamped by his presence and he will not be forgotten by those who loved him. Finally and with joy, I would summarize Roger's time on earth as "a life lived fully."

Roger with his amazing leukemia team:
Dr. Keating, Alice, and Dr. Tam.

INTRODUCTION
Written by Debbie Bennett

This book is a labor of love. It is a collaboration of two people who, with the prayers and love of countless others, weathered many storms. Roger called these our "Midnights," and from that darkness, we emerged into the light of the Savior's everlasting love and grace. This particular journey would span over 11 ½ years, and would give hope and encouragement not only to the two of us and our families, but to many others. It is a journey of hopes and dreams; of fears and bewilderment; of feeling invincible, and of mortality; of feeling useless, and of being used.

Over the years, and particularly during the last years of Roger's life, when he endured three separate bone marrow (stem cell) transplants, we kept a journal online, and much of this compilation comes from that journal. When he first told me of his idea to keep that journal, we both thought it would be more or less a tool to keep people informed of his condition while he was unable to travel with Legacy Five, his Southern Gospel music group. We quickly learned, though, that through the responses we received from its readers, we were being blessed over and over! It seemed that the more we "gave," the more we "got." Isn't that the way the Lord works?

Here and there in this book, in addition to some entries from Roger's early journals, I have added a few writings that were either published elsewhere, or that have been found in his effects after he left this earth for his Heavenly reward. What treasures! Roger, for all of his comedic ways, was a very deep thinker, and a very spiritual person. His gift was in being able to share Christ in ways that made it "real" to the average person. He walked the walk. People were drawn to him for his encouraging words, and his unique personality. Almost everyone he came in contact with has a "Roger story" to tell of how he made a difference in their lives. If you were privileged to know him, he made an indelible impression on you – and he did it in an unassuming way, never judging or condemning, but always loving and uplifting.

Over the years of our "Midnights," we would have many peaks and valleys. The first time Roger went into remission in 1996, it lasted over 3 ½ years. Following that first relapse, there were many more relapses, remissions, and changes in disease, that eventually necessitated the first bone marrow transplant in early 2004... then the second in 2005... and the third in 2006. I have never seen a braver fight than Roger fought. He endured so much, yet kept his witness, his faith, his dignity through it all. His battle was noticed by other patients, and by doctors, nurses, and staff who became more like family to us over the years. His presence in the hospital and clinic was welcomed, and was actually looked forward to by most. He was on a first name basis with nurses, technicians, and other staff, and no one ever left his side without a smile. By that same token, his absence was felt deeply by those same people who were by his side for his final battles.

During those battles, Roger was a man on a mission. I have often said that I saw that mission become more real to him with each successive transplant or treatment. He urgently wanted to share Christ with anyone who would listen. He actively sought out those who he felt were most in need. If he was too weak to walk the halls, he would have me push him in a wheelchair, or he would "hold court" from his hospital bed, as people would seek him out.

Roger Bennett left a great legacy. His songs, recordings, writings, and his memories will live on in our hearts. His message will be heard for generations to come. I would say to him, "Mission accomplished."

4

This book is but a small part of his legacy. It is, however, a part that will offer encouragement to many who are facing their own trials. Our journey through cancer is highlighted in these pages, both the good days, and the bad days. But, this is not only a book about cancer; it is a testament to God's grace, and His faithfulness in our lives.

Roger had a signature phrase, which I have also adopted in these writings. He would sign most of his posts, letters, etc., with it, and I hope that you, like he, can say that even in your own "Midnights," you are safely and securely,

"In His Grip."

WRITINGS FROM THE AUDIO "MIDNIGHT MEDITATIONS"

This journal began as a short devotional accompanying the CD and cassette of *Midnight Meditations* in 1998. Each song on the recording had a page with a short devotional applying to the song. The following are the entries for each song.

SWEET HOUR OF PRAYER

> Praying always with all prayer and
> supplication in the spirit, and watching
> there unto with all perseverance and
> supplication for all saints...
>
> -Ephesians 6:18

Sweet hour of prayer, sweet hour of prayer
That calls me from a world of care...

Prayer is truly one of the essential keys to our spiritual
life. Sadly, it is also one of the most neglected. Many
times during those first chaotic days after my diagnosis, I
would find myself in the middle of incredible stress,
exhausted and afraid. Suddenly it would hit me: "I
haven't prayed today!" There, in the midst of the storm, I
would cry out to Jesus and He would respond. I wasn't
magically transformed out of my storm, but somehow I
found peace in the midst of it.

In seasons of distress and grief,
My soul has often found relief...

It seems as if this were written specifically for me. I'll
bet that you can say the same. You may be in the middle
of a season of distress and grief, but take it from me – your
soul can find relief! Believe His Word and trust His grace.
Cast on Him your every care, and wait for the Sweet Hour
of Prayer.

"Father, thank you for the privilege of prayer... not just
empty words to unhearing ears, but the cry of our hearts to
a loving, concerned Father! Amen."

HE LEADETH ME / GOD LEADS US ALONG

Thus saith the Lord, thy Redeemer, the
Holy One of Israel: I am the Lord thy God,
which teacheth thee to profit, which leadeth
thee by the way that thou shouldest go.

-Isaiah 48:17

I became a Christian at the age of nine. I'm convinced
that God saved me on that day. I became an heir to His
riches, and the Holy Spirit became my Comforter! In other
words, I got the full shot! But I still didn't understand it
all. I was just a kid. Salvation is a moment that affects
eternity. Growing in God takes a lifetime. For example, I
knew the words to the 23rd Psalm and Isaiah 48:17, but, in
truth, I didn't get it. Until the turning point in my life
came, I didn't really understand the leading of God. Oh, I
knew that He had led me before. He led me to my
ministry with the Cathedral Quartet. He led me to my
wife, Debbie. But old think-head Bennett still didn't have
a clue! You see, people get married every day, take jobs,
buy homes, and a host of other things without thinking
twice about God's leading. Put me in that number!

However, it all became real to me when I was faced
with cancer. Oh, yeah, now I'm interested in God's
leading! How patient He is to stand in line waiting for His
preoccupied children to "snap out of it." These two songs
are some of my favorites because, when we do decide to
follow...

He leadeth me, He leadeth me
By His own hand He leadeth me.
His faithful follower I will be
For by His hand He leadeth me!

Some through the water, some through the flood
Some through the fire, but all through His love
Some through great sorrow, but God gives the song
In the night seasons and all the day long!

"Father, there is no more comfortable place than in Your leading. Lead on! Amen."

REDEEMED

> Blessed be the Lord God of Israel; for He
> hath visited and redeemed His people.
>
> -Luke 1:68

I've always thought this song was so perfect. Joyous, yet reverent. Simple, yet so deep! *Redeemed, how I love to proclaim it!* The last line of the song says it all: *His child and forever I am!* I can face life's ups and downs because of this statement. If I win the daily battle, great! If I lose one now and then, fine! I'm still His child. The bottom line! I'm His child!

Cancer has the power to make you focus on the short-term. Will I get a good report? Will the chemo arrest the disease's progress? What if I die? These are all important concerns. But when viewed through the lens of eternity, the real issue is this: What have I done with Jesus? Have I made my choice to trust Him as my Savior? If I've done that, cancer can do no long term damage!

Cancer can do a lot of things. It can affect your muscles, your bones. It can eat away at the tissues of your body. It can rob you of your strength. Yes, cancer has the power to do many things. But there are many more things it cannot do. It can't steal your joy, alter your memory. It can't steal your relationship with your savior! It can't cancel your reservations in heaven. Cancer is impotent in the things eternal! *His child and forever I am!*

"Lord, my biggest joy in life is to know undeniably that I'm redeemed. Thank you for Calvary. Amen."

THERE IS A FOUNTAIN / NOTHING BUT THE BLOOD

> ...In Whom we have redemption through
> His blood, the forgiveness of sins, according
> to the riches of His grace.
>
> -Ephesians 1:7

In my youth, our church sang a lot of "blood songs." "Power in the Blood," "There is a Fountain," "Nothing But the Blood," "The Blood Will Never Lose Its Power," and many others! I never viewed them as controversial. They were just a part of my education in the faith. I had a great respect for the concept of the blood of Jesus. I didn't fully understand the notion of its atoning power, but I knew that it was a cornerstone of our faith. Fast-forward to today. Many churches have made the decision to remove all references to the blood from their hymnals. More distressing, they've also removed the blood from their pulpits! Lord, help us!

Their argument follows. May I offer my humble answers?

"It's a bloody Gospel." Yes, it is.
"It's repulsive to people." So is sin to God.
"It's not necessary to talk about the blood to know Jesus." Without the shedding of blood, there is no remission for sin (Hebrews 9:22).
"It's not very sophisticated." So what?

We get in trouble when we try to "package" the Gospel. It is not meant to be sanitized and or made "presentable." It is what it is – a glorious plan to restore man to God. There are not multitudes of paths to heaven. There is only one narrow road. That road leads to the foot of an ugly, blood stained, and hideously cruel cross! This cross bore our Savior while He bore our sins! Scholars say that the death of Jesus was one of the most brutal a man could die; certainly one of the most painful. I fail to see a way to make that palatable to people! On a spiritual level though, it is one of the loveliest events in history!

Don't be ashamed of the blood!! It deserves our highest respect! Every precious drop came through the very heart of God's perfect Lamb!!

What can wash away my sins?
Nothing but the blood of Jesus!

"Lord, help us as your children always to hold dear the blood of Your Son! Amen."

My Jesus, I Love Thee

I will love Thee, O Lord my strength.

-Psalm 18:1

Sometimes, "simple" escapes me. I try to keep in mind that the simple things in life are often the deeper, richer experiences. But still, in a lot of instances, I needlessly complicate things. This seems to happen in all areas. In music, many times I'll search for the longest time for that unusual chord or difficult run when, in the end, after much wasted time, the solution was the most simple choice. Relationships are another area that usually benefit from a good dose of "simple." The phrase "I love you" conveys a depth of feeling that is hard to match even with the most elaborate sonnet ever created. Simple says it all!

I've found this to be true in my relationship with God. Please don't misunderstand. It's often difficult to follow His leading. However, this is always MY fault. God's plan for our salvation and our growth couldn't be simpler: "Follow Me!" He simply beckons! The way has been paid! Sacrifice made! Calvary won and now our part is easy! Follow! This is the essence of simplicity!

"Lord, I don't understand life. I can't begin to know all I need to know. But You do! So, I trust; I follow! You see the sparrow fall. I know that You see me!"

14

This song has always summed up my testimony in the most simple of terms:

My Jesus, I love Thee. I know Thou art mine.
For Thee all the follies of sin I resign.
My gracious Redeemer, my Savior art Thou;
If ever I loved Thee, my Jesus, 'tis now.

"Lord, so simple is Your love, yet I'm baffled by it! That You'd love a world that doesn't love You back! Thank You for the sacrifice that You made. Help me never to forget that this plan was bought with a price that was anything but simple. The cross cost your Son everything!! Let me always be grateful! Amen."

Turn Your Eyes upon Jesus

Mine eyes are ever toward the Lord; for He
shall pluck my feet out of the net.

-Psalm 25:15

And the things of earth will grow strangely dim...

Your response to that line might be a snort of "Yeah,
right." The things of earth have a nasty tendency to do
anything but grow strangely dim. In my life, it was like
the things of earth were in sharp Technicolor focus! As a
matter of fact, there were times the things of earth had a
chokehold on me. One of those times taught me the
wisdom of this song. Suddenly, I remembered the lyrics:

Look full in His wonderful face...

As usual, my focus was on the temporary. As
important as it seemed to me at the time, my
circumstances would eventually change. If I focus on what
will change, my life will be in a constant state of change.
But I learned that, by focusing on the one thing that never
changes, I could find a strong anchor that would hold me
secure even when things around me were shifting!

"Lord, help me to seek your face, to keep my eyes on Your
face. Amen"

GREAT IS THY FAITHFULNESS

> It is of the Lord's mercies that we are not
> consumed, because His compassions fail
> not. They are new every morning: great is
> Thy faithfulness.
>
> -Lamentations 3:22, 23

Jeremiah was a man who understood heartache. I am sure there were many times he could hardly face the day. Yet, somehow, he spoke the words that inspired David Chisholm to write this hymn.

Morning by morning new mercies I see.

I remember many times in the days of my chemotherapy treatment when I really felt like my strength was expended...gone! There would be no fighting tomorrow. But the next day, when it came time to fight again, I fought. I remember thinking, only minutes before the chemicals entered my system, "I don't have it in me today. I am just too weak to fight." But then the miracle of mercy would take place and I would find that:

All I have needed, Thy hand has provided.
Great is Thy faithfulness, Lord, unto me!

Like the children of Israel in the wilderness, I would find fresh manna from Heaven each day. That's what I've learned about grace: there is no need to hoard it; there is an inexhaustible supply! Grace will never be rationed, but, like the Israelites, we cannot live on past supplies. We have to seek a fresh serving of grace each day. It is so critical not to let our prayer life suffer or dry up. Our communication with God is essential for our growth. Our very survival depends on it! Let me encourage you to remain in the spirit of prayer. Keep those lines open. Then, relax in the promise that God's mercies are new each morning.

"Lord, Your faithfulness truly is great. Even in our unfaithfulness and apathy, You don't waiver! You are so worthy of our praise! Amen."

THE OLD RUGGED CROSS

But He was wounded for our transgressions, He was bruised for our iniquities: the chastisement of our peace was upon Him; and with His stripes we are healed.

-Isaiah 53:5

The defining moment in my life with cancer was the instant when I realized that I could easily die from this disease – that I might not make it, that I could be gone in a matter of months. What then? Did I really believe the songs I sang about Heaven? Was I really sure that there was something waiting for me? Satan's hobby is this kind of mind game for Christians. He loves to confuse and rattle the children of God because, let's face it, that's all he has left! Our souls are safe! Our minds, however, are still susceptible to his darts. It was during one of these little battles that God put an end to the liar's attack. These words started running through not only my mind, but my very soul:

To the old rugged cross I will ever be true
Its shame and reproach gladly bear
Then He'll call me someday to my home far away
Where His glory forever I'll share!

So, I'll cherish the old rugged cross
'Til my trophies at last I lay down
I will cling to the old rugged cross
And exchange it someday for a crown!

Try as you might, Satan, you cannot explain away or laugh into oblivion the significance of the cross of Calvary. It was on this cross that Jesus forever flung open the doors of Heaven for "whosoever will." That means the entire human race can gain admittance through Jesus. Satan, you lost! When I remembered the cross and what Jesus purchased there, any doubts about eternity vanished! The cross guarantees that death's sting has been plucked, and the grave's victory has been snatched away!

"Jesus, thank You for enduring the cross. It is a constant reminder to me that Your love for us conquers death, Hell, and the grave! Amen."

BLESSED ASSURANCE

> For our Gospel came not unto you in word
> only, but also in power, and in the Holy
> Ghost, and in much assurance; as ye know
> what manner of men we were among you
> for your sake.
>
> -1 Thessalonians 1:5

Some days are just made for praise. Oh, I know that every day should be filled with praise for God's grace; but I must admit that I allow many of these opportunities to pass me by. The day will be gone, and I haven't uttered one word of praise or thankfulness. But there are those days when, from the time my head leaves the pillow until its return, my mouth is full of praise! Those are awesome times! It seems that I'm more mindful of the many blessings God has poured out on me. It feels like Heaven is just above my ceiling, and if I listen closely, I can almost hear the angels sing. It's easy to praise Him then. It's almost too easy. If I made the rules, I might not even let those days count! It's in the time of darkness that light shines brightest. The true grace-filled heart will spring forth in joy at the most surprising times.

In one of my darkest days this lesson was taught to me. It was on an airplane trip to Houston to find out how far my cancer had progressed. I was at the bottom – no, let me rephrase – I had to look up and squint to see the bottom. Debbie and I weren't able to sit together on the plane, so I was sitting alone, and feeling afraid. My heart was filled with dread. I tried to pray, and couldn't; I tried to read, and couldn't. I laid my head back and closed my eyes. In a moment, I started singing "Awesome God," then "Blessed Assurance." I sang them over and over. (I'm sure my neighbors appreciated the concert!) Suddenly a peace came over me. I kept singing. A few minutes later, a new feeling came over me: joy! Peace didn't leave; God made room in my heart for both! Joy and peace flooded me. I was completely at rest. My entire state of mind changed. The valley became a blessed place for me. God did restore my soul there!

Perfect submission, all is at rest
I, in my Savior, am happy and blessed
Watching and waiting, looking above
Filled with His goodness, lost in His love

"God, thank You so much for the valley of restoration! I want to stay 'lost in Your love.' Amen."

JUST AS I AM

Come unto me, all ye that labour and are
heavy laden, and I will give you rest.

-Matthew 11:28

I fail a lot. In fact, I probably miss the mark more often
than I hit it. I'm not trying to gain sympathy by saying
that, or to seem super humble; it's just that, when it comes
to serving God, I've got a long way to go. I might as well
be honest. The only One that really matters already knows
that I fail. Through His power, I have many victories; but,
when held up to our model (Jesus Christ), I am found
wanting.

Lest you think that this is a bummer of a thought, let
me continue by saying that I thank God for my failures
and weaknesses. It is through my weakness that His
power is made perfect. The Father is not in need of
perfection; if that was His benchmark, all of Heaven is
available. He loves to use broken, weak vessels to
accomplish astounding things. When Jesus issued the
invitation to "come unto Me," He didn't beckon to the
strong, perfect people. He specifically addressed the
"heavy laden," those in need of rest, those who carried a
great burden... another example of a perfect God choosing
to love an imperfect people. Amazing! So don't say, "I've
got a few things to work on," or, "I'm trying to get
straightened out, and then You can use me, Lord." Come
now! Bring all of your "messes" to God. Stand back and
watch Him work through you – just as you are.

Oh, Lamb of God, I come, I come.

"Father, how do you do it? You use a habitually needy
people to build Your kingdom! I don't fully understand,
but I am thankful to be in that crowd! Amen."

23

Amazing Grace

> And He said unto me, "My grace is sufficient for thee, for My strength is made perfect in weakness. Most gladly, therefore, will I rather glory in my infirmities, that the power of Christ may rest upon me.
> -II Corinthians 12:9

I talk a lot about grace. I have heard that the more a certain subject comes out of your mouth, the more you need it. I believe this. You see, without grace, to put it bluntly, we would be sunk: no lifeboat, no rescue ship – sunk! The grace of God is our lifeboat. One of the great discoveries of my life has been grace. Humans don't naturally understand grace. Grace means loving someone whom you would just as soon avoid. In other words, grace is hard! But, good news: it is not too hard for God! God excels in grace. His grace abounds in the most unlikely places: in the war zone, in the gutters of despair, in the crack house, and in the cancer wards of the world! The most amazing thing about grace, though, is that it is free! Salvation's plan is available without cost to you. It did, however, cost Jesus the ultimate price. The suffering He endured on Calvary was the most hideous death imaginable. The culmination of this, though, was the morning He vacated the tomb. Because of that act, grace was set loose on the world! Romans 5:8 tells us that while we were yet sinners, Christ died for us. AMAZING!

John Newton, the writer of this great hymn, was saved from the life of a debauched slave trader. He was utterly transformed by grace. Shortly before his death at the age of eighty-two, he was heard to say, "My memory is nearly gone, but I remember two things: that I am a great sinner, and that Christ is a great Savior!"

"Lord, how can I not praise You! My lips will never grow tired of telling about Your grace! Amen."

HE HIDETH MY SOUL

In Thee, O Lord, do I put my trust; let me
never be ashamed: deliver me in Thy
righteousness.

-Psalm 31:1

One of the most repeated comments I receive is this:
"Keep your chin up – a positive mental attitude is
everything!" To an extent, I believe that. Studies have
proven that patients with a good attitude tend to do better
with their illnesses than those who "give up." Separated
from the spiritual aspect, though, a good attitude only
goes so far. Medically, a good outlook can speed recovery,
build the immune system, etc. However, at the point of
illness where it becomes clear that survival is not possible,
a good attitude's medical benefits are moot. At that point,
the positive outlook that is based on full confidence in
Jesus is just kicking in! You see, I believe in Healing! I
believe that all that it requires is a mere glance from God. I
also believe that all healing is temporary. Oh, our health
may last seventy more years, but eventually we will all
die. Hebrews 9:27 says, "And as it is appointed unto men
once to die, but after this the judgment." It is at that
moment that a good outlook based on some false god or
simply being good is not at all adequate! At the moments
of my passing, I want to be sheltered under the covering of
God's strong hand. His grace and power not only show us
how to live, but also how to die!

When clothed in His brightness, transported I'll rise
To meet Him in clouds of the sky
His perfect salvation, His wonderful love,
I'll shout with the millions on high!

"Lord, I'll live Your way; and when my time comes, I'll die Your way! I have perfect confidence in Your love. Amen."

JESUS LOVES ME / JESUS LOVES THE LITTLE CHILDREN

Verily, I say unto you, whosoever shall not
receive the kingdom of God as a little child,
he shall not enter therein.

-Mark 10:15

Since day one of my "midnight," I have had to deal
with cancer issues on two levels: physical and spiritual.
On the physical level, I have become quite good in the
jargon of cancer. I can talk to you for hours about bone
marrow, lymphocyte levels, and about various treatment
theories. I can discuss with doctors and nurses my latest
test results in pure scientific terms: white blood cells,
chemotherapy, anti-nausea drugs, remission lengths, bone
marrow harvesting, and transplants. I have become a
reluctant student of medicine. I think that is why I have
tried desperately to simplify my life. I get so caught up in
the physical science of my illness that I long for the
simplicity conveyed in these lines:

Jesus loves me, this I know
For the Bible tells me so

Our Father has never made coming to Him a difficult
thing. You don't have to understand the workings of the
universe to have a personal relationship with its Creator!
His bidding is, "Come unto Me." It doesn't get any
simpler than that! I think Karl Barth, one of the great
theologians of our time, summed up my argument for the
simple Gospel best when he was asked to summarize the
essence of his studies of the Bible. He responded, "Jesus
loves me, this I know, For the Bible tells me so!" I couldn't
agree more. Of all the things I think I must know in this
world, the most important thing that I do know is the title
of this great song!

28

"Father, I know that we are all precious in Your sight. Regardless of our race or background, Jesus' sacrifice at Calvary rings out through time the message of His love for the world. Thank You! Amen."

THIS IS MY FATHER'S WORLD /
JOYFUL, JOYFUL, WE ADORE THEE

He loveth righteousness and judgment: the
earth is full of the goodness of the Lord.

-Psalm 33:5

One of my most prized possessions is my porch. It is
one of those big ole country jobs that stretches the length
of our house. It's my favorite place to be! Our neighbor,
Brent King, has a pond across the lane, and as I am writing
this, a flock of eighteen Canada geese just came in on their
final approach. It was a loud, rowdy, honking, joyful
landing! It moved me. You see, this morning, when I took
the kids to school, the pond was dark and misty. It was
still beautiful, but not joyful. As my squadron of geese
made their noisy arrival, the sky behind them was alive
with the colors of sunrise. That was joyful, too! I was
reminded all over again that God is the ultimate artist, the
ultimate builder – the Ultimate! From my vantage point
on my porch, I get to see creation – not random evolution,
but joyful creation! What a great gift God gave us. How
often we miss it. If we all could make time to notice His
creation daily and let it move us, the mental therapy
business would wither. I think there is no better therapy
than just being a witness to the handiwork of God!

This is my father's world, and to my listening ears
All nature sings, and 'round me rings
The music of the spheres
This is my Father's world! I rest me in the thought
Of rocks and trees, of skies and seas
His hand the wonders wrought!

Joyful, joyful we adore Thee
God of glory, Lord of love
Hearts unfold like flowers before Thee,
Hail Thee as the sun above.
Melt the clouds of sin and sadness
Drive the dark of doubt away.
Giver of immortal gladness
Fill us with the light of day!

"Lord, thank You for my porch! I love the lessons that You teach me there! Amen."

Written by Roger Bennett
(This writing was found in his effects after his death.)

In late June of 1995 during a recording session, I reached up to rub some tension from my neck. What I found caused more tension than relieving it. There was a 1½" x 3" knot on my neck. The cliché about time standing still was suddenly the very best way to describe the feeling in my heart.

I knew that this was new (can't be good). The group that I played piano for, The Cathedrals, were scheduled to start a tour to the Bahamas in a couple of days. There was no time right then to see the doctor. Then, in the next moment, I realized that after returning from the Bahamas, and before heading home, we had scheduled a family vacation in Florida. It would be a minimum of three weeks before I could see a doctor. The thought hit me, "I don't have time to be sick."

The way my mind works, I figured that would be three weeks of pure spiritual battle. It was. With every piece of wisdom God sent my way, the enemy was waiting with a barrage of messages that, at best, God was not up to this task, or, at worst, that God was not there.

The Push for a Secular War

It is in these times of testing that our enemy retreats inside this safe little room. He is no longer the "devil" (the devil, he says, is just a figment); he is a kind teacher who has emerged from the swamp of good and enlightenment, and has found himself standing on the firm ground of secular humanism. It is at this point that our "friend" is at his most soothing and dangerous.

Having conquered the fireside superstitions – angels, mangers, crosses, empty tombs, – he calmly falls back on your personal environment: the overbearing mother or father, poverty, injustice, etc.

That is why we are miserable! Case closed. On to the next conversation: *"Excuse me, may I speak?"*....A small crack in the smile, then stiffly answered, *"Of course."* *"Well, it seems to me the only things you've given us are reasons NOT to believe. Sure, with simple debate tools, any argument can collapse into a point/counterpoint discussion."* The enemy smiles. But, when confronted with irrefutable facts, there is a shift in the debate, and when the believer's answers are rooted in "Thus Sayeth the Lord," faith burns brighter; the darkness in the room has to flee to make room for the sudden, unseen guest: our Defender, who was waiting for the signal to drive the darkness away...

I felt all of this happen before I was diagnosed three weeks later with CLL (Chronic Lymphocytic Leukemia). But even though the *outlook* was grim, the *uplook* had unlimited visibility!

This is a story of ups and downs. It is my intent to show you both extremes. As I am writing this, I am 45 days out from my second Bone Marrow (stem cell) Transplant. I am on top of the world! But, it wasn't always so...my prayer is that even now, God is preparing *you* for your own "Midnight Meditations," whatever they may be. It could be the very best time you spend this side of Heaven.

INTRODUCTION
Written by Roger Bennett

There have been times in my life when I thought I was in "midnight." They were the usual: financial setbacks, arguments with family members, or a myriad of other "important at the time" crises. But on Monday, August 7, 1995, I found myself in true midnight. All of the other false midnights paled in comparison. "Roger, it's cancer, and it doesn't look good." The doctor's voice on the phone line was pleasant, caring, and professional – not at all the type of voice you might associate with what I considered a death sentence. It was three o'clock in the afternoon on a beautiful summer day, but in my heart, it was midnight.

The typical view of midnight is a lonely time of darkness. Midnight in the soul is infinitely worse. That afternoon, I had people around me who love me and were steadfastly lifting me up, but I was no less alone. My heart couldn't be reached by them. Try as they might, the part of me that was wounded deepest was hidden in a place that could only be reached by One! I found at that moment that, not only was Jesus able to come to my rescue; He wanted to gather me in His arms and minister His grace to me. By the time my family and friends finished their first prayers for me that afternoon, the Holy Spirit of God had already begun to comfort and to strengthen me. By that same evening, I had the assurance in my heart that, sick or well, I would not be out of His grip! What tremendous peace that gave me!

Don't misunderstand. Midnight was not over for me. I still had many miles of uncertain road ahead. There would be days of intense pain and uncertainty. There would be days that I would have almost unbelievable joy, and my face would ache from laughing! But the common golden thread woven through each day was the gentle lessons that the Father was teaching.

35

He was showing me joy in the midst of pain, peace in the midst of suffering, and certain love in the midst of the uncertainties of life. I call these my Midnight Meditations.

Monday, August 7, 1995
Day One - The Diagnosis

Abnormal cells! An abnormal population of Lymphocytes. In Laymen's terms, Cancer! Cancer! I was expecting an entirely different call. The biopsy that I had last Friday initially showed encouraging news. In fact, I went on the road feeling very up and confident. The Pathologist looked at the cells and said that it looked like a "reactive lymph node."

This would suggest an infection. "Great. That, I can live with." But he wanted to send out another sample to a different lab. "You should know the results on Monday," he said, smiling. That was the first good news I'd had all day.

Then, this afternoon at 3:00, all that changed. Deb, Scott Fowler, and Kelly Howard were with me. I can't describe the numbing shock I felt. You know that feeling that you are in reality, but in a dream as well? I remember staring out the window for a long time and not seeing anything.

Thank God, the kids were in Indiana filming another Gaither kids video. I don't think I could have faced them today.

Scott, Debbie and I were to have left at 6:00 a.m. tomorrow for Hawaii. We were hosting a tour of about forty people, but of course now Debbie and I are grounded. Scott will take on our burden of the tour and continue. He's either a great friend, or he really, really wanted to go to Hawaii!

Deb got on the phone to Sherry at Templeton Tours to explain why we couldn't make the trip. When I overheard her say to Sherry, "Roger has cancer," it really came crashing down on me. It wasn't a dream; it was me in the here and now, and "Roger has cancer."

We started calling all of our family to alert them, and this broke me up pretty bad. Mom called my grandmother to tell her the news. When she heard it, she had some sort of heart incident, and they had to call 911. That didn't make me feel better.

Later in the evening, Scott Fowler and his folks came over. They had a lot of cancer experience in their family and wanted to offer me help. They really encouraged us to go to M.D. Anderson Cancer Center in Houston, TX. (Actually, they insisted.) I had heard great things about the place and promised to think it over.

We had a sweet time of prayer and, surprisingly, I slept like a baby!

August 8, 1995
Day Two – Frustration

Having made the decision during the night to pursue going to M.D. Anderson, Deb and I woke to attack the day. My first job was to call our family doctor, give him the diagnosis, and get him to refer me to Anderson. The receptionist informed me that it was his day off and he couldn't be bothered. I felt as if I were in a bad soap opera. Then she asked me what was the hurry? I told her that I'd just been diagnosed with cancer and needed him to give me a referral to M.D. Anderson. Her answer to this was, "Well, maybe you can get a phone book and look up his home number." I was very frustrated – angry. I just couldn't believe it. I had already learned, in my two days as a cancer patient, that waiting was excruciating.

But my Mom came to the rescue. She had gotten the admission number at MDA from a friend and called me right away. I didn't have much hope of getting in without a family doctor, but I decided to try.

"M.D. Anderson Cancer Center. This is Sandra; can I help you?" said a voice of an angel. Long story short: I called on Tuesday, and Sandra was able to work me in on the next Friday, only three days away! Now we're getting somewhere.

I bought a devotional book at the mall today. It says that people who keep a journal throughout their disease live longer. So, after a quick trip out again, I returned with enough blank journals to last longer than I probably would have lived with no cancer!

August 9, 1995
Day 3 – A New Ministry?

Went to the library today. Checked out three books on "C." Everything I read led me to believe that I'm in the early stages of Lymphoma. I don't have ANY of the symptoms that indicate that the disease has spread. None. So that was a lift. Of course, I know that every case is different, but I needed a little good news.

Debbie is great! She's handling so much of the planning that I don't have to worry about anything.

The phone is ringing off the hook with friends who are praying for me.

I'm holding up OK. We went to dinner and a movie with Rick and Cindy Busby and laughed a lot. Buz loaned me a new "You Might Be a Redneck" tape and we laughed some more!

Then we checked the answering machine. I was still chuckling when Chelsea's voice came on the machine, followed by Jordan's. I was no longer fine. I lost it. They didn't know anything yet and I didn't want my sickness to change the sweet, normal eleven- and nine-year-old voices I was hearing.

Throughout these last few days, the thought that chills me most is of leaving them. I think I can handle the fight, but I really want to live to see them grow up.

Glen Payne's wife, Van, told me that I'm gonna make it 'cause my ministry is not over yet. The thought occurred to me that my ministry may in fact change forever because of this! I'm not sure in what way, but I feel like God is going to give me a whole new assignment. That's exciting.

Later. I'm tired.

Roger Bennett
Cancer Patient

August 10, 1995
Day 4 – Singing for Free!

I visited the Hair Club for Men today! I laugh just writing about it. Here's what happened. A friend of mine called me today. He'd been thinking about bald Roger and evidently was grossed out at the prospect! He said, "I'll pay for everything; you just go get measured." He was insistent that I go. So I went, and it really wasn't for me. I told my friend that a hat would be cheaper, so buy me a hat! He did.

That was a fun way to start the day, but we had another appointment that I dreaded with all my heart. We were to pick up Chelsea and Jordan at the airport and break the news to them. We took them to lunch and brought them up to date. They are incredible troopers, though, and took in stride as much as they could. We told them that God was in control of all of our futures. They believed us and made it through just fine. Thank God!

Deb and I flew out to Houston that night at 6:45. Rick and Cindy Busby took us to the airport. We flew

Southwest and couldn't get seats together. My seat faced a lady with the loudest and most annoying laugh I've ever heard: a cross between a donkey and a lawnmower. I got used to it – tuned it out – and began to relax.

At one point I started singing to myself, "Our God Is an Awesome God," "The Old Rugged Cross," "Great Is Thy Faithfulness," and others. It was such a sweet time of worship for me. It was the first time I've sung with such conviction and worship and not been paid for it, at least in many years. A humbling thought. I'm much too busy in life. No time in the schedule for singing just to sing! But there's plenty of time to sing on stage. God forgive that attitude. You ARE awesome, and I should sing it without end.

We are now at M.D. Anderson. I think great things are going to happen here.

Friday, August 11, 1995
Let the Prodding Begin

The other night a pastor shared something with me. He was basically at a loss for words, but he did say something that caused me to think. He said, "Roger, God is going to send people to bless you and support you during this valley. It may be financial; it may be just running errands. I want you to remember that you are not in charge all of the time – let people bless you!"

Sure enough, the first person that God sent to us has really been a rock. His name is Mark Joye. I met him at a concert and he's unbelievable. He and his assistant Betty met us at the airport. They took us out for a meal, and today Mark met us at MDA at 7:00 a.m. and stayed eight

41

and a half hours! What a support he's been for Deb while I was taking all the tests.

My doctor's name is Alejandro Preti from Venezuela. I like him. He told me about all the tests I could expect. Again he asked me about my symptoms; again, I had none. He said that was a good sign that I'm in the early stages of whatever I have.

I have a very full week of tests coming up: blood tests, x-rays, nuclear imaging (I may glow in the dark), body scans, CT scans, two bone marrow aspirations (not looking forward to that), and a meeting with the Head and Neck doctor to discuss the removal of the largest lump in my neck for biopsy.

Then, nothing for the weekend! I think we are going to take in a movie tonight. Dwight and Sandy Wood are coming down this weekend. They are old-time friends of ours from East Texas. It should be fun! We are also going to see David Ring preach Sunday night. He told me something on the phone the other night that touched me. He said, "God will not more on you than you can be *trusted with.*" I was expecting him to say, "...more than you can bear." But "*trusted* with" – God trusts *me*! What a thought! He trusts me to bring glory to Him through this. I've been learning to trust Him all my life; now *He's* trusting *me*!

> Our God is an awesome God!
> He reigns from Heaven above,
> With wisdom, power and love.
> Our God is an awesome God!

The weekend in summary:

Saturday, August 12, 1995 –
We went to the Galleria and bought me some "Big Boy pants." I left mine at home and brought only shorts. After we ate a nice meal, we came back to our temporary home. David Ring and Danny DeArmas came by for a short visit. It was a really neat time. Dwight and Sandy arrived. It is really great to see them again. They are so funny and we laugh a lot when we are together.

Sunday, August 13, 1995 –
We slept in this morning! Today we went to a *huge* bookstore and I spent $70. It was very cool. I am sure Scott would have laughed at that – he thinks I spend way too much time and money in bookstores as it is! I am feeling pretty good. We had brunch at Papadeaux, my new favorite restaurant. Cajun seafood – mmmm, mmmm! Tonight, we went to see David Ring at a Pentecostal church in Houston. It was a wonderful service, and we made lots of new memories there.

Monday, August 14, 1995

Can't believe it's just been a week since my whole world changed. What a whirlwind. I had my full body scan today – not bad! I also had a 3-D chest-imaging test – bad! I had thought it would be a breeze. Not so. I had to lay on my back with my arms contorted over my head for thirty minutes. By the end of the test, I had visions of the medieval torture rack! I honestly had a tough time with it, but tomorrow is a day off, although I don't think I really need it. I am ready to get going. Then, on Wednesday, the

"Biggy" – bone marrow aspiration. Maybe a funny movie would help...

Wednesday, August 16, 1995

Head and Neck CT Scan: a breeze.
Bone Marrow Aspiration: a hurricane!
I asked for a pre-op sedative. They gave me two Ativan pills. They kicked in one hour *after* the procedure!
Words can't express how this thing felt. A few seconds of sharp pain, followed by a few minutes of intense agony. They did a bi-lateral – which means both sides – two times! Probably the most alien feeling was the sensation of pulling when they actually removed the marrow. But the good news is, it's over.
While I took a nap, Deb went to the grocery store and got some more supplies for us. All in all, I am hanging in there.

Thursday, August 17, 1995

Today I had three CT scans: Chest, Abdomen, and Pelvis. I felt like I was in a Marx Brothers movie! I sat in a little room for three and a half hours in one of M.D. Anderson's plush gown and robe sets. During that time, I had to drink three barium solutions in preparation for the test.   To add insult to injury, the television set in the waiting room was tuned to Jerry Springer, and I had to listen to and watch that. He is one of the worst daytime talk show personalities out there, in my opinion. Today, he was talking to folks who wanted to swap mates with their friends. How pathetic. Actually, now that I think about it, the barium was a lot better than Springer.

When I finally got back to the testing room, my IV came out – not once, but *four* times! The first time it happened, the iodine solution was squirting out of my arm, literally hitting the ceiling... hitting me in the face... unbelievable! That happened a second time. Then, twice, I was bleeding like crazy. There were doctors and nurses running around, all speaking fast in their native tongues. It was a real hoot!

Now, I wait for my appointment with the Head and Neck doctor. The waiting is the worst part, I think.

Friday, August 18, 1995
Good News/Disappointing News

Disappointing News: My surgery cannot be done until Tuesday of next week. More waiting. Deliver me!

Good News: The kids are here! It is so great to see them. They are the greatest. They are by far the best medicine I have had. We relaxed the instant we got to have them in our arms.

It looks like we are going to be here three weeks, instead of two. Mark Joye has offered us his home for a week while he is out of town. That will save us a lot of money. The dollars are adding up. He also has two golden retriever pups we can pet while we are there.

I am waiting to see Dr. Preti for the first time since my appointment a week ago. I got a look at some of my results this morning. If I read them correctly, all areas of my body appear to be clear of cancer, except for my neck. Praise God!

45

Vestal Goodman called last night. She is so encouraging and uplifting. She says that God has assured her, or given her peace, that I am going to be fine. I agree!

We are sitting in a waiting room, as usual. My appointment to see Dr. Preti was for 10:00. It's now 11:20. There is some comic relief, however. A guy in the waiting room has "befriended" us. He is *very* talkative, and seems to have millions of KBs of information on everything from bagels, Budweiser, snow in Texas, unemployment, cancer, BMWs, etc., etc. Mark is being extremely patient, while I, on the other hand, continue to seriously write in this journal!

They just called my name... more later.

Well, well, the first good news: the tests show that the cancer has *not* spread to any other part of my body. I was all tensed up, waiting for the "but...." However, there are some signs of abnormality in the lining of my bones – not the marrow, but the lining. This indicates that my diagnosis will probably be small cell, slow-growing lymphoma/leukemia. Dr. Preti says that some patients live for decades with this diagnosis with no change whatsoever! We will still do the surgery on Tuesday to biopsy the growth, but if it's what he thinks, I will come to MDA every three months or so for tests to watch it. If the cancer changes at all, he will zap it, he says, "before anyone else would know it was there!"

It's great news, but it does mean more waiting...

The Weekend Off

Saturday, August 19 -
Scott and Kelly Howard came down to visit us this weekend and we had a ball! Scott is like a brother to me. He is also one of the funniest humans I know. The kids were here, too, and that added to a great weekend. We went swimming twice – just Jordan and me. He is a hoot! Jordan learned to dive in and swim to the other side under water. That's big news for him! We all went to see *A Kid in King Arthur's Court*. It's a cute family movie.

Sunday, August 20 –
Okay, Papadeaux again! I had the best crawfish I have ever eaten. This is definitely my new favorite seafood place. We took Chelsea and Jordan to the airport to go home this afternoon. They have school tomorrow. Chelsea starts sixth grade (middle school) and Jordan will be in third grade. We are all very anxious. Wish we could be there with them...

Monday, August 21, 1995

It's another day off. Chelsea's first day of middle school was an *awful* day. She had fever and threw up at school. She spent the biggest part of the day in the office lying down. Then on the way home, she got sick again. I know she felt as bad about all of that as she did about actually being sick. Our heart is heavy for her, and we want to be with her. She is so smart, talented, and wonderful. I am sure nerves, coupled with all that is going on, had a lot to do with it. We have just made her a more diligent matter of prayer.

47

Jordan is doing fine so far. He is still in the same school as last year. His good news is that his best friend Jonathan is still in his class. But even more surprising is that Mrs. Puckett, his second grade teacher, whom he really liked, has moved up to third grade; so he has the same teacher as last year. He is happy.

Tomorrow is surgery day...

Friday, August 25, 1995

I met with Dr. Preti today. It turns out I *do* have Lymphocytic Leukemia. This really stunned me. I knew there was a possibility of this being the case, but I guess I was just hoping to hear something else. He said that he wanted to refer me to Dr. Michael Keating. Dr. Keating is supposed to be one of the top leukemia doctors in the world. I have an appointment with him at 1:00 p.m.

7:30 p.m. –

I hope the Lord understands, but I am really low right now. Dr. Keating ordered more blood work. He is almost positive that it is leukemia. And it is going to require treatment sooner than I expected. Maybe even a bone marrow transplant down the road.

On one hand, he has given me hope, and on the other hand, it doesn't sound too good. He told me that, using the older statistics, my survival chances are 50 – 60% for ten years. But, he also said that new advances are being made *every day*, so just hang in there. This disease is rare among people my age; it usually strikes people who are at least sixty-five to seventy years old. I always knew I was special!

I just feel real bad tonight. We are on our way home. We just took off on the plane. I just feel as if I have been kicked. My mind is mush. I will write more later...

> When the world says it's over,
> The Master says, "No, I've just begun."
> In your darkest of times,
> Whether rain or in sunshine,
> Don't be afraid!

As I was closing my journal, Deb pointed out the most beautiful sunset outside my window. It was very moody-looking, just right for my mood. Then, we climbed above the clouds and it became so incredibly bright and beautiful! What appeared to be one thing was suddenly another. That may be what God wants me to know. Sometimes, when it appears to be sundown, it's really just the beginning! Sunrise!!

Lord, help me to keep my eyes open for blessings like this!

Monday, September 18, 1995

It's the first day of National Quartet Convention. It is shaping up to be a tough week, physically. Everybody knows about my sickness, and even though they are well meaning, the constant questions really are taking a toll on me already. Gina (Younce) Eroskey told me to just stay away (and also to wash my hands often!).

There are many neat things to tell, though. God is drawing me near and giving me abundant grace. I really haven't had many bad days with this – just a couple. I feel that He is going to heal me in a way that will give great glory to Him. A friend suggested to me that that may be the reason the chemotherapy is not scheduled to begin until December: to give enough time for people's (and my) faith to be strengthened. Then, when I go in, the cancer will be healed! I know it's totally possible with my Father!

Friday, September 22, 1995

What a huge week! Wednesday night, the Cathedrals flew to New York City. *The Today Show* invited us to sing on live television on Thursday morning. That was a huge deal. It was the first time a Southern Gospel group has sung on network TV in years. It went very well. Scott, Ernie, and I walked around NYC and saw Times Square, the Ed Sullivan Theater, etc. It was great. They called even before we got back to NQC to ask us to come back in December to do some Christmas music! This has been a great open door!

More good news: At the Voice Awards this year, I was voted "Instrumentalist of the Year." I was in total shock that I won!

More good news III: At the Singing News Fan Awards, the Cathedrals were voted favorites in all of our categories, and "Jesus Has Risen" was voted "Song of the Year!"

This makes three years in a row that I have won "Favorite Musician" at the fan awards. I truly am shocked every year. Lord, help me to never think more of the awards than I should. It is a compliment from the fans, and nothing more.

I am very, very tired. Good night!

Sunday, October 8, 1995

I am en route to Nashville from Chicago. It has been a while since I have written. I am doing fine. I am able to be on the road with no noticeable side effects, except fatigue. I just have to go to the bus and chill if I start feeling too tired.

George Younce is having me give my testimony every night on stage. That's good in one way, but it feels a little weird in another.

I am glad to be able to share the goodness of the Lord, and hopefully to be an inspiration to someone else that might be struggling with sickness.

The concerning part is, I don't want this cancer to *define* me. I don't want to become "Cancer Boy." I don't want to get a standing ovation because of this disease. I want to continue to grow in the Lord, and share *that* process, too. I am just praying for wisdom.

I have been shocked with the outpouring of support from people! There are too many cards to count! The phone calls have slacked off some, and that's good. I really don't like to talk about it all the time.

I have been told about so many remedies!! There are people who are pushing me to become a total vegetarian. A man in East Tennessee has a place called "Hallelujah Acres." He had colon cancer seventeen years ago. He started researching the Old Testament diet and put it into practice. He is still alive and thriving. I must admit, it is a compelling argument, but I am not sure it is for me. I am going to seek God about it, though.

Then, a lady told me the other night that, unless I called this doctor she knew, I would die! *Die!* That kind of ticked me off. I know that she meant well, but I believe that it will be God, and not her, who will decide when it is my time.

On a non-cancer note, Scott Fowler and I just bought an office condo that we are going to move our studio and mail-order office into. After fourteen years of marriage, our office is finally out of our house! Debbie and I may move some stuff in today. The studio part will need some remodeling, so it won't be functional until December.

We are landing, more later!

November 7, 1995
In the Air to Nashville

Scott, Glen, and I flew out of Phoenix this morning. We should be landing in a few minutes. I slept well last night, even if it was only for five and a half hours. Our long West Coast trip is over and we now have ten days off. I will be so glad to get home to my family.

The night before I left on this trip, the kids were going to bed. I told them "bye" and Chelsea said, "Will you kiss us bye before you leave in the morning?" I said, "Yes," but I didn't really want to disturb their sleep, and I figured they'd never know anyway. Well, the next morning at 6 a.m., I went upstairs for something and thought I'd pop in their rooms and give them a peck. When I walked into Chelsea's room, she was lying there, eyes closed, with her glasses on. I thought, "Bless her heart, she went to sleep reading." As I bent over to kiss her, those beautiful eyes opened and I said, "Honey, you went to sleep with your glasses on." She said, "No, I just got up to use the bathroom, and I was waiting for you!" Boy, my heart jumped. What if I had just assumed they were asleep? She would have lain there for an hour waiting for her kiss. Another lesson learned: Keep your promises, no matter how small they seem!

Late November, 1995
En route to New Orleans

My white count is up. Last month, it was down. I was
very happy. But today, I called to get my results and the
count was 9.9. Last month it was 8.6. Seems a little
depressing...

Sunday, December 10, 1995

I am on my way to Houston to start my treatments.
This is where the rubber meets the road!

All of the remedies that have been sent to me are
sitting home, unopened. Some may say it's
procrastination; some may say it's God's moving.
Anyway, now it's just God. That's definitely the way I
want it! He has led me this far and I sincerely trust Him to
lead me on! I am safely In His Grip.

The last entry of my journal was rather depressing. I
had just started having some "down" days, some really
tough times. Satan had been playing mind games with
me, and I was feeling too weak to fight him off. He really
kicked me around for a while! But today in church as we
were singing "He's All I Need," the Holy Spirit gently
touched me, and I feel so renewed! So refreshed, so ready
to face this! I wonder how Satan is feeling right about
now.

The difference is the anointing of God. Within myself,
I am not up to the challenge; but, almost like a tag team
match, when I touch the hand of the Father during the heat
of the battle, He flies into the ring and the tide is turned!
Praise the Lord!

My faith should be stronger – but God is using this
trial to strengthen it. I expect great things this week!

We are staying at Mark's house again, and Papadeaux is calling. Crayfish tonight!

Mom and Dad came up to Tennessee to stay with the kids while we are gone. Chelsea made us the most beautiful card today. She was being very brave, but she teared up at the airport. She is so sweet and sensitive.

I have faith that I will be writing great news later...

Friday, December 15, 1995

I am sitting in a wheel chair, waiting to board the flight to Nashville after my first round of chemo treatments. It has been quite a week. And I don't think I will be able to even think about Papadeaux for a while. I got so sick after my chemo, and I had made the mistake of having a great meal there before the sickness hit me.

A really tough week, but we are on our way home for Christmas now. Things will get better, I know.

Sunday, January 14, 1996

It has been nearly a month since my last entry. I was so incredibly sick the last time that I tried to write, I literally didn't have it in me to continue. Needless to say, the chemo made me very sick. On the third day, the sickness just *smashed* me! I woke up at midnight and stayed awake until 7 a.m., with sick spells on the hour.

When we got home from Houston, I stayed in bed for three days. I was hoping to avoid this part of it. Dr. Keating thought I might, but it was not to be.

At this writing, I have finished my second round of treatments. I was able to take the second round of chemo here in Franklin, TN – we will have to see how that is going to work out. There were a few problems there. Dr. Keating also said I wouldn't get sick on the second round... two for two, Doc!

On another happy note, my hair has been coming out in greater amounts. In the shower and on the pillow... maybe I won't lose it all!

I got sick so bad this time that I had to miss a concert in Tulsa, OK. I did fly out to Des Moines, IA, to make a concert that was a big one. I felt well enough to travel. I am on the way home now from Chicago!

Thursday, March 14, 1996

I am trying to form the words... the word that is hardest to form is *Remission!* Dr. Keating called this morning at 7 a.m. I was in the shower, so Debbie answered the phone and then gave me the news. He said there was NO sign of cancer in my body – totally clean! I was in such shock. I am embarrassed that I am surprised. So many people have prayed and believed and yet I am still in shock.

Dr. Keating says I will still need to have my last two months of chemo and then they will harvest my bone marrow, clean it up some more, and keep it in storage in the event that the cancer should return.

The word is "remission" instead of "cure" with leukemia. I think my personality will do better with this. My spirit will still need to lean on God and depend on His sustaining. Each treatment could bring the news of recurrence. So I continue to trust and pray.

REMISSION! Totally clean! "Healing!"

April 14, 1996

6:30 a.m.

I am sitting in the Charlotte airport waiting to board yet another plane to Nashville. I just finished another round of chemo. I am having to take them in Houston again, due to some problems we incurred in TN.

I really despise the treatments. This time I had some sort of nerve attack. I was sitting in my hospital bed, and all of a sudden, the most miserable feeling came over me. I felt such despair! I tried to pray and couldn't. I just said the words and left the rest to God. I don't remember ever feeling so bad. Eventually, I dozed off; and when I woke, the feeling had passed. Thank God! It sure felt like a spiritual battle that I was losing.

I feel as if I have let my walk with God "slip" a little in the past few months. I am very disturbed about it. I want it back.

I have the hiccups so bad it's hard to write right now. I had them on stage the other night, and had to testify and sing with them – not fun. I think I overdid it this week by going on the road. I don't feel great, and I went out one day after chemo. I will try not to let that happen again.

May 16, 1996

I am en route to Cleveland, OH. We sold our house! We are going to move into an apartment in Franklin and we are getting ready to build! Those two sentences describe an amazing turn of events.

To elaborate, Debbie and I have always wanted to build a house, and have never had the right opportunity. One of the men in our office condo is a realtor, and we had him looking for land for us. In the meantime, I mentioned to an engineer friend of mine about our search. He told me about a twenty-eight acre farm he had just bought, and said that there were just over twenty-one acres available adjoining it. He said it was beautiful and that we should see it. We did, and it was! It has rolling hills, pasture, and a three-bedroom house with a barn. We asked Scott and Kelly Howard, who had decided to move to Nashville anyway, if they were interested in looking at the house and five acres. They were, and they loved it, long story short. We asked the Lord if we could have it. If yes, just open the doors; and, if not, make it so hard that we would know it was not His will. Almost from that instant, things progressed at an incredible pace. The bank approved the loan. Our offer price was accepted. Scott and Kelly are moving up. And the coolest thing is the story of the sale of our current house. Debbie mentioned during church prayer and praise time that we are putting our house up for sale, and the next day a friend from church called and said she knew someone who wanted to buy a house in our area. They came by the next day, said they were interested, and made an offer even before we had to list with a realtor – and we accepted it! We are so excited. We close in two weeks, move into an apartment that day, and hopefully start building sometime in June.

We just landed, so I need to go get back into the whirlwind. We just figured we didn't have enough excitement in our lives lately!

August 2, 1996

I am still in remission! My bone marrow lymphocyte count dropped another three points to 8% this last testing period. It was just a year ago that I had the biopsy on the lump in my neck. What a year: fear, dread, numbness, joy, pain, relief, excitement, defeat, and victory. I have had varying amounts of all of these emotions. I feel that numbness now. I know that the remission is good news and I am very thankful and relieved, but honestly, I worry about it recurring. I guess it still might be feelings of unworthiness. I don't know...

I am set to have my marrow harvested this month. It will take about five days for the procedure, from start to finish. Then, I guess it will just be regular check-ups.

I seem to again be drifting in my walk with God. I just don't seem to have the desire for His face that I want to have. That is ridiculous! After the massive amounts of grace He has poured out on me, I don't hunger after Him – God help me! I DO love Him, and He is my source, my strength. I just have neglected Him, my first love. This is heavy on my heart now.

Monday, September 2, 1996

Two weeks post-bone marrow harvest – what an ordeal! Over 200 punctures in the hipbones! I was completely out during the surgery but, when I came to, it was pure pain! I am sure I have never been that sore. I ran a fever for four or five days afterward, and I am still a little tender.

Mom and Dad are here for a visit, and NQC is next week. Time is really flying by!

I am still not where I should be with God. It is not a matter of open rebellion in the sense of living in sin; it is in the area of priorities. So, I guess in the definitive sense, it really *is* rebellion. I just need to make time for God. I feel as if I am shutting Him out sometimes. I seem to be so preoccupied with other things at times; I may even be shutting my family out. "Father, I DO love You..."

I heard a pastor say once, "Don't forget in the darkness what you learned in the light." I thought that was a cool thought. But since this sickness, I think for me it should be, "Don't forget in the light what you learned in the darkness."

I never want to lose the feeling of utter dependence on God. But I think that, as my condition improves, I tend to forget that "leaning" feeling. This is so dangerous. We tend to cry out to God in our desperation – then in times of ease, we forget to even thank Him! Lord, don't let me forget in the light what I learned in the darkness!

Thursday, November 21, 1996

I am en route to Chicago – again. I am feeling pretty good! I will be going back to Houston for another bone marrow test in January. This will tell me if I am still in remission or not.

I guess I am in a time of "trusting" right now. This should be a continuous state.

Thanksgiving is coming up. I've got so much to be thankful for! If I had been diagnosed with a more deadly form of cancer, I could have already been gone! God has preserved me. I pray that it is so that I can be of some kind of special service to Him. I will keep listening...

Tuesday, January 28, 1997
En route to Nashville

I am no longer in remission. I had my tests this morning in Houston. The blood work came back normal, but the bone marrow biopsy showed an increase in cancer cells. I was definitely not expecting that. Because the bone marrow biopsy I had this morning didn't give a really good sample, Dr. Keating asked me to have another biopsy this afternoon. You can't get much more fun than that! I will know the results of this one on Friday.

It's real again! The time in remission gave me a false sense of security – almost like it was over. To paraphrase an old saying: "You're only as clean as your last exam." I will start another round of chemotherapy soon. Scheduling will come later. All this comes around a projected move-in date of about four weeks to our new house.

My faith is *not* shaken. I have preached nightly from the stage that God is God in sickness or health. Now it's time to put that into practice – again. I fall so short of the mark, but I can rely on Him *never* to miss the mark.

I don't want to die. I have been so blessed, and I want to live to enjoy that blessing. There is so much on my mind right now. I am going to try to put it all aside and focus on Him. I want to not be distracted from His leading.

> Some through the water,
> Some through the flood,
> Some through the fire,
> But all through the Blood.
> Some through great sorrow,
> But God gives the song,
> In the night season,
> And all the day long.

Amen.

Monday, April 21, 1997
Tulsa, OK, 7:20 a.m.

The tests came back showing that I am still in remission! Three long days of waiting, and then the call! I have been so busy that I haven't written lately, but so much has happened.

Besides the chemo, we moved into our new house at the end of February. What a blessing. After nine months in a two-bedroom apartment, the house seems palatial! Huge. I think everyone building a house should have to live in a small apartment. That would ensure that they would really appreciate it.

I had a solo date in Tulsa last night at Friendship Baptist Church. What a good time. I heard a great illustration yesterday:

During Napoleon's time, there was a private in the French army who was also named Napoleon. He was a good young man, in every area except one. It seems that he was a coward in battle. When the fighting started, he would run away. The story goes that, one day, he was called in to see the emperor Napoleon. The emperor looked at the young man and said, "Son, either change your name or live up to it!"

How many times could Jesus have said the same to me regarding His name, "Christian"? I could never live up to His great name, but by grace, I will try to represent Him well!

Tuesday, April 22, 1997

We have the week off. Our next concert is on Friday.
I can't believe how time is so swiftly passing – April 21
already! Deb and the kids are doing fine. The Lord is
blessing me more than I deserve.
I flipped back a few pages and read, even though I
write very sporadically anymore. I am so glad I have kept
this journal. It is a good record of the peaks and valleys I
have been through, but even more, it is a great reminder of
God's grace!

Sunday, April 27, 1997
Charlotte, NC

We worked with Bill Gaither the last two nights. Even
with the big crowds, they were tough nights. The
Cathedrals are used to more intimate settings, but it was
good anyway. While sitting in the green room before we
went on, I was listening to Gloria Gaither. She is an
amazing woman – very deep. Some things she said made
me think again how God is moved by the prayers of His
children. He loves to hear us pray.
We have some time off. I plan to spend it with my
family. Jordan got his hair cut the other day in a
"military" cut. It looks good on him. Chelsea won an
award in Band!! I am very proud of my kids.

Wednesday, May 7, 1997

I am en route to Fresno, CA for the West Coast NQC. I have been looking at my calendar and I am amazed by how busy life is. I have tried to cut back, but it is very hard. There are so many opportunities, and I have a hard time saying no.

Chelsea realized a life-long dream this week. We bought a horse! He is named Banks (his full name is "Bank on It"). He is an older horse, very experienced, and well trained. He should be perfect for us. I hope it is a good experience.

September 30, 1997

We are en route to Nashville from – get this – Belfast, Northern Ireland! We just spent six days in Great Britain. Who would have thought that a boy from Strawberry, AR, would get to travel that far? This was a trip with the Cathedrals (except George). We had one concert in Glasgow, Scotland, and two in Belfast. Debbie got to go with us, and it was the absolute *best* trip we have ever taken! The concerts were great, the scenery unreal; but the most wonderful part of the whole experience was the people.

Our hosts: Ian McDowell; Campbell Tweedie and wife Eleanor; Gordon Halliday and wife May, sons Gareth and Graham. They became precious to us almost instantly. It's so hard to describe, but I know the Lord was in it. We were treated royally and we got to see a lot of great locations – castles, lochs, etc. The concerts were at capacity, and God blessed each one. All in all, it was really a "magical" trip!

George was unable to go because of a mild heart attack he suffered on July 7. He is recovering well, but his doctors didn't want him to tax his body with the travel and jet lag. I agree. We are exhausted! A six hour time difference between our country and theirs, and several nineteen hour days: it all adds up to a lot of fatigue!

This entire summer has been full speed from June until now. I am so ready to be at home for a while.

For summer vacation, Deb, the kids, and I went to California for ten days. We flew in and drove up the coast, visiting many cities. It was a great trip, but tiring. This, added to the usual two cruises we work and a heavy concert schedule, and the body becomes weary. NQC was six days of non-stop going, but it was a great time, too.

The kids are back in school. Maybe now we will all settle down into routine again, and get some rest this fall.

My tests show I am still in remission, with no sign of disease. Praise to God!

July 31, 2000 (forgotten journal entry)
Estes Park, CO

Legacy Five sang at a Christian music seminar here in Estes Park today. It was mostly adult contemporary Christian rock artists, and we were the only Southern Gospel group here. Tore it up! It was great! I ran some fever earlier in the evening, but I feel better now. Things are going extremely well for Legacy Five, and we are much farther along at this point than we projected. We are in the midst of negotiating a new record contract. I am not sure where we will land, but it should be decided soon.

Now, to VACATION! Scott and Taryn Fowler, Scott and Kelly Howard, and my family are going to Buena

Vista, CO to Ken Davis' cabin for a few days of R&R. Rest, fun, beauty, friends, family... the best things in life!

August 4, 2000 (forgotten journal entry)
Denver, CO

We came down from the cabin today. We are at the Denver airport Red Roof Inn, waiting to fly out tomorrow for home. We had a great time, and the kids really loved it. Their favorite was the four-wheeling. We went up several steep trails, and Chelsea and Jordan got to drive on their own; I was just there for back-up. We also took a float trip to ride the rapids of the Arkansas River – WILD RIDE! At one point, Chelsea almost ended up in the river, but she held tight to a rope and was pulled to safety. In spite of all that, she loved it!

We talked a lot about the future, and dreamed a lot of dreams. I wrote a song, we had two business meetings, and played a lot of cards and games! Now, back to the real world... home tomorrow. I am feeling better. One more month of chemo. I am in remission again. (The cancer came back last November.)

August 11, 2000 (forgotten journal entry)
Pensacola, FL

What a tough night – the crowd worked us hard. There was a three year old kid tonight who was allowed to run at will on the front row. He was very distracting to me. Last night in Arab, AL, I thought the concert started at 7:30, so I started getting dressed about 7:00. Scott Howard came out to get me at 7:00 and told me the program was starting. I missed the first song! Glen Payne would have killed me. I guess that's one of the advantages of owning the group – HA!

Jordan and his friend Graham are on the road with me this weekend. They're having fun. Jordan starts back to public school this week. After one year of being homeschooled, he's really anxious to get back. He misses his friends. I'm a little worried about him getting back into the swing of things. He was bullied a little bit in the 6th grade (mostly we just didn't like the principal and her attitude). I'm praying for an easy transition for him. He's a great kid!

Chelsea is as well – she is amazing! I couldn't be more proud of her. She is very into the band, and was elected to serve as Secretary. She turned 16 this year. We were able to buy her a '98 Mustang. It's deep green and she loves it! I know now the rush that parents get when it's time to buy the first car. It was so much fun for us.

I'm so blessed. My wife loves me, and I love her. We have the two greatest kids in the world. AND, they both can tolerate us (pretty well)!

August 17, 2000 (forgotten journal entry)
En Route, 3 a.m.

No air conditioning on the bus! Today the temperature was 102 degrees, and we got no A/C. We've had nothing but trouble with this bus.

The kids started school yesterday. I'm worried about Jordan. This is his first year back to public school. I'm sure he'll be fine, but I worry sometimes that he's TOO good.

It's too hot to sleep, but I've got to try!

September 3, 2000 (forgotten journal entry)
Lilburn, GA

Three years have passed since my last entry. The reason is that my cancer stayed in remission all that time. Unfortunately, it's back now, and a little more aggressive. It's requiring a stronger round of chemo.

Kids are doing well in school. Both seem to be adjusting fine. This is Chelsea's first year to drive, and during the first week of school she had a wreck. A roadgrater didn't see her, and pulled right into the side of her car. She was uninjured, but trapped. Deb and I were in Houston finishing up my chemo when the phone rang. It was Chelsea from inside the car, very scared. I nearly slipped into a coma myself. Thank God Scott Howard was home and could go down and be a daddy for her. She's fine, and the construction company is paying all damages and more. So I guess "all's well" and all that. Jordan is with me on the road this weekend.

August 20, 2000
Home

I went for my latest check-up this week. It doesn't look good. My CLL may be back. I have an elevated white blood count and my marrow has lymphocytes in it. The definitive test results will be back tomorrow.

If it is back, I'll probably have to start chemo in two months. To top it off, I've got shingles again!

I'm trying very hard to stay positive and trust God. I'm having to walk the walk. I sing and write about fear so much. I try to encourage others not to be afraid, and now I've got to prove it as my condition worsens.

My fears?

…That I'll die young and leave my family

…That my family's life will be disrupted.

…That somehow I'll dishonor the call of God on my life.

I seem to fear all the things that I say grace covers! Fear or no fear, though, I WILL keep trusting. I'm in His grip and, until He wants me home, I'm not going anywhere!

I may be surprised by tomorrow's results, but I have a feeling that I'm about to enter another battle.

FYI

I won't go into details, but it was bad news, and there was a very tough fight that didn't work. You'll see that some of the next few entries deal with something very strange in my system, and me moving slowly but surely to the biggest battles of my life.

November 18, 2000 (forgotten journal entry)
En Route from London, England to Little Rock, AR

My mom is on life support, and not expected to live. She had been steadily declining during the past couple of years. She was diagnosed with an incurable lung disease, and really started dying then. She had a few good days off and on, but the breathing became more and more difficult. I guess I was in denial; I knew that it was bad, but I never thought it would happen this quickly. Another situation is compounding the problem: My dad just had emergency open heart surgery and has had so many mental complications. He is so weak and sometimes just out of his head. Although he is home now, and slowly getting better, I really wonder if the stress of Dad's condition worsened Mom's. You really couldn't write a story like the one we have been through lately...

My family and I have been in Belfast, Northern Ireland for a Legacy Five tour. I always called Mom from there in the afternoon, and then again at midnight, to check on things. This worked out to be the best timing, due to the six hour time difference. Yesterday morning, I talked to her, and she sounded bad, because she had just been up and to the restroom. She could hardly breathe. She was very concerned about Dad's weakness. He had fallen during the night, and Mom had to call the neighbors to help get him up. I told her to rest, and that I loved her, and would call later. When I did call back, their neighbor Don answered the phone. I thought this was odd. He told me Mom was in the hospital, and he put his wife on the phone. She told me the bad news.

I talked to Dad, and he seemed coherent most of the time. I realized that things were happening quickly. I then called Uncle Mike's house, and the news got worse. I was told that Mom had actually gone into cardiac arrest; her heart had stopped for 15 minutes. They were able to revive her (get her heart re-started), but they think she may be brain dead. They won't know for sure for 24 – 72 hours. I called home just now from the plane, and she has now started having seizures. I can't believe it. She has been so strong, and such a fighter, that this seems unreal. It's a sad, tragic situation.

Deb and I rushed to fly home. The kids are still in Northern Ireland with Deb's parents. We will make their plans when we get home and see the situation.

The Bible says that God will not put on you more than you can bear, but this feels close. I'm... a little shaken right now.

The last concert in Northern Ireland was great. I said a lot of things about "grace". It now seems that I was talking to myself. I remember saying that as lonely and as desperate as times can get, that's just when God's grace takes over. Let it be so.

November 21, 2000 (forgotten journal entry)
Postscript

Mom is gone. She died yesterday. How can this be? When Debbie and I finally made it to the hospital in Batesville, AR, the situation was so grave. Her vital signs were so bad, that the doctors told us that most likely, she was beyond hope....probably severely brain damaged, and her heart and lungs beyond repair. We basically started a vigil at the hospital, along with many other family members. I knew that the decision to remove her from life support was coming, and that it would be me who had to make it; Dad wasn't able to. We tried to get her to wake up, but she didn't respond at all. It was pitiful. Machines keeping my Mom alive. After 48 hours had passed, we were told that it would be a miracle for her to come out of it. A signature on a piece of paper, a switch flipped off, and in a matter of moments, I lost my mom. It's amazing to me that at 41 years old, I can still feel like an orphan...

June 5, 2001 (forgotten journal entry)
On a Plane

My family is on a plane returning from a 10 day vacation in California. It was supposed to be 12 days, but we all were ready to come home, so we changed our tickets, and we will be home tonight at 6 pm! We really had fun. We spent some time in San Diego, Los Angeles, San Francisco, and drove through Yosemite. We drove up the coast along the way. It was breathtaking! The kids seemed to enjoy (for the most part) spending so much time with the "old folks"!   (Speaking of, Deb turns 40 tomorrow. She's doing fine!)

It's been seven months since Mom died. I still miss her terribly. I am hiding a lot inside, but it's all I know to do. I don't know what else to do. If I talk until I am blue in the face, she is still gone.

Chelsea will be 17 next month. College applications and choices are coming up soon! I am just praying that she will go close to home. I don't expect it, but that's what I'm praying. Jordan is 14 and going into the 9th grade. He is doing great, as well. His grades are wonderful.

Deb and I are hanging in there. We are sitting next to a young boy on a plane who is getting married this week. He is approximately 19. So many experiences are ahead for him! Deb and I will celebrate *twenty* this year. There have been lots of good time, and a few bad… in a nutshell, life. I wouldn't change partners for anything.

August 9, 2003 (forgotten journal entry)
Home

    Well, it's been almost a year since I have written. I *did* enter a storm. The cancer was back. I started an aggressive round of chemo the week before Thanksgiving, and stayed at M.D. Anderson for nearly 30 days. The treatments were hard. I had severe reactions. Dr. Keating called it "shake and bake" (chills and fever). The kids came and spent Thanksgiving with us. What a blessing – our friend Judy had arranged to get us two rooms at the Rotary House for the entire month. Scott and Taryn Fowler also got to come for a visit during that time. I finished the treatments in time to come home for Christmas, and we had a really sweet time together.

    As the weeks passed, and I got back into the schedule of touring, I began to notice that I wasn't feeling well for a good portion of the day. I had a lot of symptoms like bronchitis. After three months, we finally figured out that I had contracted a staph infection! Not good. It took forever to clear up.

Then, about three months ago, a familiar set of symptoms made a repeat performance: fever, chills, and fatigue. It has felt like I was taking chemo again, and suffering all of those side effects. I am worried this time. It can't be good. I guess it's just a question of *how* bad!

    This time, I am scared. I have made my peace with God, and I feel totally safe (even if it means a young death). I hope that's not the outcome, but a man must be prepared. To quote George Younce, "My house is all in order. I'm packed and ready to go."

    Deb and the kids are great.

II Corinthians 4:16-18.

September 23, 2003
Home

Well, sir, it seems as if it's time for the CLL Traveling Road Show to make its annual stop on Little Pond Lane.

About a month ago, the tests revealed Salmonella poison in my blood. It's a bad infection that is rare in the blood. It is usually picked up OUTSIDE the USA. Go figure. Dr. Keating wants me in Houston ASAP for more aggressive chemo. Less than a year between major treatments and the beat goes on! The chemo this time will consist of all of the different kinds I have had before, only all together at once. Can you say "Cancer patient look"? This might just be the time that I start looking like a cancer patient. My weakness will be more of a factor this time, too. My faith has never been more important.

I'd like to articulate a little about the "more"...

At the end of a short cold, a nasty letter of goodbye... You say, "There's got to be 'more'."

Your boss makes a few changes around the office, and the first change is, unhappily, *you*... "There's surely 'more'!"

Standing, looking at the body of the person who raised you, lying on a bed in the ICU... When you are willing her to speak, move, twitch, something... When hands place a clip board in your lap for your signature... When time speeds up as her breathing slows down... When the moment you have dreaded all your life arrives, and you feel alone, afraid to face the world without her...

It is then that you are glad to *know* that there *is* more.

September 29, 2003
Home

I believe we are at war with an ancient enemy. I'm convinced that it is a spiritual war. The enemy is Satan, the fallen. He's been given this world. We are on enemy ground. He is sly, cunning, ruthless, and completely without pity. His goal is to rob Heaven of as many souls as possible. I believe this.

My entire life has been lived in the balance between God's plan and Satan's goal.

Satan's weapon against me is simple but deadly: the word "why." To a person inclined to ask "why"... God is either interested in humanity or He isn't. Black or white. My enemy knows that I don't like the brutality of this world and would stop it if I could. But that is only half the story.

Evil exists. Evil is active. Our world groans under the powerful pull of evil. Since Eden, evil has been growing like a cancer cell in an otherwise healthy body. I must realize that, as the cancer of Satan's plan grows, so grows evil in the world.

Here's the good news: God's plan is to counteract evil with love, to shine light into darkness, to invade the cold depths of despair with the warmth of His spirit.

My job is to remain focused on the Word, immersed in prayerful listening for the prompts or nudging of the spirit. I must not be seduced by the easy, humanistic worldview that says, "Evil strikes the innocent, so there must not be a God." Heaven forbid. Easy to embrace, difficult to believe.

I don't have all the answers. But it's not about me; it's about a plan that spans eternity. It is for me to study, to become less like me and more like Him!

I want to live like a Believer!

FYI

Time passed and Roger's condition worsened. It was decided that his only chance for life was a complete Bone Marrow Transplant.

At this point in the story, we move to his online journal. Roger started the "blog" to keep his friends and prayer partners updated on his condition; but it quickly became much more that that. Roger began to write from his heart about the most personal, painful experience of his life in hopes that someone in cyberspace who was going through a similar valley could find some hope in his writings.

The list grew at an unbelievable rate. Thousands of individuals read "Midnight Meditations" daily, and many ARE finding the comfort that Roger hoped he could provide.

We begin with Roger and Debbie relocating to Houston.

January 7, 2004
Tuesday in Houston

Well, I had my first official stress test today. (I thought I'd had a lifetime of stress tests! Haha.) I did OK. Didn't pass out! I'll get the results tomorrow along with some other tests. I'm hanging in there. Still no word on a bone marrow donor. I have an appointment with that doctor on Thursday. I'll keep you posted. I hope you enjoy this web journal. I'll try to keep it up to date.

Legacy Five is doing well. I've had to miss the last few dates, but look forward to getting back on the road ASAP.

January 7, 2004
3:00 a.m., and sleep is nowhere to be seen.

It's now 3 a.m. I've had my meds and am not finding sleep at all. One good thing is that I get to sleep in tomorrow!

I spent a lot of time in the past few days in places unfamiliar to me in the cancer center. One in particular was in the ER. I watched people literally cry out from the pain. At one point it sounded like something out of a horror movie. Sometimes they stopped, and sometimes they WERE stopped. Funny how a little needle full of liquid can settle all differences.

My heart bled for their lives. I longed to hear all of their stories, but many of them were just too sick. They were grimly going about the business of dying, a process that we will all go through sometime soon. Those hours in the ER gave me a new yearning to live every minute to the fullest, to try to love my family and friends more; but, most of all, to tell the story of Jesus in more creative ways, and to tell it often. Just think how many we could rescue from the brink, if we only took time to share the story that saved us.

Let that be our New Year's commitment!

Love you, it's so late and I've GOT to get some sleep,

January 9, 2004
Home!

Been a little sick today, but I did make it home fine. Family is gathered around watching a few tapes that make us laugh the most.

No real news today...

They are just looking for the bone-marrow donor. I feel that we'll be closing in on it real soon. My spirit is fine, and God is answering prayers on a minute-by-minute basis. He loves us so much that He'll send blessings after blessings our way. I'm not naive enough to think that every prayer gets answered in the way that we want, but I am CONFIDENT that His Will will work for our good.

A simple truth that I've been taught since Mrs. Saffell's Sunday School class: He wants to do exceedingly, abundantly more that we ever hoped. Now, much of it will have to wait until Heaven, but when has God ever failed us? I don't even have to answer that. His Will is for our good.

Not always the way we want it, but I'm totally convinced that His ways are better than mine!

Hope you are having a great New Year and that you are enjoying this web log that I call my Midnight Meditations. I will walk you through everything that I will face during the next year and let you see for yourself the blessings of God.

January 10, 2004 -- Resting is hard!

Have you ever had a doctor tell you to rest, or else? I thought, "No big deal." Boy, was I wrong. I hope to get the hang of it. I thought I knew how; but I realize now that, even before when I thought I was resting, I was actually continuing to do stuff. The last 24 hours, I've done nothing. I don't like it! Just 168 more hours to go!

January 11, 2004
Talk to the Troubled

I'm sure you've seen the faces. You know the ones I mean. They have that tendency to look over you or through you. Never quite making eye contact. A little too quick to tell you that they are doing "great." Nothing about their countenance says "great," but they insist that it is so.

I know how to describe this person because I've been one of them. The feeling is, if you make each encounter with your friends or family a short one, then they'll never see the emptiness in your eyes or words. I know this because I have said those empty words.

Let me tell you what the "troubled" need. They need their friends to push just a little. Not in an aggressive or confrontational manner, but just a little push. "Are you sure you're fine?" or maybe, "I hear what you say, but your eyes and spirit don't say the same thing." Another good door opener can be, "I know there is something wrong. You may not be able to talk right now, but just remember I am here, and the minute you do want to talk, I'll still be here."

This is all pretty simple stuff; and the truth is, you may not be able to help in much of a physical way. You can't cure the cancer, repair the marriage, or calm the fears of growing old. But you can be in the room! You can touch the shoulder. You can drink a cup of coffee and listen. You know what? That's enough! What your troubled friend needs is a friend. Not all the answers; just someone to point them toward the answer.

The last thing you're gonna need is patience. Believe me, I know that in the "fix it now" world we live in, what we want is instant healing so that we can move on with our too-busy lives. Yet the truth is that troubles aren't always fixed with the immediacy that we're used to. I know this because, eight years ago when I was diagnosed with cancer, I wanted the "fix" immediately. I scheduled my chemo ASAP. I kept working hard and expecting any day to be through with this inconvenience. I just knew that any day now I could put it behind me and get on with life. Well, it's been eight years and five months, and the toughest days for me appear to be ahead. My attitude today as opposed to eight years ago is, "Lord, Your will be done." I may have to fight this battle for years but now, I've been taught to enjoy even the times of waiting.

I've been blessed. I've got family and friends who know how to minister to the troubled. I want to encourage you to learn the same skill!

January 13, 2004
Shoot the wounded?

When I started these Midnight Meditations, I didn't think that the posts would really be at midnight! But here we are at 12:39 a.m. central time, and it's just me in a quiet house. The only sound other than my typing is the snoring of my twelve-year-old Australian Shepherd, Maggie. Oh, I've tried to sleep... I lay in bed for quite a while struggling with the thought in my head. Finally, after much prayer, the only peace I found was when I determined to get up and write.

My prayers lately have been for many of my friends and family members who are hurting. Don't get me wrong – I pray a lot about my cancer and my future, but so much of the time the Lord is laying someone else on my mind. I realized tonight that much of the trouble that our wounded Christians have to deal with is the condemnation from within their own fellowship.

If you have ever seen any kind of military movie, I'm sure you have noticed the same thing that I have. When a member of the outfit is wounded, the entire mission changes to include getting that soldier out. I think the phrase I hear a lot is "no one left behind." What pride it always stirs in my heart to see those men and women risk all to get their wounded buddy back to safety and care. You know something else I noticed? I never heard one of the rescuers say while bringing that wounded brother or sister back, "You were so stupid to get shot up like that!" or, "I ought to just leave you out there on the battle field. You brought this all on yourself."

Now, I've never been on a physical battlefield, but I've been on plenty of spiritual ones. So it's from this perspective that I speak.

How many times have we seen our brothers or sisters in the body of Christ make mistakes? Plenty. It turns my

81

stomach to admit that, at times, I've been in the "you brought it on yourself" crowd. But it shouldn't be this way. The sinner knows more about his or her sins than you or I ever will. The One who really counts – Jesus – knows more about the sinner's sins than the sinner does! But what is His example? Does Jesus say, "You had it coming," or, "You brought that on yourself?" God forbid.

I'm sure that the woman in the Bible who was discovered in her sin expected a much different answer than the one that Jesus gave. Instead of picking up a stone, He made the statement that every sinner since has longed to hear. "You without sin, cast the first stone." What a Savior! What an example. (John 8:4-10)

Don't misunderstand – I'm not "pro-sin;" I'm pro-Jesus. Those of us who have sinned (and all have) need mercy the most. It's not justice that we cry for in the midnight hours of our life. It's mercy. And every time, mercy is extended from our Father. "His mercies, they fail NOT ... Great is Thy faithfulness, Lord, unto me."

We Christians know what the wages of sin are. And, if left untreated, the full payment of our sin will be dealt out to us. But thank God for the treatment! The blood that was shed for us on Calvary has the power to cover ALL our sin! I'll pause to give you time to shout your praise to God for this great love He has for all of us who are wounded!

These musings about grace are not meant for one person, but many who are on my heart tonight. If you know someone who is wounded and almost to the point of giving up, make a phone call today. You aren't condoning their sin by saying, "I love you." You are opening the door to restoration! What a powerful thought. God uses ordinary people like me and you to extend an extraordinary Grace.

I'm not talking about doctrinal issues or even disagreements on scriptural interpretations. I'm talking about a much simpler scenario: that of a broken believer having encouragement from another member of the body. Remember, OUR potter doesn't throw the clay away!

So, to close, I'll just say, the rocks that are in my sling will not be aimed at my fellow believers. I'm aiming at that giant in front of me!

If our need had been money, a banker would have come. If our need had been shelter, a carpenter would have come. But our greatest need was forgiveness, so only a Savior would do!

"Thank You, God, for sending Your greatest gift: Jesus."

January 14, 2004
"Thanks" is not a big enough word!

I've had a lot of time on my hands during the last week. For those of you who don't know, the doctor put me on at least eight days of bed rest. It seems that the high white count and the years of fighting this cancer have taken a toll on my body, so I've had my wings clipped for a while. Legacy Five are on a Bible study cruise to Mexico this week, so all the times I've been sitting in my chair taking my meds and temp, I've been thinking about those guys being on the beach and eating themselves straight up (a George Younce statement)!

But the good thing about this forced idleness has been the time that it's given me to reflect on God's goodness in my life. As most of you know, I'm facing a bone-marrow transplant in the near future, and my insurance denied the claim. So my partner Scott Fowler took it on himself to start raising the money, and the response has been overwhelming. In less than two months, over $600,000 has come into the benefit fund. The majority of the donations were less than $100.00 each. Do the math and you'll see why I use the word "overwhelming." My life literally has been changed in the wake of this experience. I know that the upcoming days will be hard, but my spirit has been so blessed – not only by the donations, but by each of the letters that came along with the donations. I'm working on posting many of them on the Legacy Five website. I think you'll be blessed by reading them. God's people exhibiting God's love is one of the most awesome things you will ever see.

So the meaning of this long note is to try and say thanks. One of the biggest problems that I have is trying to come up with a way to say thanks that really gets it said. I've yet to find the words. So, to all of you folks who donated: thanks from the bottom of my heart. To all of my friends in Southern Gospel who rallied around this cause: thanks from the bottom of my heart. To those of you who wrote and said, "I'm not able to give financially right now, but I'm praying for you:" the money is not the only way to send a blessing, and thanks to you from the bottom of my heart.

I hope that the language of heaven will one day let me express my family's gratefulness to all of you.

January 16, 2004
The Cry of His Child

There is a great Southern Gospel song that my dear friends the Hoppers sing. It's called "The Cry of His Child." I remember the first time I heard it. It was on one of the great Singing at Sea Cruises. (Nothing but Southern Gospel and Food!) (Oh yeah – great scenery and fun, too.) Most of the time throughout the year, Legacy Five works alone on our concert dates, so it's a treat to actually sit out in the crowd and watch a group sing an entire stand. Brings back memories of me as a kid going to Southern Gospel concerts. Anyway, The Hoppers started this great song. The gist is that Jesus was asleep in the boat during the storm. The winds and waves were crashing. (According to weather gurus, the sea they were on experiences some of the most fearsome storms in the world.) But there was Jesus, sleeping through it all.

The song goes on to say that it wasn't the howling wind or rolling thunder that woke Jesus. It was the cry of His Children! Amazing? Yes indeed. What a comfort to know that our Lord never gets distracted. His ear is tuned to the cry of His child. I know that many who are in the valley right now may not be able to summon the joy of this thought. You may feel as if the exact opposite has occurred and that you dare not even speak the words lest you be labeled "unbeliever." Well let me give you good news on a personal note.

I've lost the confidence that I once had in my health. With the current state of affairs, I can't commit to doing much in the way of physical exertion. This has been hard for me. My kids love to do stuff occasionally that requires more of me than sitting on the couch or in a movie theater. And lately I've had to pass on these things. I can't even lift boxes of Christmas decorations to put away for my wife this year. (Don't laugh... that might tax even the most buff among you. Every year it looks like Christmas has exploded in our house! Ha.) I've been so discouraged that I wondered if my prayers were getting through.

Here's what I've found out. Though it doesn't seem so at times, our Lord hears every prayer we make, every anguished cry from our mouth. The Word says He even understands the groaning of our hearts. Be encouraged! God has a plan for you. It may include periods of "dark days." It will most assuredly include some waiting, but it HAS to include JOY! He cannot go against His Word and

He says without stuttering, "I came that they have life, and have it abundantly!" Remember that during your troubled times. When you lay in your bed of sickness, instead of feeling sorry for yourself (like we are all prone to do), start counting your blessings! No matter how insignificant some might seem, start naming out loud to God what you are thankful for in your life. I can tell you that this works for me every time.

I don't mean to say I'm healed at that moment, but I'm given that "new grace" to get me through that trial.

And this knowledge all started with me hearing one of my favorite groups sing a song that changed me!

"Thank You, Jesus, that You still hear the cry of Your children."

Well, it's 5:15 a.m., and yet again it's just me and Maggie (my dog) awake in the Bennett house. It's unusual – I have trouble sleeping until I write, and then most of the time I fall right off to dream land. Tonight I dreamed I was doing a concert with Legacy Five, and someone had dipped the piano keys in the "Blooming Onion" batter from Outback Steakhouse! They said it would make my hands just slip across those keys! Ugg... I can still smell what that keyboard smelled like!

On that weird note, goodnight; and remember: "You're never too old to cry out to your heavenly Father."

January 16, 2004
Two Big Days Coming Up!

Two of the biggest days in any Southern Gospel lover's history are upon us!

Before I go any farther, you need to remember that the first twenty years of my involvement in this music was playing the piano for the Cathedral Quartet. There's been no better time in my musical life. I had more fun sitting around listening to George Younce and Glen Payne talk and laugh. I also learned a lot about how to treat people. I learned how to treat folks like friends instead of fans. This post would be too long if I continued listing the benefits of being a Cathedral.

So, back to the two special days. January 18, 1944. A seventeen-year-old boy named Glen Weldon Payne stood shivering in the cold of a Dallas winter morning. It was 5:45 a.m. and he was waiting for his ride. The ride was to come at 5:45, but Glen was terrified of being late, so he had been standing on the corner since 5:00 a.m. just in case. (I would later learn the hard way that Glen insisted on promptness!) The ride he was waiting for was a car full of quartet men from the famous Stamps Quartet. They were heroes to many in Texas and around the country because of their highly popular morning radio show on the powerful KRLD radio in Dallas.

Glen was too nervous to eat. He was standing on one leg and then the other to stay warm, when finally the big black car slowly made its way down his street. The back door swung open, and Glen crawled in. In about five minutes, he made his first radio appearance, and a giant was discovered.

For the next fifty-five years, Glen Payne set the standard as to what a lead singer should sound like. I say this with the authority of having played for him night after night – there was no other like him who had it all.

He had excitement, both in his voice and in his stage presence. He was a real southern gentleman who believed in standards, both in his music and in his life. In short, he was the man! Period. In his last days before passing away, Debbie and I were over at Glen and Van's house. He was very weak and lying on the couch. We'd had a great visit and, at the end, Glen wanted to sing again. And sing he did! This is not written as a fan but as a person who's heard a lot of lead singing. He was as good as he ever had been! Big rich tones, a little "edge" to his voice (but not too much), and more importantly, you still felt the anointing in the voice. He was one of the greatest men I've known. So Happy January 18. You won't hear about it on the news, but that day changed Southern Gospel Music forever!

Now let's look at the second important date, February 22. The town is actually outside of a beautiful town in the North Carolina mountains called Lenoir. On that day in 1930, a happy little baby boy was born to Mr. and Mrs. Tom Younce. They named him George Wilson Younce. The fledgling Southern Gospel music world didn't know it on that day, but another giant was born in North Carolina.

George was a happy kid. His specialty was entertaining the other kids with his antics. (He even made an appearance on the "Little Rascals" program.) This natural comic skill would serve him well in 1964 when he became the bass singer for a new group called the Cathedral Quartet.

If I had to describe Younce with one word, I'd use the word "heart," followed closely by "desire." George NEVER stopped learning. Even in retirement now, he has a recording studio set up in his house and is constantly singing just to keep his voice in shape.

I remember the first time I heard George sing. The year was 1975, the city was Jonesboro, AR, and the setting was the beautiful Forum Theater. I was blown away! I didn't know which had impressed me most: his singing or his mastery of the stage. I decided to be impressed by both. What he did seemed effortless. I would find four years later when I joined the group that a TON of work went into making it seem effortless. George is a craftsman, both vocally and from an MC's point of view. He took it seriously. I can't tell you the nights that I sat up front in the bus and listened to George vocalize while he drove our Silver Eagle in the middle of the night. Not just one night or even twice a week; EVERY night he drove, he was working on his tone and rhythm.

I am so thankful that there is such a huge body of recordings of both George and Glen, not only for our blessing but also for our instruction. My advice to any bass singer in this business is to get your hands on every George Younce recording that you can. Solo or Quartet, it makes no difference; he gives a clinic on every song! Young lead singers, get any recording that Glen is on. If you still want your voice to sound fresh and strong, listen very carefully to this artist who knew the difference between singing and yelling!

So this year while you're celebrating George Washington's birthday, don't forget to take a moment and remember the living legend: George Younce!

One last memory before I try to sleep again. The first rehearsal I had with the Cathedrals was at Glen's house. I had flown in earlier in the day. (My first flight!) Glen picked me up and took me to Bob Evan's for breakfast. (My first Bob Evan's!) Then he took me to Diamond's, an exclusive men's clothing store, had me fitted for my quartet suits, and bought me two new white dress shirts. (I was so nervous that I ended up leaving them at Glen's house and had to buy two more the next day in Winston-Salem, NC.) That afternoon the group gathered at Glen's for our rehearsal. The first song I played with them was "Holy Is Thy Name." My ears were pinned back listening to the blend, and at the end of the first chorus George went down and hit the most solid "A" I have ever heard! I literally stopped playing and gawked at him. (I'll bet he was thinking, "What kind of redneck kid have we hired?!") I stopped again when Glen locked in on the high note at the end. It was so loud and bright I was, yet again, stunned. I thought, "I'm in WAY over my head! I'll never make it!"

But you know what those guys did for me? They gave me time to become my own person, musically. I didn't sound like anyone else and that was fine with them. Those two men had patience with me and showed me what I needed to know to become a quartet pianist. I will never be able to repay them for that. Literally everything I have is because of the Lord using George and Glen in my life. So, gentlemen: thank you for everything!

Happy January 18 and February 22! Take the day off!

January 19, 2004
Weakness vs. Strength

I'm getting ready to take my bucket full of pills for the night and pondering the virtue of weakness. One observation: it seems that, for most of our lives, we are conditioned to be strong. Eat all your veggies, take your vitamins, exercise, an apple a day... you get the drift. That's all good and I'm for it. But I want to tell you just a little bit of what I've learned about weakness.

Physical weakness, for me, has been a time where God has shown me that He is totally dependable. The times where I literally had to put aside any hope of winning the battle in my own strength were the times that His strength came to the forefront. I know this is not a new concept.

How many of us have sung the song "Jesus Loves Me" without a thought of what we were really saying? "I am weak, but He is strong." In our society, we're taught that any show of weakness is a mistake. We should display confidence in every aspect of our lives. Again, I think that's fine. But the key to real strength, I've found, is in knowing the source of that strength.

Years ago, I wrote a song called "Strong in the Strength of Someone Else." It sat on the shelf for years. When I wrote it, I was healthy and cancer-free. After we recorded it, I had been diagnosed with leukemia for a while, and it seemed like a whole new song for me. Just to quote a short passage: "Living a life of spiritual wealth, Strong in the strength of Someone else." God's timing is amazing! The very moment in my life that I needed to learn about weakness and strength, He sent me a valley that demanded that I get strength from Him.

It's not been an easy lesson for me to learn. Even today I find myself trying to take over and unintentionally pushing God out of the driver's seat of my life. Every time I do, I bring more burdens into my life. The old bumper sticker couldn't have been more off-base. God is not my co-pilot – He is my pilot!

I don't know whose bell I'm ringing right now, but if you've reached the end of your strength, I say GREAT! There is more strength and power than you can believe just waiting to be given to you. Trust Him. He knows our beginning and our end, and He knows how much strength we need. As the Word says, "His strength is made perfect in our weakness." It's a liberating feeling to know that the source of our strength comes from an unending supply!

On a personal note, I've felt stronger today than I did yesterday. This is the first day in a while that I have felt a little improvement. Thank God for His sustaining power.

January 21, 2004
Focus

I think that, sometimes in our lives, we are anesthetized to reality. Our own struggles, whether they be physical or emotional, tend to take our minds off the things that matter. I certainly was that way nearly nine years ago when I was cancer-free. Oh, I loved my life and family; but I was so busy that it never occurred to me that it could be over in a heartbeat. Cancer focused me to the reality of the blessings of my life.

The reason for this subject is a sad one. Deb and I were just getting ready for our day this morning when the phone rang. A friend of ours from church was killed last night while going to the mall. She was trying to change lanes and a fast driver plowed into her. Her car was flipped and she was killed instantly. She'll be missed. The suddenness and violence of her death was breathtaking. I'm sure the last thing on her mind when she was making her way to the mall was that, in a matter of moments, her life would be over.

Don't misunderstand. I'm not trying to scare you or be morbid in any way. But what I take away from this tragedy is this: Don't wait to enjoy your life. Don't put off the thing you were going to do with your kids. Don't live in the fog of a busy life while missing the fun that you can have in your own living room.

Reclaim your life with a vengeance. Don't allow fatigue or worries to become your master. Focus on the important, eternal things in your life, and enjoy them to the fullest. We've all heard the old phrase, "You can't take it with you when you go." Very true. However, there are SOME things you do take with you: your faith in Christ, and your memories of your family. The Word says we'll be known as we are known. So I believe that our little times together as family are eternal things that transfer when we do!

I know this is second nature to many of you, but it's just a reminder from one who's been on both sides. Don't let tragedy be the force that focuses your life – focus now and enjoy!

January 23, 2004
I Made It!

I made it through my first concert since having my wings clipped a few weeks ago! I felt weak and looked pale (according to Deb), but it felt so good to be back. Thanks for your prayers. We are in Weatherford, TX, tonight, and then Deb and I head to Houston for more follow-ups with my doctors on Monday.

January 26, 2004
The Little Pager That Could

I've just come back from my latest consultation at M.D. Anderson. Labs at 7:30 a.m., Dr. Lenihan (a cardio specialist) at 8:30 a.m., and then Dr. Keating and Co. (for the leukemia) at 11:30 a.m. As you can deduce, I spent a lot of time in waiting rooms today. I have this theory that a cancer patient can spot another cancer patient. Of course it's easy at a Cancer Center like MDA, but it's interesting to watch. When the new patient comes into the room, there is an immediate sizing up that takes place. I do it as well. You look for the tell-tale signs: any obvious lines or ports in the veins, complexion variations, or hair loss. It's not an uncomfortable thing; it is just the way it is. I don't think there's any more honest place in the world than a cancer waiting room. The conversations that take place are no frills and always contain terms that the average healthy person is unfamiliar with: CBC, neutrophils, aspiration, and a host of other things that might not be discussed so openly in another place are right out in the open in the waiting room.

One of the other rituals that takes place is identifying the patient. Many times this is not a problem, in that the patient is obviously sick and a companion is there for support. However, there are patients like myself who look healthy on the outside and are accompanied by a healthy companion. You can see it in the eyes as the two people are judged and the decision made. Sometimes you're right and sometimes not.

I was wrong today. I wasn't feeling quite up to par this morning, and in one of the waiting rooms I fell asleep. The room was empty except for Debbie and myself when I dozed off. But soon, a quiet conversation roused me. I heard talk about pain management, etc. I woke to see a very young mother and what looked to be her father in the room with us. I quietly listened to Debbie talk with them. I made my choice: It was the dad who was sick, and the daughter was his caregiver. She looked so healthy and vital. I was wrong. This young woman, a mother of two small kids, was the patient. She has a rare form of bone cancer and is in for the fight of her life. It broke my heart.

During our talk, I kept hearing a vibrating sound, like a cell phone's alarm. Every few minutes, sometimes more than once a minute, this little pager would make its noisy announcement. I thought, "Boy, she's a busy lady." Then she told me the story of the pager. It seems her prayer group at church gave her the pager and, every time anyone at church prayed for her, they would page her just to remind her of their love and support! She didn't have to talk to anyone. No one wanted a call back. This was just to encourage her that her friends had not forgotten her! I got cold chills every time that little pager vibrated! And I could see that she found strength with every vibration! What a great idea and what a picture of grace.

I know firsthand the power of prayer and how important it is to your spiritual health. And I saw firsthand the power of reminders today in the face of this beautiful young cancer patient. Her friends were remembering her, and that reminded her that God remembers, too!

It doesn't have to be a pager. A little card will do the trick. Sometimes a voice mail is better than a phone call. It depends on the day, but sometimes when you're sick, it helps just to listen and not to have to talk. Whatever form you choose, let your sick friend know that you are remembering him or her.

"Lord, I thank You for teaching me these little lessons in the most unusual places!"

January 29, 2004
A Proud Dad

I just got back from a concert by the orchestra at my daughter's university. Chelsea has always been a great musician and was always involved in band in high school, but this was a little different. Tonight she was a part of an orchestra that included members of the Memphis Symphony and the Chattanooga Symphony, as well as a ton of talented young people from the University of the South. It was a great night, with extremely difficult music played by extremely talented people. I must confess that one of my dreams for Chelsea was for her to be a part of a group like this, so you can imagine how her Mom and I felt as we sat in that audience. I know that when she reads this she will not be happy with me, but I have a bigger point to make.

During the intermission tonight, as I was trying hard not to be the embarrassing dad and point out to everyone that that was MY daughter up there, I realized something else. Can you imagine, if we can love someone with that level of intensity, how much more our heavenly Father loves us? When we react to events in a way that pleases Him, how much joy He must feel. He loves us with that much power even when we don't please Him! What a thought! That while we were yet sinners, He sent his Son to die in our place. As deep as my love is (and I can't imagine it being deeper) for my kids, He loves us all so much more. That should make us ready for any valley we face. I certainly don't understand it – but I don't have to! He loves us. Unconditionally, without measure, He loves us!

I know that many of you read this journal to keep up with my health, and there'll be time for health updates in many entries to follow. I just wanted to take the time tonight to remind you that you are loved and that love is stronger than ANY struggle you face.

"For God so loved the world that He gave His Son...."

February 3, 2004
Heartbeat

Do you remember when you became aware of your own heartbeat? That day came for me about a month ago. I had always had this deal with my heart: "You keep beating, and I'll keep moving." I know, kind of a lopsided deal for the heart. You beat your 2.5 billion times, and I'll keep eating what I want until you give up. Now don't bother me! Well, about a month ago, that attitude all changed.

Legacy Five was getting ready to hit the road for the weekend, and I was getting some CDs and songbooks together to load onto the bus. I realized that I was suddenly having trouble breathing. My condition worsened very quickly to the point that I knew I was in trouble. It was midnight and my one thought was to get on the bus, and after a good night's sleep I would be fine. Long story short, I wasn't. During the night, I had another episode – this time, a little worse. The next morning, I called my doctor at M.D. Anderson, and he told me to get to an emergency room ASAP.

The final result was that I had had a light heart attack, and that yet more tests had to be run in Houston. They tell me that the attack was brought on due to my long fight with leukemia, that the damage is light, and that the function of my heart looks and sounds fine. I don't have heart disease, but the danger is still there because of the effects of the cancer. When I was cleared to leave Houston, it was with the assurance that I would go home and REST for a couple of weeks.

It was during that time that this journal came into being. The defining moment for me during this new trial was not the heart attack or the ER visit. It was during a routine echocardiogram in Houston. You see, I had never had a look at my heart before. As I lay on that table and watched the monitor of my heart beating away, I was struck at how fragile it looked. To be honest, it gave me the willies! That little blob in my chest didn't look like it was doing too well. The flaps that opened up to allow the blood in looked downright flimsy, and I found myself pulling for the thing to work. "Come on buddy! Keep it up! You can do it!" Pitiful, I know. I think it's still part of the process of facing my mortality. The cancer was always out in the future somewhere and seemed somehow removed from me when I wasn't in chemo. But this heart thing... I mean, looking at it through that monitor, I could see how it could just stop any time. It still sort of creeps me out to think about it. I don't live in fear, but I do have a deeper feeling about the fragility of life.

I know there will be a lot more times like this during the coming days, so I'm adding a new request to my prayers. I want the Lord to give me clarity of thought. I don't want to just coast through these days and miss the little spots of joy along the way. I want to be present in every moment. I want every heartbeat to take me to the next good thing that God has for me.

As I was thinking about this entry, for some reason my thoughts turned to the heart of Jesus. Not the spiritual heart that is eternal, but the heart that beat in His human body. The heart that increased the beats to keep up with Him when He was playing as a boy. The heart that nearly burst from the stress of the beatings He endured before the crucifixion, and that struggled to supply blood to His body as that precious blood was spilled out on the Cross. The heart that quietly stopped when its owner cried, "It is Finished." I'm sure that Satan and his demons were overjoyed to hear the silence that echoed through the spirit realm when that tortured heart fell still. The stillness lasted for only three days. To His followers, it seemed an eternity; but something wondrous happened on the third morning. A new sound blasted through the spirit world! A deep strong pulse that had never been heard before – a resurrected pulse! I like to think that Satan was interrupted at his party and his head turned to look toward the tomb. I think he knew at that moment that the best he could hope for was to sow confusion in the world, because Christ had won and the door to heaven was opened to "whosoever!!!"

So, with that in mind, it really ends the worry about how long our heart will beat in these earthly bodies. Two and a half billion beats, they tell me, is about seventy-five years – a good, full life, but not even a second in the span of eternity that we are guaranteed because the heart of our Savior still beats today!

Make sure that you have a spiritual heart by-pass. Make sure that you are grafted into the heart that will never stop again.

God is good, Jesus saves, and we are... In His Grip!

February 9, 2004
As Far as Faith Will Take Me

It's about 4:30 a.m. on Monday. Deb and I are on the way to the airport for a quick trip to Houston, and then back home this afternoon. I'm feeling really well right now. Just the usual symptoms, but no heart hiccups or fever, so it's a good day.

"As Far as Faith Can Take Me" is one of my favorite new songs, sung by my friends, the Martins. It's a great thought. But, as usual, I started twisting the theme around and looking at it from different angles. It occurred to me that many of us sick people go as far as attitude and positive thinking can take us. All fine notions, but there is something much deeper here.

I am inundated with self-help books about defeating cancer, and I've read many of them. They all center around a "PMA" (positive mental attitude). This, according to the experts (?), is the cornerstone to fighting this deadly disease. Again, a great thought, and I know that it's useful. But it only goes so far.

If attitude is our fortress, it will eventually fall. The invaders (cancer cells, a weak heart, diabetes, etc.) will eventually wear us down and our PMA will falter. It stands to reason that, at some point during our weakness or sickness, the stress of keeping our chin up will make us crack.

Enter Faith! This is where the supernatural power of God takes over. See, good attitude is outcome-based. We'll keep smiling because we can see an eventual end to our valley. The problem comes in when the enemy we face will not give up. Faith, however, lets us rest in God's Word. Not having to understand, not having to explain to our friends and family, we rest in faith, knowing that He has our interest at heart.

Can I promise that you'll have no suffering? Not at all. Can I promise tough days someday? Absolutely. You can't get around the fact that we live in a fallen world. Our bodies eventually want to quit. But with a life-view based on faith, your foundations – while sometimes shaken – can never be brought down. The PMA benefits stop the moment you stop having a PMA. Faith in Christ is still there even when you may be too sick to fight. At that point, count your blessings. Thank God for loving you and keep believing.

> My hope is built on nothing less
> Than Jesus' blood and righteousness.
> I dare not trust the sweetest frame,
> Yet wholly lean on Jesus' name!
> On Christ the solid rock I stand,
> All other ground is sinking sand.
> All other ground is sinking sand.

One more unrelated thing. Many of you have heard about my best friend Scott Fowler's heroic efforts on my behalf. I've assembled all of his letters and updates on

Legacy Five's homepage. I got cold chills putting the page up, and I think you'll be blessed to see how the grace of God was poured out through a friend. It continues to be the most inspiring thing that has happened to me in a long time.

February 10, 2004
Update from Houston

My check-up yesterday showed that my white blood count has risen to 261,000. My doctor decided that I need to start chemo today. It was not the news I had expected, but I am glad that we are going to take action against it. Deb and I came to Houston yesterday expecting to be here for a few hours, and now we're not sure how long we'll be here.

So many of you ask about what to pray for specifically, so here it is:

1. Pray that my reaction to the treatment is light. I usually make it fine, but the side effects are the toughest part.

2. Pray for strength for Debbie and the kids. I'm not the only one that this affects. My peace of mind is tied directly to their peace of mind.

3. Pray that my heart will remain strong during the treatments. It still is not at 100%.

That's it. I didn't bring my computer this trip (thinking it was a one day check-up) so I can update only when a computer is available here. I'll do my best to keep you posted.

I am weak but He is strong!

February 11, 2004
Chemo Crash

When I last wrote, I was extremely excited about getting my treatment started. When I did finally get going, five minutes into the treatment, my body said, "No, no!" I developed a severe reaction to the medicine and spent the next seventeen hours in the ER. Not a great night. Good news however: they learned that the premeds they gave me were not strong enough, so they hot-rodded the premeds and today I went through an eight hour treatment and made it just fine.

That's all for now. I'll be glad to get back to writing in my "Journal" mode and not so much "sick" mode. Love to all you wonderful friends who really care.

February 12, 2004
Huge News, I Hope You're Sitting Down

I've always tried to be real honest about this cancer experience. When I had bad days, I told it. When they were good days, you knew that as well. As you know, this week started out with more than its share of bad news. The terrible reaction that I had to the chemo was the most serious episode in the last eight years of this fight. Bad news. Then the next day I was able to tolerate eight hours of treatment with no ill effects. Good news!

But I was not prepared for the news I got today!

My bone marrow coordinator asked to see Debbie and me this afternoon. She sat down across from me and, with tears in her eyes, said, "Roger, your dad is a 100% match for your marrow! The chances of this happening are less than 1%." She continued by dropping another bombshell: "Your son Jordan is almost as close a match! Again, less than a 1% chance of this happening!" What news! What a shouting time we had. There are several reasons that this is huge news:

1. The chances of your body rejecting a related donor are much less.
2. This means that we can get the ball rolling right now! I'm literally weeks away from starting the transplant.
3. It's my DAD!!! He helped give me life in the beginning. He was my best man in my wedding and now, at the age of seventy-one, he is literally saving my life! I can't tell you the joy that's in all of my family's heart right now.

I wish you could have heard Dad on the phone when I broke the news to him. He'd prayed to be the donor, but knew the chances were almost too slim to even mention. We cried and laughed for thirty minutes on the phone. Talk about a time of rejoicing!

I'm still so excited that I can't seem to form these words. I'll write more later, but please, share this with as many people as you can! God met my needs financially through thousands of you folks who responded to Scott Fowler's appeal. Now God has met my physical need through the most unexpected person – my dad! My spirit is so high right now. I know that many tough days are ahead for me with this transplant, but I feel that God has done such a mighty work through this sickness that I can face whatever comes my way.

Oh, by the way, the word "miracle" was used many times today at M.D. Anderson Medical Center. I think it is very appropriate!

February 17, 2004
Planes, Trains and Automobiles

I'm still a little speechless over my last bit of news. My dad has not even started to come down off his cloud! He's out walking, trying to be in the best shape possible so that this transplant goes off without a hitch. My current physical state is kinda "blaahh." I can feel the effects of the treatments on my body, but my spirit is soaring. I've been able to appear at every L5 concert in the last few weeks. This weekend in Lansing, IL, Bloomington, IL, and Eau Claire, WS, we had exceptional services. We laughed so hard we ended up crying, and then sometimes we cried so hard we ended up laughing! This is one of my lifelines to a normal life, traveling and singing our songs. Pray that I'll be able to keep it up until the last possible moment.

I'll bet you're wondering about the title of this post?

Well, it seems now that the big news has been delivered, Deb and I are dealing with the mundane things involved in preparing. Flight schedules, car rentals, hotel and apartment hunting – stuff you can do with your eyes closed. If I'm not careful, this can numb me to what's really going on around me. I don't want to be lulled to sleep with these preparations so that I miss the "God Things" happening all around me. And there are hundreds of them or more!

I'm working on a major overhaul of L5's website. And on this new version, I'm gonna list many of the letters that Deb and I are going through right now related to my transplant. I predict that page will be the most popular on the site. Coming soon! I ask for your patience with this. My energy is real low and I try to accomplish my tasks ASAP, but ASAP for me is different now than earlier in my life! OK, that's my whine for the day. I'll make it happen soon.

It's nearly 2 a.m.; I'm not sleepy, but I think I saw a box of Girl Scout cookies on the counter and those Samoas are calling my name. Maybe that will make me sleepy! Have a great day! I love you a lot, but God loves you more!

February 18, 2004
Mute, Please!

I'm a habitual "muter." If it's in my control, I almost always hit the mute button on my TV remote when it's commercial time. It's one of my pet peeves I guess – the shrill and over-the-top way in which we are told which soap to use, which car to drive, and how to whiten our teeth is something that I don't want to hear. So, I mute. It's one of the perks of having the remote.

I think one of the reasons this is on my mind is I had another chemo treatment today. (It was my first one in Nashville and it went quite well!) During the long hours of waiting, TV is one of the distractions we "chemo-ites" have at our disposal. I don't know if it's just me, but reading is sometimes hard for me during treatments. I think it is the tendency of my mind to wander that keeps me from being able to focus on a book. Anyway, back to the mute. I've found that sometimes I even mute real life! Debbie has always said that I have selective hearing, and a lot of the times I "select" not to hear her! I disagree. (I think.) While tuning out of tough or uncomfortable situations is easy, I want to do my best not to mute the moments that are special. I find myself stepping back from the uncomfortable moments and then, out of habit, I forget to "un-mute." The danger in this is that I might miss something God is trying to tell me.

So, in this spirit, I'm trying to grow more comfortable in the silence of waiting on God's still, small voice. I guess

105

you could say I'm going to use my mute power for good. I'm gonna mute the distractions of this world and tune in stronger to signal of Heaven. There are some amazing things waiting for us just outside of our sight – things that can't be forced into our lives, but must be revealed. I'm finding these moments happen when I spend time in His Word or in prayer. I'm trying to learn not to "bend God's ear," but to let Him bend mine!

OK, I'm through for the night. Feel free to mute any and all commercials on TV, but try to un-mute the whispers of God.

February 24, 2004
Feeling great – then the injection!

Today started out quite well for me. The L5-Mobile dropped me off early this morning at the Jacksonville, FL, airport for a quick hop to Houston for check-ups and a little splash of chemo! (So refreshing!) Then the bad weather hit New Orleans and shut it down. We circled for an hour and quickly decided that the fuel situation would need to be addressed rather soon, so we diverted into Birmingham to wait it out. Still no problem – I bummed a cell phone off of a new friend and let Deb know I would be late into Houston.

I finally arrived, 4 hours late but glad to see my baby. We took in a movie and then headed back to the room for an early night. We came back to the room early mostly because it's shot day for me. I have to take this real hoity-toity shot three days a week that's supposed to really help me build up immunity. I noticed at the entry points of earlier shots there was a little bit of rash and itching. No big deal to me! I've seen every John (THE DUKE) Wayne movie made! I know how a man is supposed to handle something with which he is unfamiliar.

Duke Rule #1: Ignore the warning signs and proceed at full speed into danger. Here's how it went down: I gave myself the shot in my leg, and about three minutes later my old head felt like an overripe mush melon. I had no feeling at all in my face, and shortly my palms broke out into white whelps! At this point, my Debbie is in her high alert mode. Her eyes bugged out with that expression that says, "If I don't see an improvement in five seconds, it's 911 time for the Strawberry Flash." (Don't ask... It's an old nickname that Glen Payne gave me.)

I rebuked her non-submissive ways and said, "Woman, I've seen every John Wayne movie made. When THE DUKE was injured, he didn't run to the ER; he just dipped mud out of a puddle, applied it to the gaping gunshot wound, and was back up on Ole Roscoe before you could say, 'HAYYYOOOOOOO!'"

So I lay in my bed, feeling weirder by the minute, also wondering how to keep my manly pride intact while saying to Deb, "You know, Sugarbunch, John Wayne wasn't giving himself shots in a hotel room – he was GETTING shot in a hotel room. Maybe we ought to keep an eye on it. If you want."

Gradually, over the next two hours, I leveled off, and am now sure that it was just a delayed reaction to the latest miracle drug. I'm fine as I write this. It was a false alarm, and we can all now go back to our campfires and tell lies with John Wayne about how brave indeed we men are!

In all the silliness, there is one lesson for you tough guys out there. Braveness only goes so far. Don't be a hero. If you're having dizziness, shortness of breath, and any sort of chest pains, GO TO THE ER!!! My Docs tell me that, in the case of the heart, you literally count the seconds till you get the treatment you need. Sorry guys, but that's my speech to you tonight. But don't get too much of a big head, ladies; I'm sure I'll have lots of opportunities to preach to you in a little bit!

All in good fun, of course... I love you all. I know that I've been hard to reach lately, and I'm behind on e-mail responses, but I'm slowly digging out from the bottom of the pile.

Big meetings with all doctors tomorrow. I'll post again tomorrow night with details.

February 28, 2004
Update from Roger

Just a quick update. First, for those of you who have been scolding me about the injection: I'm fine. The medicine was changed the next day and I've given myself several more shots with no ill effects at all. Thanks for your concern, but I'm really fine.

The schedule is falling into place. I will let you know the particulars as soon as I know, but it looks like pretty soon I'm going to get on the road to recovery!

My dad told me yesterday that he's almost become a hermit because he doesn't want to get sick before the harvesting of his stem cells. Ha. We are still so excited about his match.

God is good and is sustaining me. I'm out on the road with the troops (L5, not the army) and feeling fine. It seems that my wish to sing and play right until the last minute is going to happen. Thank God for His strength.

OK, I'll run. No big long post this time, just a few lines to let you know the latest. I love you all very much and I also want to thank you for making this journal such a success. Evidently you are forwarding it to friends, and so are they. The numbers of people reading are just unreal. That was my dream in the beginning – not to have a lot of traffic for traffic's sake, but to get the word out to as many of my friends as possible. Thanks for helping!

March 3, 2004
Heavy Days

I think that the best explanation of a "heavy spirit" has happened to me in the last few days. On one hand, everything should be well. I should be light as a feather. But I'm not. On the other side, one of my favorite uncles underwent lung surgery today after finding cancer a few days before. He's my dad's sister's husband, Bart Voyles. Uncle Bart has a great attitude, but this is a scary time. The closest thing to a sister I will ever have are Bart's daughters, Bev and Donna. My heart hurts for them and my Aunt Betty. "Aint Bet" (that's Arkansas pronunciation) is one of the funniest people I know, and I'm praying so hard that the entire Voyles family is restored and refreshed very soon.

My hero, George Younce, is in the critical care unit in Akron. The family is by his side and is seeing a few glimpses of the old George. He is able to respond to commands; he can't speak yet, but the family is thrilled with this turn for the better.

When I have these sad days and need encouraging, I think of this old hymn. You may not be familiar with it, but Legacy Five will have it recorded on some future recording. I think this will bless you!

Begone, unbelief! My Savior is near
And for my relief will surely appear,
By Faith let me wrestle,
And He will perform
With Christ in my vessel,
I smile at the storm!

Words written almost 500 years ago that are as correct today as the day they leapt from the pen.

March 6, 2004
Good news regarding my previous post

I'm doing great. We are getting things packed for my time in Houston for the transplant. I'll have a date for you soon. My donor, dad, is still in the clouds about being a 100% match for me. His excitement is contagious and I'm feeling pumped up as well!

Please forgive the delay in this post. When I'm on the road, it's a little more difficult to get computer time. I'll work hard at keeping you all up to date.

March 10, 2004
45 down and 45 to go!

First of all thanks to all, of you who e-mailed and snail-mailed birthday wishes to me. I certainly appreciate it. Forty-five years ago today, a little girl (she was twenty-one years old) brought a tall, skinny baby into this world and named him Roger Douglas. She was a fierce mama from the start. The doctor that delivered me said to her, "He's an ugly little devil, ain't he?" She, needless to say, found no humor in this statement. I guess I caused havoc from the beginning. As many of you may have heard me say, telephones were not the norm in those days, and my grandmother had to go to an electric company on the outskirts of Strawberry, AR, to use their phone to alert the doctor that Mom was on her way. My grandmother was so bent out of shape with the impending birth of her first grandchild that she put her dress on wrong side out to make this trip to the phone. I never let her forget it.

Birthdays never seemed like a big deal to me, except for the presents. Until recently, I never gave age a thought. I don't know if it's a boy thing or not, but I couldn't care less about whether I'm thirty-nine or forty. But since my illness, I've quietly celebrated each passing birthday with thankfulness. I count it as another year of God's faithfulness to me.

I got to spend the day with my son. We went to music stores and bookshops. Then we went and ate way too much Italian food. Tonight, my daughter is coming home, and I get to spend some time with her. I'm not into parties that much, so this is my favorite way to spend a birthday. I hope I have a lot more of these days. I'd like to take my "*grand-rugrats*" out for my birthday. I feel sure that I will. I find that the longer I live the more I'm into the little things. Now, don't get me wrong – I still like presents and cake, but my favorite gift is time. How 'bout you? Do you have a tendency to run the rat race? Remember that the only winners in a rat race are rats!

My prayer for you is for less stress and more time to enjoy your blessings.

Happy Birthday to you too!

March 13, 2004
My Bone Marrow Transplant Schedule

Now that the time is at hand, I feel that I'm of two minds. On one hand, I'm excited to get going and whip this thing (with God's help); and, on the other hand, my heart is heavy at the thought of being away from my kids for this long a time. Chelsea and Jordan, hopefully, will be able to come to Houston for a visit before I start feeling the bad effects of the transplant.

So here are the bottom line prayer needs:

1. Strength for Debbie. She is my 100% caregiver during the entire 100 days. This is a real big-time deal. The manual of medical stuff and instructions for her is huge. I know she is up to the task, though. She has been my rock during this eight-plus year battle.

2. Comfort for Chelsea and Jordan. They are filled with faith and are confident that I'm gonna be fine, but I want them to have as much prayer support as possible.

3. Comfort for my extended family: in-laws, out-laws, grandpa, uncles, aunts, cousins, and friends.

4. Strength and determination for Legacy Five. If you want to really help me feel relaxed, add L5 to your prayer list and go see them at every opportunity. Scott and the boys are taking this added burden on their shoulders and have never flinched. Pray for great days for them.

5. My health, both mental and physical. There are several factors that influence both of these areas, including medication and isolation. I can't control either of them, so my prayer is that I don't go nuts! I'm sure that, as much as I like to read, I'll have a lot of time to catch up. Deb has packed a trunk full of books and videos to keep me occupied, so I'm sure that I can keep what little mind I have engaged!

6. My doctors, nurses, and all the medical staff. I pray for them to be used by God to bring about a great conclusion to this transplant.

That's it. I love you all so much. Your encouragement has been a lifesaver for me and the family. From your financial outpouring at Scott's request to your prayers and notes, this has been so vital to my peace of mind.

So I'll close now and be in touch very soon. I'll miss you. You will be in my thoughts daily. Scott is going to try to call me every night that it's possible during their concerts and let me say hello to you. I look forward to that.

Remember, God is not dead, nor is He asleep. He has our good in mind.

March 15, 2004
My conversation with George Younce

I was sitting down today, getting a list together of things that I need to do, when my phone rang. Caller ID said "Younce." I answered, thinking that I would hear George's daughter, Gina, on the phone with an update on George's health. I was stunned to hear that familiar bass voice on the other end saying, "How's it going, Doc?"

I can't tell you what it did for me! I was stunned. The last I had heard, George was indeed home, but I thought he would be out of commission for quite some time following his latest ordeal. Was I wrong!

We laughed and talked for about fifteen minutes, and my heart was so much lighter after our talk. Younce always has a way of lifting spirits. Let me share with you part of what he told me. His latest heart attack nearly did him in. His daughter Dana had to perform CPR for fifteen minutes until the paramedics arrived. That night, the doctors shocked his heart six times before it would beat on its own. They put him on a respirator and told the family that it would be cruel to shock him any more, and they recommended removing George from life support. I've been faced with that decision, and my heart broke for the Younce family.

They didn't have a peace about allowing him to be removed from the machine so, like many times before, they gathered around George's bed to pray. They asked God for direction and for His peace in the matter. When the prayer ended and they raised their heads, just outside George's window was the most beautiful double rainbow in the sky! Coincidence? They didn't think so (and neither do I). They told the doctors that they were going to keep George on life support. Long story short – my phone rang today, and my friend who supported me and my family for years was there on the other end, supporting me again and encouraging me for the days ahead! God is so good!

I've always said that George's body was made up mostly of HEART (and a pair of cowboy boots). Not the small heart that beats in his chest, but the giant spiritual heart that beats in his soul. Many times the doctors have given a grim prognosis regarding George; a few days later, my phone would ring and I would be treated to the latest "George Joke." I love doctors, but I'm glad that they don't always have the last word.

I just felt that you would love to have this kind of update about George. Keep praying for him.

Long live George Younce!

March 16, 2004
"Roger, are you scared?"

I'm asked a lot of questions regarding this upcoming Bone Marrow Transplant.

"Will it hurt?" Probably not. Not in the sense of sharp pain. I've been told that the actual transplanting of the marrow is pretty pain-free.

"Will you be sick?" For sure. Chemo is never easy, and the side effects are sometimes brutal.

"Will you lose your hair?" 'Fraid so, but not 100% sure. I hope not. I'm afraid I might have a lumpy head!

The most frequent question is, "Are you scared?"

Of course I am.

My earthly eyes can't help but see the fight ahead in a physical sense. But my spirit eyes see a completely different view. When I'm afraid, I remember the words of Jesus concerning fear. So many times He encouraged His followers not to be afraid. It's hard sometimes, even after all I've learned about God's faithfulness, not to be afraid. My eyes look at the storm instead of the Master of the storm. So, yes – there are times when I'm filled with dread for the coming days. But it's in those times when I glory in my weakness and fear. I know the Master of the wind and whether I'm here or in Heaven, I can't lose.

I'm a little skeptical when I hear people say, "My wife and I have been married thirty years and NEVER had a cross word!" My first thought is, "You must not have uttered many words in thirty years." Debbie and I had our first big fight the night of our wedding rehearsal dinner. But we loved each other then, as we do now, twenty-two years and many cross words later!

I'm equally skeptical to hear a Christian loudly proclaim that they are never afraid, or unsure, or lonely. If we were never in fear, doubt or dread, why would we need a Savior? This Savior who said, "Come to Me, all

115

who are weary and heavy-laden [burdened], and I will give you rest." Jesus knows that there will be days when we don't have the courage that we need within ourselves. That's why He sent a comforter: His sweet Holy Spirit to minister peace to His children who sometimes have small faith and are prone to look at the storm around us rather than look to the "Storm Calmer." Thank You, Lord, for knowing us better than we know ourselves! Being sure of THAT fills me with confidence and strength.

Are you ever afraid? It's OK if you are. Jesus is bigger than any fear you have. He is more than enough for your need. Cast your cares on Him. He is able.

March 21, 2004

First Night in Houston

Well, we are in Houston, and all tucked in for our 100-plus day stay. It feels funny to know that I'm not gonna just be out of town for the weekend. I usually feel like I've left something important at home when I leave for only a weekend; you can only imagine how I felt knowing that I'm leaving home for four months! My head hurts to think about it!

I will keep you posted often as the process moves forward. Nothing really new today so I'll close and get to bed early.

Here we go!!!

March 23, 2004
Get Ready, Get Set...

Go! I started my morning out with a 3 hour PET scan. No, I didn't have Maggie (my Australian Shepherd) with me! (I know you people.) The PET scan is not a new veterinarian procedure. It's a spanking-new (for me) body scan. Much more detailed, I guess. Anyway, I made it fine. Dad had a few tests, but the fun stuff for him is coming in the next couple of days.

My daughter Chelsea is coming down for a few days over her spring break, and Deb and I are so looking forward to seeing her. She lights up my world.

I had a meeting with the social worker today.

It's a mandatory thing before a transplant. She taught me something that made me happy. She commented that I had a good attitude. She said, from talking to me, she could tell that my good attitude is because of my faith and not because I thought I would benefit from a good attitude. She said that my attitude came before the thoughts of benefiting from a good outlook. I'd never thought about that, but I guess it teaches us that trust is more important than expectation of reward.

Kind of deep thoughts, but I think they're worth exploring. Do we have good attitudes when troubles come because Oprah and Dr. Phil say that we'll do better and will have a better outcome if we have a positive mental attitude? OR, do we have faith and display a calm spirit because we have been told by our Father that He has our good in mind, and that liberates us to trust regardless of the outcome! I don't know if I'm ringing anybody else's bell here or not, but it's blessing me to think that we need to "be of good cheer," not because of what we expect out of it (that's a fringe benefit); but to "be of good cheer" because HE has overcome the world! With that in mind, it's hard NOT to have a smile on my face tonight!

March 29, 2004
Reality

I'm supposed to be asleep. I've been scolded once already, but I can't seem to "turn it off." Tomorrow is a big day. It starts a big week for me. Bright and early, I'll have a bone marrow aspiration, which is medical speak for "HURTS-QUITE-A-LOT." On Tuesday, I'm literally running from place to place for some last minute tests; and then, Wednesday, I'm getting fitted with a brand new Port. I guess this will be the "landmark of beginning" for me. Up until now, anytime I've had treatments, they were administered through an IV. You know, a temporary solution to the problem. In two or three days, the treatments were over, the IV came out, and I went along my merry way. Not this time.

The dreaded Port. A constant reminder of the disease. A constant reminder of my weakness in body. You know what I've decided? Bring it on! I am going to try to let it be a constant reminder of my total dependence on my Father. I know my heart – if left unfocused, I might fall back into the days of denial in which I've sometimes lived, those days when I felt as if I'd never had a diagnosis of cancer. Those days were fun. No doubt; much more care-free. But yet, not reality.

You see, I've got a disease that is tenacious. It wants to kill my body. It doesn't make sense. I mean, think about it. If the cancer has its way, I'll die, and so will it. In killing me, it kills itself. Not too smart. My treatment has, at times, put it into remission, but it never really left. This time, we are going for the throat, so to speak. With God's help, this time it will be totally eradicated. But not without a fight. Some tough days are ahead, tougher than I've ever faced. But I will face them. There will be posts to this journal when I will tell you in totally honest words that I don't feel like I'm making progress. I hope that's OK. I didn't start this journal to gloss over my experience. And please don't feel as if you have to comment to every post to cheer me up. I know that, many times, there are no words to say, so don't force a response. I understand. Treating this process like this will make the day even more sweet when I get to tell you that I'm coming home and feeling better.

I believe that day will come. Will it last? No. Even if I'm totally healed of CLL, it's temporary. It's unrealistic to think that, somehow, when it comes to death, an exception will be made in my case! I hope it's a long time off. I want to live and am fighting to do so. But my investment isn't in the permanence of this body. I'm gonna work hard to keep it in "showroom" condition. (My dad's a car dealer.) But it's a depreciating asset. Someday I'll trade it in for a new model! One with an eternal warranty! I don't know how many miles I'll have on me when I make that trade. I hope several more million; but, regardless, I only dread the process, not the transaction! I don't look forward to the crossing, but the instant I see Jesus, all thoughts of dread will leave me and I'll be home.

I hope that I don't alarm you with all this talk of "crossings" and such. I'm not hiding anything from you. I haven't received bad news that you don't know about. I'm just awake and thinking about the future. You know what? It's bright either way!

I gotta go – I just got scolded again for not being asleep. That woman's gonna push me too far one of these days!

April 1, 2004

The port install was no big deal. I'm slowly getting used to it. I just work at ignoring it.

My dad is hanging in there. The shots that he's taking before the marrow draw are making him feel pretty sick. He's trying not to let it show, but I know how bad he feels. The good news is that tomorrow is the big day for him. Hopefully, by this time tomorrow night, the extra cells that are making him feel sick will be in a freezer at M.D. Anderson waiting for me. I like to picture them nestled in that big freezer next to the butter beans and corn. I wonder what the nutritional label on the package would contain! I know – gross!

I'll let you know how Dad makes it.

By the way, several of you have made me aware of a twenty-four-hour prayer chain that is taking place for me on GaitherNet. I've been overwhelmed with that news. I know that I should never be surprised by the graciousness of God's children but, once again, I'm so appreciative. I hope one day to be able to make some grand statement of thanks, but until God gives me those words, I'll just say thanks so much for remembering me and my family in your prayers. You will never know until Heaven how much all you do means to me.

April 2, 2004
Collection Complete!

My dad made it through his tough day with flying colors! It was a long, stressful procedure, but it's finished. When we left the hospital today after nine hours, we were told to wait until tonight for news of whether there were enough cells collected during the procedure. If they didn't get enough, it would mean another long day tomorrow. But, as I said, the news was good, and today's mission was accomplished!

I'm so glad that it worked out this way. Now Dad's work is done and he can head home to Arkansas next week. Thanks to all of you for the extra prayers for him today. We truly felt them! All the Bennett bunch will sleep well tonight, and we hope the same for you.

April 8, 2004
Test Results

I'm lying in bed right now taking my first treatment. I guess this is day "minus thirteen." I will be admitted into the hospital next Wednesday.

I received my test results from the latest lymph node biopsy. The news wasn't what I'd hoped for. It seems that my leukemia has transformed into lymphoma. Apparently, it is a more aggressive form of cancer than CLL. This will not change the bone marrow transplant, except that I guess the stakes are higher now. Lymphoma, if not controlled quickly, can have a more serious outcome.

Of course, this is not the news that we wanted; but I promise you that my trust is intact. If I believed God could bring me through my first diagnosis nearly nine years ago, I have to believe that He will get me through this most recent trial.

I know many of you have been waiting to hear the results and will be upset with this report, but let me encourage you to trust God. I've been blessed too much to think that God has anything but my good in store either way.

I've heard the poetic expression, "My faith still holds." True, but at times like these when my vision is blurred by the bad news of today, it's not about me or my performance with my faith. It's about His power to "hold me."

I will be taking this treatment until at least 3 a.m. My shadow (Debbie) is right here taking every hit that I take, so pray for her strength tonight as well.

Still In His Grip!

April 9, 2004
With All Thy Mercies

I found this verse of a hymn. I thought of how perfect it is for me and certainly for many of you.

> When worn with sickness, oft hast Thou
> With health renewed my face
> And, when in sins and sorrows sunk
> Revived my soul with grace
>
> **Through every period of my life**
> **Thy goodness I'll pursue**
> **And, after death, in distant worlds**
> **The glorious theme renew**
>
> When nature fails, and day and night
> Divide Thy works no more
> My ever grateful heart, O Lord
> Thy mercy shall adore

What joy to know that sickness cannot separate the believer from the mercies of God. I didn't want the last post of my night to be the one that shared bad news. God brought me this far; His grace will lead me home!

April 10, 2004
Easter 2004

In the shadow of the Cross, our troubles cease to trouble. They don't disappear, but appear in their proper importance. Passing, temporary things.

This night before Easter all those years ago, Hell's party was in full swing. The Son still lay still in His borrowed tomb, His followers stunned and, seemingly, defeated; and the world not even knowing that Salvation's plan was about to be accomplished!

Then, in the early morning hours of that first Easter, the crowning moment of the greatest three days the world would know happened! His eyes opened, He folded the grave clothes, and vacated the tomb! All of Heaven knew that the manger in Bethlehem was a prelude to this moment; Heaven knew that the Cross, in all its hideous cruelty, was yet a prelude to this moment. Many babies were born in a manger; many men were killed on a cross... but this one was different. No other had defeated death and ripped out its stinger. No other had stolen its victory. But this man did. The world changed forever in those early morning hours. Satan knew that, now that he had lost the war, his only weapons would be confusion and lies. But those of us who know the Truth – the Truth embodied in Jesus – we know that death has lost and life has won!

This Easter, let me encourage you to turn your eyes upon Jesus. The things of earth really do grow strangely dim in the light of His glory and grace!

He is Risen... He is Risen Indeed!

April 14, 2004
Today's the Day

Just a quick post to let you know that I'll be admitted into the hospital today. Normally I'm doing my taxes on this day! Treatments start Thursday. I'll be in touch. Spirits are high... I'm ready to get this behind me.

April 15, 2004
Shut In

Well, my first night in the hospital is behind me! Through yet more scheduling problems, I ended up being admitted at about ten o'clock last night. Another little shock was I was put in the "Protected Environment" area. Masks, gloves, shoe booties – and that's just the clothing. I think another one of their weapons against infection must be COLD! I, who normally sleep on a bus that is about sixty-two degrees at night, had to ask for extra cover last night! But I'd sure rather sleep cool than stuffy, so that's not a complaint!

The staff here have been so wonderful. Even with the short time that I've been here, I feel very comfortable and totally relaxed about the level of care I'm getting.

They started my first treatment just a few minutes ago and, so far, there's been no reaction.

One day soon I'll post a new photo of myself after my "chemo haircut." The day before I was admitted, I went to a barber and said, "I'm gonna be in the hospital for thirty days and don't want to worry about big gobs of hair falling out." I did a pre-emptive strike. It's as short now as it was when I was a three-year-old! It sure doesn't take a lot of primping!

I'm all wired and connected to the internet, so keeping you updated should be easy.

April 16, 2004

Had a nine hour treatment today with no ill effects! The only problem I'm having is that I can't remember that I'm tethered to an IV! I have almost turned my cart many times today! I wish I had a video camera set up! More home movies!

April 17, 2004
Blessed

I've been going through my e-mail tonight. I thought that, during this time in the hospital, I would catch up on it all. I see now that it is a very optimistic dream! I may never get to answer each one of you, but please know I read them all and am so encouraged by your love. I've had a good day – a new round of chemo this morning with no reaction. I can tell that there are things going on in my body, but I've made it fine so far.

Quite honestly, I have had one negative side effect... I miss my kids. This being day 3 of 100 seems a little daunting to me when I'm thinking about them. We talk on the phone and IM each other, but I am missing my "couch time" with them. My prayer is for their well-being, and that this time will fly by in that regard.

Still, I feel so blessed. I don't want you to misunderstand – this is not some cakewalk that I'm in denial about. I don't like being in a small room with a window; but it's better than being in a small room without a window! I'm not enjoying this – big shock – but I'm still blessed. God has not moved away from me during this time. To the contrary, I feel a peace that I can't explain. I guess what I'm trying to say tonight is that this situation is a real and raw as they come, and yet I feel hopeful and convinced that God is here.

Little moments of faith and joy are the norm. My day is pretty mundane in the physical sense. I have chemo, and then I don't. My location doesn't change, but my perspective does. Debbie is here most of the day (until I send her home to rest), and we laugh sometimes; sometimes we read, and not a word is spoken. My joke today was to remind her of our vows made twenty-two years ago – the whole "in sickness and in health" thing. This little gem of humor was delivered as she realized that the rubber gloves she has to wear anytime she's in my room are causing an allergic reaction! And that the mask she has to wear all day long makes it hard to take a deep breath. She won't complain and won't be happy that I even mentioned it, but as I watched her reading today all decked out in mask and gloves, I realized how much I love her and how my life would not be complete without her in it. I tried to make her think that I was looking out the window, but I wasn't. I was looking at her and being glad she said yes twenty-two years ago. That's why I'm blessed.

Pretty mushy, I know. I didn't even know what I was gonna write tonight. I started to tell you about how I've learned to gargle the Star Spangled Banner, or how I am three-for-four in the "candy wrapper in the trashcan" three-point shoot-out, but somehow it evolved to my thankfulness.

All in all, it's been a good day.

April 20, 2004
Update from Debbie Bennett

This will be my first post on Roger's "Midnight Meditations," not because he is unable, but because I thought I would give my perspective on how things are going at this point. Right now, I am sitting in the hospital room with Roger, typing this in rubber gloves. Needless to say, I am having to do a lot of corrections! We have been in Houston for one month now, and Roger has been in the hospital for almost a week. He has been through several rounds of chemotherapy and anti-rejection drugs, preparing him for the transplant tomorrow. I asked the doctor today how long the actual transplant would take, and he said only about one hour. Roger and I looked at each other, thinking the same thing: "Such a short amount of time for such a big event." We have both learned a lot about our faith and values, during this week especially. The main thing is that, no matter how "prepared" you think you are for the really big challenges in your life, you still can't handle them without God. HE has had to be our strength when we didn't think we had any left.

In spite of the excellent care Roger has received here, being confined is not an easy thing for him. There are times that his "midnight" becomes very real to him. His physical and mental states have gone through the wringer, and there will be many more days ahead of the same. I can't say I am coming through totally unscathed, either. It is very hard to be away from our families for such a long time, but we are so thankful for phones and internet to keep in touch. I must confess that I am going through animal withdrawal, as well! Many of you who know us well know that we are pet-lovers deluxe, and leaving our menagerie behind in Tennessee was hard, too.

Now, having said all of that, I must now say how blessed we really feel through all of this. God keeps reminding us of the countless prayers going up on our behalf. We get so many cards and e-mails that it is impossible to count them all. We KNOW that God is still in control, and we can't wait to see how He works throughout this entire process. We are so grateful for the love and support our many friends and loved ones provide for us. Daily, we can look around here and see so many who are worse off than we are, and we often question how people get through this experience without the hope that God provides. We are also thankful for the opportunities we get to share with others how God is at work in our lives. They come in many unexpected forms, from technicians in test labs to random encounters in gift shop check-out lines. The next entry will be post-transplant, so look for a new and improved Roger to check in later! Until then, our prayer is that God will keep us in perfect peace while our minds are stayed on Him.

I am also in His very capable grip,
Debbie

April 21, 2004
Day Zero

Well, I never thought that I'd be writing a post tonight... But that shows what happens when I think!

My transplant happened today at about 1:00 p.m., and was completed around 1:30 p.m. I kept waiting for something else to happen when the technicians said, "That's it!" The actual process was surprisingly quick and painless. At the moment the stem cells entered my system, I felt a real strange sensation that lasted throughout the transplant; but it really didn't feel any different than the usual chemo side-effects. Thank God!

This will be short. My counts are at an all-time low for me (which is what the docs want) and I'm pretty tired. I just wanted to let you hear from me today. Didn't Debbie do a great job with last night's post? She's a great writer and always seems to capture the moment so well.

It seems a little strange to think about the fact that Deb and I have been in Houston for about a month and everything has been leading up to this day. Day Zero... Only 100 more to go!

"His grace has brought me safe thus far, and grace will lead me Home!"

April 23, 2004
Day 3

"So far, so good." That's what a nurse said to me earlier today. That pretty much sums it up. As my counts continue to fall, I feel weaker. However, given the circumstances, I'm doing great.

As you know, I will be in Houston for at least the next ninety-seven days. When I'm released from the hospital, that is really just the beginning of my time here. The doctors tell me that I will still come to the clinic every day for about four to six hours in the days after my release, but I can spend the rest of my time in our apartment. This will be a big milestone.

I continue to be blessed by Psalm 116. I've heard critics say that Christians are misguided people who use such scriptures as wishful thinking. That's sad to me. Their "wishful thinking" is our faith in the unseen, all-seeing God of the Bible. Faith. What a comforting word. Faith, that God is on the throne and His Word is a divine record of His great love to us and His plan for our eternity!

Read Psalm 116 when you can. I think that, instead of wishful thinking on David's part, you'll find the thoughts of a man who was convinced of God's power in his life.

April 23, 2004
Day 4

Still doing fine! Debbie and I had our lunch today over a John Wayne Movie. The Doc is pleased with my progress. His quote today was, "We want this part to be boring. Boring is good."

I was able to take a couple of walks around the Protected Environment Floor. They encourage us to walk as much as possible. It feels good to be moving around.

My goals for each day are to stay out of the bed as much as possible and to not turn on the TV until a certain time. Staying out of the bed is for my physical well-being. Keeping the TV off is for my emotional well-being. I can just about quote every "lawyer" and "go back to school" commercial I've seen. I don't know how it is in your town, but daytime TV is a wasteland! I guess I'm becoming a grumpy old man! Haha.

April 27, 2004
Day 6

Still feeling fine. The only side-effect that I'm having so far is fatigue. It's worse in the early morning and late afternoon, but it soon passes and I'm feeling better. The design that God used to create our bodies is incredible. Evidently, right now is a very critical time for me. My body is making its choice as to whether it will accept my dad's stem cells, but I don't feel a thing. It's amazing to think that this change is being made without any input from me at all. I like it that way. It's in God's hands and not mine!

I just hung up the phone with Scott Fowler. Legacy Five (Four) is on a ten-day trip out West. He calls me every night from the stage and I'm able to talk to the folks at the concert. It makes me feel great to hear the crowd and to say hello, but it also makes me miss being on stage with those guys. They are in Wyoming tonight and I'm sure they'll have a great time

One more thing. Thanks to all of you who fasted (or are fasting) in my behalf. What a great encouragement it is to me. I will never be able to say thanks enough. My attitude is bolstered when I think about the prayers and love you are sending my way.

Gotta run – medicine time. You'll hear from me again soon. I love you all.

April 28, 2004
Day 7

No news is good news. I'm still doing fine. One new development today is that I was given a shot of Neupogen. It's meant to encourage my marrow to produce white blood cells. I'm amazed at the precision of the treatment, but I'm even more amazed with the precision of the human body. God is the ultimate engineer.

Today's entry is short and boring but, as my doctor said, "In these cases, boring is good!"

April 29, 2004
Day 8 – Eternal Perspective

More treatments today. I'm having small blood pressure problems, but that seems to be an expected side effect. Legacy Five are in Fresno for the West Coast Quartet Convention. I really miss being out on the road with them. I'm so looking forward to crawling back on that bus.

The treatment I had today is a drug I've had before called Rituxan. It's an incredible compound that sniffs out abnormal cells and attacks them. It softens them up and allows the good cells to kill them. It makes me feel bad at first, but then I bounce right back. Amazing.

I'm feeling fine. Still blessed, still happy and still redeemed! Let me warn you against what I call "moment stealers." They are those things that come into our lives that distract us from the moments: those moments of glory, moments of quiet joy that light your life – moments that the enemy hates!! The enemy will stop at nothing to steal these moments. He wants you to focus on the little picture in your life. The sickness, the pain, the stress. Non-God moments. I've been the victim of this type of theft lately. I've let my circumstances dictate my happiness. I'll be honest: during moments of great sickness or stress, I find it hard to think about my happiness. This has a two-part effect. First, you just feel horrible with no relief in sight. Second, you feel guilty because in your heart you know better; you know that you should be spiritually mature enough to overcome this weakness.

I've learned something through these trials. You can take this to the bank. Here it is: Ride it out! As the song says, "It didn't come to stay; it came to pass." And it will. Our spirits are tied to our bodies, no way around it. The health of these "jars of clay" directly affects the way you

132

feel, but our future and spiritual health is NOT tied to this prison of flesh. My favorite scripture is 2 Corinthians 4:16-18:

> Therefore, we do not lose heart. Though outwardly we are wasting away, yet inwardly we are being renewed day by day. For our light and momentary troubles are achieving for us an eternal glory that far outweighs them all. So we fix our eyes not on what is seen, but what is unseen. For what is seen is temporary, but what is unseen is eternal.

What a hope we have! It's not a new thought, but my goal is not to let my "light and momentary troubles" steal my joy. If you go through a deep valley, don't feel guilty if you feel you're not up to the test. You're not, but He is! Your relief may not come when you feel it should. "Weeping may endure for the night, but joy's gonna come in the morning!" I'll meet you in the morning!

May 1, 2004
Day 10

I was on pins and needles waiting for the doctor today. I had convinced myself that I needed confirmation of the good news he told me yesterday. I got it! He told me today that my counts were indeed moving up, and he expected "the first part of next week" to release me from the hospital! I will then start my daily outpatient program. That will include a daily visit to M.D. Anderson that will last anywhere from four to six hours. These daily visits will monitor my counts to make sure that nothing is happening to undermine the transplant and infusion of any nutrients that I might be lacking. This could last quite a while, but at least I'll be out of the protected environment.

I know that many more tough days could be ahead, but I'm so thankful for this news. I hope that this means that my body is responding as hoped to the transplant and that I might be released completely sometime in late June or early July.

It's about time for my evening meds, so I'll close. Have a great day... I know I have!

May 3, 2004
Day 12 – Set Free (kinda)

Great news! I will be released from protected environment tomorrow! I'm very excited. I spent quite a bit of time today being briefed on the days ahead. I won't go into all the details, but I will have an appointment every day that will last four to six hours, at which time they will monitor my counts and give me IV medication. The thing to watch for now is Graft vs. Host disease. This is a disease that is sometimes a very serious problem in the days and months (and even years) following a transplant. I hope not to have to deal with it, but it is the reason that M.D. Anderson requires that you be in close proximity to the hospital for 100 days. I can deal with that. I am so thrilled with the prospect of freedom, however limited, that I will try not to grumble!

I can't tell you how pleased Debbie and I are with the care that I've received here at M.D. Anderson. I've been coming here for almost nine years and knew the folks here were tops; but three weeks in the P.E. ward just drove that point home to us in a big way. The doctors and nurses really take their calling seriously and they treat the patients with the utmost respect and sensitivity. (They could always be counted on for a laugh when I needed it, as well.) Thanks to all of them. I will never forget their kindness to me.

Gotta run. It's time for meds again, and then a walk around the floor. One hundred forty-four steps make a complete round, and I try to go five or six rounds per trip. I don't know why I threw in that factoid, but there you have it!

May 4, 2004
Day 13 – Home!

I'm out of the hospital and at the apartment. I can't tell you how good it felt to make the short ride from MDA to our apartment! It's a beautiful day here in Houston and I enjoyed every moment of the ride. No more hospital food! Deb had made me broasted chicken and a squash dish for lunch. It tasted like a five-star meal.

I start my outpatient treatment tomorrow morning at 9 a.m., and this will be my routine for the next ninety days or so. But that's no problem! I feel so liberated and cannot complain! Thank you all for your continued prayers. I totally feel that your prayers played a huge role in my recovery. I love you all and look forward to seeing you again at a Legacy Five concert ASAP.

God is good and I remain...
In His Grip!

May 6, 2004
Day 15 Post-Transplant

Still improving. All the indicators they watch are looking great. One side-effect I've had the last two nights has been insomnia. Right now it's 5 a.m. and I'm going strong. I have to leave for treatment in a couple of hours, so I've decided to stay up and shoot for a nap this afternoon. For some reason, my body said, "Get up," at 3 a.m. – and I said, "Sure!" I try to do what my body says – I don't want him going on strike just now.

I've been listening to one of my heroes and friends this morning: Kenny Hinson. Kenny made as big an impact on Southern Gospel Music as anyone ever has. He was an amazing singer and pastor, and my dear friend. We got to visit only a few times a year, but during those visits we had a blast. Kenny also fought cancer for many years. His battle was over on July 27, 1995. He never knew that I was waiting to hear my own diagnosis. At his funeral, my heart was so heavy for Kenny's family. A beautiful wife and two great kids had just lost a wonderful husband and dad. I couldn't help but wonder what path God would have for me in this illness. The next week, I was diagnosed with Leukemia; and over the last 8-plus years I've thought about the example Kenny was for me, though he never knew it. He continues to be an example for me and I miss him.

This morning, I'm particularly mindful of the gift of music. I've been listening to Hinson recordings that are thirty years old but still have the power and anointing to move me to tears. It's been like that for me all my life. God has used music to trigger blessings and anointing on me, second only to His Word. What a powerful force. Tomorrow night I'll probably be listening to someone else that has moved me. I'll share that with you as well. The Father inhabits the praise of His people. So praise away as often and as loud as you can! You might be alone when you start, but you won't be alone when you finish!

May 8, 2004
Day 17 – My Buzz Cut

Well, my chemo ended nearly a month ago, but yesterday I had my first major reaction! This one was no big deal. My hair started falling out in bunches. Every time I brushed it, it snowed hair. My pillow in the morning was a hair farm. Very gross. So, I decided to put an end to this foolishness. I went down to the MDA barbershop and said, "Give me the full Kojak!" (Ask your parents who Kojak is.)

I'm still doing great. Deb fixed me a huge meal of chicken and dumplins (note the Southern spelling), and I'm feeling like a short walk tonight. My counts are still fine. There have been some minor fluctuations here and there, but nothing unexpected. The doctors are watching me very closely, and God is keeping me very securely... In His Grip!

May 9, 2004 (forgotten journal entry)
Mother's Day

I am running a slight fever. I am supposed to go to the ER if it reaches 100.5 F. It got up to 100.2 F. PHEWWW! Just missed it... fingers crossed! My hair is still falling out. Tomorrow I have decided to shave it. That will be a first! The idea bothers me a little, but the grossness of seeing hair everywhere bothers me more.

Today is Mother's Day, and I miss mine. Chelsea made Deb the *best* card and emailed it to me to print for her. It had photos of Chelsea, Jordan, and all of the pets looking at a photo of Deb in the center. It was so cool!! Made Deb cry! She took it to the clinic with us, and showed everyone.

My hands are trembling a little. Side effects of the medication, or a harbinger of things to come? HA!

May 11, 2004
Day 20 – Cue Ball Bennett

I'm doing fine again today. My daily routine continues: labs at 8:00 a.m.; 9:00 a.m. starts the IV meds, and this takes about four to five hours. This is a very non-eventful process. My labs are holding up well. I'm having a few little side-effects that vary from fever and chills to fatigue. I never know when these little bonuses are going to show up, and I'm understanding more and more why I'm required to stay here for the 100 days. None of this is unexpected, and the doctors are still very positive about my recovery.

Here's another update for you. My hair continued to fall out at a fast rate, so I decided to just to REALLY buzz it. Yesterday I went back in time and got a hairstyle that I haven't had for forty-five years! Yep – I'm as bald as I was the day I was born (except for a little stubble)! I'm looking good! To be honest, it's a relief. I was so sick of being in a "hair storm" every time I scratched my head! I guess now I have a new sickness… It's called "*skinheadia!*"

On that serious note, I'll close. I wish I had something deep and profound to share today, but it is not to be.

We're told there's a time for everything; for me, today has been a time to laugh.

P.S.: Debbie wanted you to know that she thinks I'm very cute as a baldy.

May 13, 2004
The Battle for Joy

I've made a couple of observations about sickness that have intrigued me. After spending more time alone than I ever have before, I've also learned some things about myself. Some things I'm not crazy about. First, I've found that, after stealing your confidence in your health, sickness tries to steal your joy. I saw a trend developing very soon after I entered the hospital back in April. As my body started feeling the effects of the chemo and was knocked down to a low point, my joy started leaking. It was a slow leak, so slow that I didn't even notice it until I was already in big trouble. The night that I bottomed out was one I'll never forget. It was about midnight and my room was silent. Sleep had evaded me, and my thoughts were anything but joyful or confident. Physically, I was weak; but mentally and spiritually, I was weaker. I'm convinced that our enemy stalks us exactly in the way the Bible describes him, as a roaring lion. He hides in the bushes waiting for any sign of weakness, and then he strikes.

He didn't strike me physically. That had been accomplished for him by the chemo. He struck a more critical part of my being: my joy. My confidence. My hope. Every thought I turned toward Heaven fell back down to me as if it were made of brass. Every time I tried to "look on the bright side," I ended up imagining a very dark future. Then he threw his most effective dart at me: doubt. "You call yourself a Christian," he said. "What a hypocrite! You wrote, 'Don't Be Afraid,' and yet you are more afraid now than you've ever been. You wrote about Joy and yet now you are filled with despair. So much for your faith, Mr. Gospel Singer."

I feel sure that had I not been so fatigued in body this attack would have been useless. But it was not useless. It was very effective – so much so that I believed everything

140

Satan said. I tried everything I knew to pull out of it, all to no avail. I thought, "If I can just doze off, this will pass by morning." But the clock seemed to move in slow-motion. Sleep was nowhere near. I tried to lose myself in the Bible, but the words blurred to my eyes and I couldn't make sense of any of them. Every doubt I ever had sprang to my mind in terrible clarity. Doubts about my health that I hadn't thought of in years suddenly came back to life.

In real life, many stories don't have a happy ending. I know people who've had an assault on their faith and never recovered. Broken lives litter the landscape of this world. But this story does have a happy, even a joyful ending.

Suddenly, a thought sprang to my mind. Paul and Silas were in jail. It was certainly a time of testing for them. The Lord brought to my mind that, even in their midnight hour, they didn't despair. They sang! It began to dawn in my heart that their singing was not a fluke or a "throwaway" gesture. They sang, and that became their weapon. Jail bars broke and they were set free. At that moment, I knew that "singing at midnight" was no metaphor. It was a literal description of what these two men used to bring their joy!

So, in my small, dark, lonely hospital room, I began to sing. Not in my heart, but with my weak voice I sang.

"Oh, what peace we often forfeit; Oh, what needless pain we bear, All because we do not carry Everything to God in Prayer."

"...You ask me how I know He lives; He lives within my heart!"

One after another, these old songs came to my memory, and I sang them to my empty room. It wasn't a great performance from a musical standpoint. In fact, it was pretty trembly and off-pitch, but it may have been the most powerful blessing I've received in my life. I had an audience of three – Father, Son and Holy Spirit – but it felt like the whole world was listening. This is the truth if ever I spoke it: the battle turned THEN AND THERE! I sang for half an hour, cried and thanked God for the victory, then dozed off and slept like a baby. My joy was waiting for me the next morning when I awoke. The enemy was nowhere to be seen. A sense of total confidence was in the room. I had found a weapon of great power: Praise. If Paul and Silas had sung in the darkness of their prison, so could I. From the bottom of my heart I tell you, it is real and Satan hates it.

Now, let me give you both sides. I'm not saying that one night of singing will scare your troubles away. You may have to sing every day of your life until you get to Heaven. But wouldn't that be great? Christians struggling through an unfriendly world with a song on their lips is, I think, exactly what our Father had in mind.

So the lesson for today is this: Sing! Not just anything; sing the Gospel. Paul and Silas knew the secret and passed it on to us. I'm telling you from firsthand experience that, in my deepest valley yet, it worked. It transported me instantly to a place of peace, in the very presence of the Father. My heart was strengthened and my faith increased. Thank God for the song of the redeemed.

Into His Presence with Singing!

May 16, 2004
Day 25 – Time Flies

I've had a quiet weekend. Our daughter, Chelsea, came down for a short visit, and that has been good medicine for Deb and me. My counts were stable enough that the doctors gave me the freedom of a weekend with no hospital visits. They sent us home with several bags of IV meds and a pump to infuse them with, and I've made it fine. Thanks to all of you for your prayers.

I can't believe that this is day twenty-five post-transplant! In some ways time has crawled by; but in most ways it has flown by. I'm very much aware of God's blessings concerning this whole process. I know that my weakness will continue as long as it takes for my body to heal. I have no idea what waits for me tomorrow, but THIS is the day the Lord has made! I'm trying not to borrow worries from tomorrow or stagnate worrying about the past. I'm asking God to help me live in the moment. To enjoy the blessings of the present instead of carefully putting them on the shelf to be brought out sometime in the future. I want to live, love, and laugh in the NOW!

May 17, 2004
Day 26

The doctor's report today was still great. My counts have dropped a little, but that is to be expected. I feel fine. I'm still looking good with a few pitiful little hairs trying to poke their way out of my cue ball head. They remind me of our optimistic flowers in Tennessee that always bravely poke their heads out in April – only to be slammed down by a late frost! I don't know what to expect for these brave few, but I'm gonna nurture them. Baby shampoo and Sea Breeze – that's the magic potion, they tell me.

My, how the subject matter changes in these posts. Oh well, better to laugh than cry!

Concerning my "sprigs," I say, "Come on, little fellas. The worst that will happen is you'll end up getting to know the business end of my electric razor!"

By the way, for those of you who asked: Debbie did buy me a bag of Tootsie Roll Pops to complete the Kojak look. Thanks for your attention to detail! "Who loves you, Baby?" (That's a Kojak quote for you real young'uns, like my daughter, who asked Deb, "Mom, who is Kojak?")

Feeling old, but happy to be feeling.

May 19, 2004
Lessons from a Mask

One of my restrictions when going out into public is my mask. You know, the little cloth mask that surgeons wear. My immune system is very weak, and a simple cold bug in my system would be very dangerous. Thus, I look like a doctor in the operating room every time I venture outside. This is really no big deal at all. It is a simple precaution that gives me freedom and protection. Well worth the inconvenience.

But I've learned a lesson from the mask. Unexpectedly, I've found that I feel self-conscious when I wear it. When I walk into a restaurant or any other public place, I get stares. The adults make it very brief. They are shocked to see this grown man wearing a doctor's mask. Everyone from the security guards to the clerks gives me a second or third look. The kids are the funniest. They don't disguise their curiosity at all. Their eyes get big and some even point me out to other kids. I must admit that I do feel a little conspicuous. The stares get fewer the closer I am to the hospital – everyone in that world sees it every day, and it's not unusual at all. But out in the "real world," I'm an oddity.

It really doesn't bother me except for the momentary discomfort of being noticed. The lesson I've learned is that there are so many people that experience this everyday who can't solve the problem by taking off their masks – countless people who have birth defects or injuries that have scarred them for life. People who are WELL aware of their differences, but being aware of it doesn't make it possible to change it. They have to endure the stares, laughter and cruel words. My heart goes out to them now in a way that it didn't before. This is just another one of those times for me when I'm reminded again of the golden rule. I've always been soft-hearted toward any underdog, but now I've had a small, small taste of what being different feels like. My "abnormality" is a simple, small, temporary thing.

"Lord, help me to be more aware of hurting people who endure a lifetime of being different, people who endure the stares every day and do it with dignity. Help me to respond to them with the same dignity."

May 22, 2004
Day 30 – A Milestone for Me

What a day. This is day thirty post-transplant, and I'm very blessed to be so far along in my recovery. If I had thought that this day would be spent in quiet reflection and rest, I would have been wrong. This is not only a milestone in my eyes, but one in my medical team's eyes as well, and they had plans for me.

This is the day for all the re-testing. My day started at 6:45 a.m., and I finished at the hospital at about 6:45 p.m. The tests included, but were not limited to (I've been watching too much Court TV – picking up the legal lingo): Labs, X-rays, a two hour PET scan and a three hour CT scan. The CT scan itself only lasted ten minutes. It was the preparation that took almost three hours. But it's over! I got to engage in one of my new fun activities: listening to other patients talk about their stories. I find this becomes more interesting to me as time passes. A lady in one of the "holding areas" today overheard me talking about my transplant, and she very quietly asked me some questions. Turns out she's going in for the same procedure next week and was very (and understandably) nervous. We talked for about ten minutes, and both of us felt better afterwards.

That's about it. I won't have any results until sometime next week. I expect good news. I'm feeling just about the same as the last few days. I'm not quite ready to run a race yet, but feel I'm improving daily.

I've got the weekend off so I'm gonna sleep 'til supper tomorrow.

May 24, 2004
Test Results

I had a good day today. As I've told you before, one of the hardest parts of this ordeal for me is the waiting. Most cancer patients will say the same. Knowing that the results will be in any day and not knowing the outcome is hard. Today, however, I was so pleased with the doctor's visit. Only one test result was in, but it was a big one for me. The PET scan that originally had shown disease (lymphoma) in my body came back clear. The lymph nodes that were swollen a month and a half ago looked fine as of Friday! I know there are a lot of tests yet to be read, but the good news really made me feel great!

Thanks for your prayers for so long... I feel today many of them were answered.

May 28, 2004
My Mini Vacation Is Over

Well, my two-day vacation is over. I'll make my familiar trip to the clinic tomorrow for labs and medication. I've really enjoyed this little break. Tests are still looking good. The lymph nodes that were enlarged are shrinking, and I'm showing signs of the donor cells grafting nicely into my system.

Speaking of donor cells, I'm thrilled to tell you that my dad is doing just great! He's working in his yard and expecting some HUGE tomato and pepper plants from his little garden. He says to tell you thanks again for all your prayers and support.

This is a big weekend for Legacy Five. They'll be celebrating our very first "Homecoming" called Celebration 2004 this weekend at the Gaylord Opryland Hotel in Nashville. We're expecting almost 3,000 people, and the whole event is going to be incredible.

May 30, 2004
A Surprise for Everyone!

I just got back to the apartment after a whirlwind surprise trip to Nashville! I need to go back to the beginning to explain.

One of the most "bummer" things about the schedule of this bone marrow transplant was that I would not be able to attend Legacy Five's first homecoming. We called the weekend "Celebration 2004." We started planning it last year, and the response was unbelievable. We kept selling out the facilities at the Gaylord Opryland Hotel. We had to keep expanding the ballroom to accommodate the crowd. We maxed out the space at 3,000 people and quickly filled it up. Anyway, I was extremely disappointed to miss it.

I had secretly kept the hope alive that I would progress so well that my doctor would allow me to make the quick trip and come home as soon as the Sunday morning service was complete. So on Monday, May 24, during my visit with Dr. Khouri, I popped the question. I said, "Dr Khouri, I have a question." I was cringing inside as I nervously continued. "If I double-masked and double-gloved, avoided all close contact with people, could I make a quick trip to Nashville for the weekend?" He looked at my lab results for a minute and said, "Will your wife be with you at all times?" "Yes," I answered. He asked, "Will you keep to yourself as much as possible?" Again: "Yes." He said, "OK, you can go. IF your labs remain stable on Friday." I sweated it out until Friday. We bought the plane tickets just in case, alerted Scott Fowler to the possibility, and waited. Friday morning rolled around and we took our packed bags to the hospital for my check-up. I was so nervous – but the news was good! We headed for the airport and got on the Nashville flight! I was so thrilled.

That night I was waiting back stage when Scott made a fake phone call to me in Houston. I couldn't resist – I told him that I had a bad signal, and said, "Let me walk to a better place." That place was the stage. So, for the first time in over two months, I walked on stage with Legacy Five! What a night. It felt so good and was the best medicine I've had in a long time.

I won't mislead you – it was a grueling weekend for me, and I'm beat. BUT, I would not have traded the experience for anything. I got to spend some great time with my kids. I was able to personally speak to 3,000 of our best friends and thank them for all the prayers and support. I feel like a new man!

May 31, 2004
Happy Memorial Day

I'm writing this post with a thankful heart. I'm thankful for all the men and women who have dedicated their lives to serve our country in the military. Many have served, many have died; ALL deserve our gratitude.

My dad's older brother was killed in World War II. He was twenty years old with his entire life ahead of him, but it was lost in a fight against the enemies of liberty. He didn't want to die on a foreign battlefield. It was not on his list of things to do, but he fought anyway. His letters to my grandmother hinted that he knew he would not come home alive. Our family is still affected today by his loss. Obviously, I never met him, but I feel pride when I think about his sacrifice. Imagine all the stories of families across America who have lost loved ones in the various wars in which we have fought. Those stories would fill libraries to the point of bursting.

So, on this day set aside to honor those who gave the ultimate sacrifice for freedom, I say thank you. Thank you for believing in the idea of freedom enough to defend it to the death. America salutes you and will never forget.

June 6, 2004
Day 46 Update

I had lost count of how many days I am post-transplant. I was shocked when I counted it up. Forty-six days! In some ways it seems like a lot more than that, and in other ways it's flying by. I saw my doctor today and he's just real upbeat about the response of my system to the transplant. The DNA test that I had on day fourteen showed that 35% of my cells belong to my dad. Great news. This tells us that my old cells are fighting, but seem to be losing ground against my new, healthy cells. Way to go, Dad! My bone marrow test from last week indicates that the disease is in retreat on that front as well!

To top off all this good news with my body, I got some good news for my soul yesterday. Our daughter, Chelsea, came down for a week to visit with Deb and me. Our son, Jordan, will arrive on Sunday for a few days as well. It just keeps getting better!

I'm off to bed. One word of encouragement to you: TRUST! Sometimes during this valley of mine I've tried so hard to "grab the wheel," so to speak, and do the driving myself – always with terrible results. I've found that God is well aware of my needs and has both hands on the wheel. His vision reaches much farther down the road than mine ever could. So I'm letting go. This is not something that happens overnight. After a lifetime of trying to be the designated driver, it's difficult to let go; but time after time He has proven that He is a much more experienced driver than I. He knows the road of my life like the back of His hand, so I've determined to sit back and enjoy the trip!

June 10, 2004
Making Memories

A friend sent me an e-mail this morning that said, "I hope you're enjoying making memories with your kids." I thought about that phrase. Yes, I am enjoying it. In fact, it's my favorite thing to do. Making memories... every vacation, every outing, all of them are meant not to just fill up time, but to make memories. Those are the most prized possessions that I have. Possessions will come and go; unfortunately, even some friendships are not permanent. But when we get out the old photos, or sit around and talk about our time together, that's when I feel the most wealthy. My condition right now doesn't allow me to do much that involves physical activity. As well as I'm doing health-wise, it's on a different scale than any other time in my life. I'm very weak and thus very limited as far as "fun stuff" is concerned. But I'm not limited in reliving memories and making new ones.

My son reminded me of a memory of his that happened a few years ago. It was during another "weak" time with my immune system. I had to wear a mask in public. We were walking into a movie and some "smart" kid, about eighteen, looked at me and said, "What's up, Jesse James?" I had forgotten the incident, but Jordan hadn't. He remembered me making some kind of equally "smart" comeback and putting the kid in his place. I don't have a clue what I said, but Jordan is still laughing about it. That's why it's good to make memories with your kids

– they can remind you of them in a few years when you'll do well to remember your ATM code!

Have a great weekend, and try to make some memories.

I don't go back to the Dr. until tomorrow. I'll let you know if there is any change.

June 13, 2004
An Overdue Thank You

To all of you who attended Celebration 2004, I want to say thanks so much for your kind words and assurance of your prayers. Being able to attend on such short notice was very exciting, but nothing approaches the thrill I got in my spirit when I stepped on stage during Scott Fowler's "phone call!" All weekend long, if I was tired (and I was), I knew if I could just make it to the platform, I'd be all right. Most Gospel singers who've sung for many years will tell you the same story. Some call it adrenaline; those of us who've experienced it call it anointing. We serve an on-time God! Thanks to the Lord for that.

We had a great time at Celebration, but it was over all too quickly. We made a quick trip back to Houston, and now I'm back in the saddle of treatments and waiting! But what medicine it was for our souls that Deb and I got to go home for even two and a half days. You all looked great! I'm counting the days until NEXT Celebration, in 2005! It was successful beyond our dreams! The Opryland Hotel, the people, the food, NOT HAVING TO DRIVE ANYWHERE THE WHOLE WEEKEND! That was one of my favorite parts.

June 13, 2004
An Encouraging Day

I had a good day today. Debbie and I were invited to "Bone Marrow Transplant Survivor Day" at M.D. Anderson. This was an event where many survivors gathered to share their stories. I gotta tell you, I needed it. I've been a little beat the last couple of days, and when it came time to get ready this morning I almost decided not to go. Boy, I'm glad I went.

The first person I met was a lady who had her transplant thirteen years ago. I thought she might be in a small segment of people who have been through a BMT, but I was wrong. I met many ten-, twelve-, and even a couple of twenty-year-plus patients! I proudly wore my little badge that proclaimed me to be a fifty-two day survivor and secretly dreamed of the day that I could attend another such meeting as a twenty-year survivor.

One of the pioneering doctors in bone marrow transplants was there. He shared just how far they've progressed in the treatment. The story was far less positive only a few years ago, but recent advances in stem cell transplants have dramatically improved the patients' chances of long term survival.

As I said, I enjoyed the day very much. There were people of all age groups and social backgrounds. Whatever the state – rich or poor, young or old – I saw a room full of fighters, and it encouraged me to continue to do the same.

June 18, 2004
Silence

There is an old song from my young days called "The Sound of Silence." I never cared for it. For my Southern Gospel taste, it was too slow and glum. But tonight as I was waiting on the Lord to impress me with a thought to share, I became aware of the sound of silence. I remember how terrible it felt for me a few short weeks ago when I cried out to Heaven and was greeted with that sound. What a difference in the feeling that I have tonight. Instead of hearing the sound of emptiness, tonight I am simply waiting expectantly, trying to "be still and know!" I think we try so hard at times to always have something to say or think, that we often miss the message that God is trying to send.

I sit in this room tonight feeling somewhat that I'm in a "holding pattern." The drama of the actual transplant is past. I'm in a routine of treatment and tests that don't reveal any concrete answers. I'm told to be patient. That, "In time, the results will be revealed." I've found that this is a spiritually dangerous time for me. It is very typical of our enemy to attack us during the lull in the battle. It's dangerous for me because it is very mundane. It's sometimes easy to forget that I'm still in a battle for my life; easy to get lulled into a false sense of well-being and forget to cast my cares on the Father. As usual, everything that Satan throws against us is a cheap impersonation of what God's best is for us. Satan wants us in a false sense of well being; the Father promises an eternal, true sense of wholeness. Satan wants us to feel that we need to fill our lives with entertainment in order to fill the void; our Father wants to fill our life with abundance that never ceases to satisfy.

You may not feel that you are living an "abundant" life right now. You may be bored with the mundane routines that you feel make up your life. You may be trying desperately to fill up the silence with trivial, material things. I've been there, and recently. I think that my job tonight is to remind you to embrace the silent part of your day. Use it, not to write a "to do" list, but to listen for His still, small voice. He wants so much to communicate with you, to actually commune with you, to whisper into the silence, "I love you and I have a plan for you."

In the room I'm in at this writing, I physically hear the sound of a small clock on our bookcase and our neighbor's A/C unit humming outside. But with my spiritual senses, I'm listening closely for the voice of my heavenly Father. I'm excited to hear what He has to say.

Let me encourage you to let the silence in.

June 20, 2004
Shared Blessings from Debbie

Happy Father's Day to all of you wonderful Dads out there! This is Debbie again, writing an entry to salute my father, my father-in-law, and my husband for being such great examples of fatherhood.

It has been a while since I wrote in this journal, and I just wanted to share some more of my feelings with you. Every day I continue to be amazed at God's wonderful grace. It still just overwhelms me when I think of all His goodness. All I have to do is look around me to know how blessed I am. We may not say it often, but I do need to tell all of you Ropeholders and Benefit Fund contributors how God has used you to bless the Bennetts' lives.

A typical day for us here in Houston is like this: We wake up, eat a little breakfast, then head off to M.D. Anderson for lab work and IV infusions. In the afternoon,

155

we come back to the apartment, eat some lunch and rest, watch some television, read, and maybe take a walk after dinner if we can muster up the energy (!). Night time is similarly full of activity: some more TV, a little straightening up, laundry, and off to bed so we can start over again the next day.

Now, if I left it like that, you might wonder where all of the blessings come in, so I will expound. Every day when I wake up, I rise in a beautiful, well-furnished, comfortable, cool, safe apartment that is possible to stay in due to the generous contributions of many faithful friends. Breakfast is fixed in our own kitchen, and eaten in our pajamas, if we want to, instead of having to order room service, or travel out to find something each day. We were able to bring our own car to Houston, so we walk out and drive a vehicle that is familiar and safe, to park in a well-monitored, out-of-the-weather garage while we are at the clinic.

Roger's nurses and technicians are truly a blessing. God seems to have placed just the right ones in our lives. We talk about spiritual things while they attend to his physical needs. Daily we can share the many miracles in our lives with someone else. We meet many people in the same situation as we are, and we get to share advice, laughter, and needs with each other. I am even able to leave him for a while occasionally to go down and donate platelets for other patients.

We live near several great grocery stores, so I can shop for whatever we need, and come home to my own kitchen and cook it, or lay in supplies for quick snacks. I use my kitchen often to bake for the nurses and some other patients we have made friends with who don't have access to kitchen facilities. Our laundry room is in our apartment, so I don't have to leave Roger for several hours and look up a Laundromat in an area that might not be so safe. We have entertainment with us – we brought plenty of books that we hadn't yet gotten around to reading, and many videos and CDs. And, of course, we have internet access here in the apartment, so we can keep in touch with all of you and read the wonderful comments you post back to us on the web journal.

By the time we are ready for bed again at night, in a comfortable bed in a quiet neighborhood, we are so full of blessings that it is hard not to relive each day's goodness while falling asleep.

Again, we are so thankful for all of the prayers and the donations that have made this possible. I am ever conscious of the fact that you all are used of God, and ever mindful of the ones who don't have the same advantages. There are times of guilt over this, but God reminds me that He had this all planned, so we are able to minister to others without the stresses and burdens that would be here without this help. Many people at M.D. Anderson now possess Legacy Five and Roger Bennett CDs.

I hope I have not rattled on, but I just feel so blessed today, and I needed to share it with you! God bless each one of you, and if you need confirmation that your prayers are working, I can testify that they are. Roger is doing so much better than anyone had expected, and I have to say that he is being a model patient as well. We are enjoying our time together (the most we have had in our twenty-two and a half years of marriage), and we are still in love, so I am pretty sure we have made it through okay! Keep those prayers coming, and remember to say some extra ones for the people we meet here whom we are able to share with.

I'd like to leave you with a verse that has more meaning to me than it used to. Second Corinthians 12:10 says: "Therefore I take pleasure in infirmities, in reproaches, in necessities, in persecutions, in distresses for Christ's sake: for when I am weak, then am I strong." I pray that I may be a strong example of Christ's love to those around me.

Debbie Bennett

June 24, 2004
Misc. Catch-ups

I am fighting my ever-present battle with insomnia. I thought I had enough artillery to win the fight tonight, but it seems I've been bushwhacked again: 4 a.m. and I'm up for the day. I've been sitting on this couch since 2 a.m. hoping for the sandman to pay me a visit. I've used the time to work on the Legacy Five website.

I've got surgery tomorrow to remove a few moles on the head. I hope they don't get too close that massive brain in there – I'd hate to damage the blade on their "brain crusher tool."

My dad is down for a visit. He'll be here until Sunday, so we'll have a good time just being together.

Well, I just saw Captain Kangaroo run up the wall of our living room. He got to the ceiling, turned, winked at me, and said good night. In case you're not up on sleeplessness, seeing a beloved children's TV star on your wall in black and white is a big sign that it's time to try again for the bed!

One time when I stayed up too late and was groggy from the meds I'm on, I and went on *eBay*. I bought some great stuff. If I forget to write about it later, your hint is, the story has to do with my bidding strategy. You'll end up laughing at me some more! Oh well, you won't laugh any harder than Debbie or I did! It's a classic story in our family. Well, I'm getting that eBay fever so I'm off to bed.

June 28, 2004
Day 68 Report

I've taken a break during the last few days to visit with my dad and thought I'd get back to posting by giving you all an update.

First of all, my dad is doing great. He's feeling very well and is staying very busy around his house.

I've had a couple of bits of good news in the past few days:

1. My hospital visits have been reduced to twice a week. I still have treatments every day, but five days a week I have them at the apartment.
2. The MRI that I had on my brain last week came back clear! (I'll finish the joke for you: they didn't find one!)
3. The time is passing quickly. I'm at day 68 of 100. If all goes well, I'll be released in a little over a month.
4. I got to join L5 at their appearance in Houston last weekend. I had a great time and, as usual, it was great medicine for me. I can't wait to get back to work.

Debbie is doing great. She's been holding things together. I don't know what I would do without her.

I hope all is well with you and your loved ones. I pray God's blessings on each of you.

July 3, 2004
Without God

> "Without God, there is no virtue because
> there is no prompting of the conscience.
> Without God, there is a coarsening of the
> society; without God, democracy will not
> and cannot long endure... If we ever forget
> that we are One Nation Under God, then
> we will be a Nation gone under." - Ronald
> Reagan, 1984

During my time in Gospel Music, I've had the privilege to travel to many different places in the world. I've seen some beautiful sights, experienced meeting some beautiful people, and made memories that will last forever. But no matter how impressed I am with the trip, there is always a part of me that gets so excited to come home. You see, all it takes to remind me how much I love this country is to either travel abroad or, in these days, watch the news. It's so true that we have many problems in America, but it is still the most amazing country in the world. I make no apologies; I am a patriot and am thankful to God for His blessings upon our land.

Our founding fathers risked it all to help bring forth this nation. In those days, to take the stand that they took didn't get you featured on TV or the newspapers; it got you an appointment at the end of a rope. I wonder if I would have had the courage to be a part of that group. I've been reading about the consequences that many of the signers of our Declaration of Independence paid for their signatures on that document. Some say that these are "old wives' tales," or simply "legends" without a grain of truth. However, we know that the Revolutionary War is not a "legend." Many men and women gave all they had to ensure our independence, and I say thank God for them.

May we never so lose our way as a nation that we become anything but grateful to our Sovereign God for giving us this blessed land.

God Bless America!

July 9, 2004
An Ongoing Project

One of the projects that Debbie brought to our temporary home here in Houston is our collection of photos assembled during our twenty-three year marriage. I know that the average family has a ton of photos around the house; but, since my big lifelong hobby has been photography, our file cabinets are over flowing. So my Snookums got it in her head to transport twenty-three years of photos to Houston to hopefully to get them in safe albums and into some kind of order.

We are having a blast, more fun than should be allowed. Many of these family shots are sweet, some are funny, and some would make you wonder why you were ever friends with me at all!

I'm doing great. I'm in the hospital tomorrow for the last tests of the week. I'm closing in on the finishing-up phase! Thank God.

He has used you folks to lift me up in so many ways; I can't wait to get back on the road to lift you up once again!

Debbie and I send our love.

One last thing – a lot of e-mails are coming in demanding that I publish a book out of my journal so that everyone can get a glimpse into this valley that I've gone through. At first, I was against it. But, if anything, the requests are growing at a tremendous rate. So, while I can't say for sure at this time, I'll just say: the wheels are turning and some ground work is on the drawing board. Having said that, my lips are sealed (maybe).

July 11, 2004
Day 81

Well, it's now day eighty-one. Nineteen more days until the big 100. In some ways, it has been the longest time for us; and, in others, it has flown by. We came to Houston thirty days before the transplant, so really this makes 111 total days away from home. I know you already know all of this, but it does me good to look back and see how far Deb and I have come.

I am feeling fine and my spirits are high. I've been meditating on the good things God has done for me during this ordeal. If I had to pick one thing that has been the most encouraging for me, I would say it's been getting to know some of the other BMT patients. I've spent so much time talking with them in the various waiting rooms, and I always come away blessed. I've found some to be in better shape than I, and some in worse shape; but all have been a real encouragement to me. They are truly men and women that know the meaning of being refined by the fire. I thank God for each of them. It will be hard for Deb and me to leave our new friends behind.

If things go as planned, in about nine days I will begin the "re-screening" process. This means I have to take all the tests over again to see how well my body has accepted my dad's cells. I expect to get good news.

Thanks again for your faithful prayers.

July 14, 2004
Quick Update

I just wanted to let you know that I'm doing well, but some of my counts are fluctuating and I had to have some shots this week that have left me a little washed out. I'm really still doing great and feel fine. Those BMT survivors out there know exactly what I'm talking about! You feel fine until you try to do some activities – then your body says, "Not so fast, Tubby!"

The days are quickly passing! I'll have more for you soon. Stay cool and drink plenty of fluids! (See, I'm learning this doctor stuff pretty well.)

July 21, 2004
My Works or His?

It's been a few days since my last post. I wanted to let you know why. I'm at day ninety-one, and the last battery of tests has started. I've been running around like crazy for the last few days! Friday, July 23, should be the day that I hear about the schedule for my release! Needless to say, Debbie and I are very excited to hear the news. We've now been in Houston for 121 days and, while we have very much enjoyed the city and the people of Houston, we look forward to being home again soon.

It seems impossible that so much time has passed since I first knew that a Bone Marrow Transplant was in my future. We arrived in Houston on March 21 of this year, and August 1 is only days away. As I look back with the 20/20 vision that hindsight gives, I'm so blessed to see how God's faithfulness and leading have brought me through this experience. I'm reminded of the fact that God doesn't promise to take us out of our storms, but to be present in the MIDST of the storm.

I never expected to be plucked out of this valley. I knew that God was able to do so, but when it became evident that it was His will for me to experience this trial, I felt sure that He would walk me through it. I will admit that sometimes my faith was weak. In the hard days of the transplant, I couldn't always see how it would be for my good, but it always was. What I learned is that God's provision, His protection, is not based at all on my performance. It wasn't about anything that I do; it was about everything that He did. I came to realize that my relationship with God was in no way based on my being able to do anything. If that were so, it would make me an equal partner with God. Now, I don't know a lot, but I do know this: His work on the Cross is the only work that will save and sustain me. My works could never rise to that level. My hope for Heaven is based on His work, not mine! So, with the confidence that my Creator is in control, I can let go of the wheel and let Him do the driving!

I encourage you to do the same. God only asks us to believe and accept Him, to call upon the name of Jesus and be saved. Then our works are the expression of our love and thankfulness to Him for His work on Calvary.

July 24, 2004
Waiting

> "Waiting is a skill that grows easier to exercise when practiced often."

You are probably searching your memory, wondering where you heard that little nugget before. "Was it Ben

Franklin? Maybe Abe Lincoln." Let me ease your mind – I made it up. Oh, it's true; and I'm sure it's unoriginal, but I think it's one of the most profound utterances that I've had today. (But the day's not over.) Waiting is just a state that Debbie and I have learned to live in. I've spent the last 123 days for the most part within a three mile radius of the hospital. There have been days that we were so excited to hear some positive news that we actually got to the hospital early so we could hear it sooner. We did this enough days, only to be told that certain test results would be a few days late, that we naturally began to learn the skill of waiting.

What we learned is not in the waiting, but in the attitude of waiting. See, the bottom line is that everyone everywhere has to wait. That will not change. Getting bent out of shape while you wait is futile. Anger will not change the fact that the test won't be back for three weeks. A wise friend of mine once told me that life will throw punches to everyone; the secret is to learn to roll with the punches. I had heard that before but, when I actually thought about it, it made perfect sense. The knock-out punch is on the way. There is no way the intended target can stop it. He (or she) has two choices: 1. Stand firmly and take it on the chin; or, 2. Roll with the punch. Number one pretty much guarantees some damage. Number two cancels out, to some extent, the power of the punch, and extends the fight.

You may be wondering what all this talk of waiting has to do with anything. Great question. Here's the answer. During my 123 days here, I've spent time waiting in one form or the other. But, thankfully, Deb and I have learned to wait *pleasantly*. I'll admit that, in my early days of this odyssey, frustration with waiting cost me some sleep and earned me a sick stomach. I'm not sure when it happened, but the day came that we decided to occupy our time with something that we enjoyed while waiting.

For her, it might be a trip to the fabric store to browse through the crafts (or whatever they have in a fabric store!); for me, a bookstore or computer shop. We might cap it off with a whirlwind swing through our favorite: Wal-Mart! Whatever we chose, our time was occupied in a positive way (at least for us – it doesn't take a lot to entertain some people), and we found that it passed quickly and without much damage.

What I've just described will work for anyone anywhere. I don't have to know anything about you to dispense this advice. It's a simple but powerful truth that works universally. But, as with any situation in life, if we know Jesus, there is a spiritual version that is far deeper and far more powerful.

> *But they that wait upon the LORD shall renew their strength; they shall mount up with wings as eagles; they shall run, and not be weary; and they shall walk, and not faint. – Isaiah 40:31*

I found in a very personal way that waiting upon the Lord is a sure way to weather any storm. With the promise of renewed strength and supernatural energy, how can I go wrong? I'm gonna see the world from an eagle's point of view! Waiting is definitely worth it!

The reason I'm writing about waiting is that I'm having to practice what I'm preaching (so to speak) right now. Yesterday, July 23, was to be a big day for me. I expected to get my walking papers. I thought that I would leave the hospital with the news that I only had one more week to go. As with every situation, it wasn't that black and white. I may get released next Friday (July 29), but I may not. There are a few tests that we don't have the results for yet, and my doctor says, "We'll have to wait and see." So we fell into our "waiting routine." Only this time, before we went out for fabric, books, or Wal-Mart, we reminded ourselves that God has brought us safe through this trial and it will soon be behind us. What's a few more days? It will give our waiting renewed strength and a view from eagles' wings!

Thank You, Lord, for teaching me the value of waiting.

July 27, 2004
Changes

This is Debbie writing again. I am sure that Roger has told you we have been involved in a project while here in Houston, sorting through many years' worth of photographs. We have had many laughs, I can assure you of that! Most of them were at our own expense ("What were we thinking?"), but a few were at the expense of others – maybe even some of you reading this! Don't worry, though. Whether we were laughing or just reminiscing, we were enjoying the memories. Of course, my comments changed over the course of looking at the photos of myself, from "Wow, I was really thin then," to "Let's just throw that one out."

All of the reviewing of photos got me thinking about the many changes in my life. Yes, I would love to be that thin girl of twenty who married Roger, but I have come to the conclusion that life experiences, at least in my case, must weigh a lot – and I would rather be forty-three and have learned all I have learned than twenty with all of it ahead of me. I can compare my youth and my, uh, shall we say, *maturity*, and I can truly say that the maturity will have to win out. When I was twenty and thought I knew a lot, sure, the body was in better shape; but the mind and spirit had a long way to go. Now that I am older and,

167

hopefully, wiser, I realize that it's what is on the inside that really matters. Time has a way of teaching things that youth cannot, or will not, be still enough to learn. Some twenty-three years later, I have experienced the delights of motherhood to two of the most wonderful kids God could have gifted me with; I have spent almost twenty-three years walking hand in hand with a wonderful husband; I have learned that, no matter the trial or test, God is always with me; I am at least a little more practiced at patience (and still learning that lesson on a daily basis); I have a greater sense of compassion for others; I value the little things in life in a way I could not have imagined in years gone by; I know the worth of true friendship; and I realize now that I will never know it all, but it's okay, because I don't ever have to stop learning.

Those are just some musings gleaned from sifting through images of the past – but I am still trying to lose some of that weight. Wisdom surely can't weigh that much!! Take some time to review some of your memories. It is time well spent.

Still changing,
Debbie

July 30, 2004 (forgotten journal entry)
DAY 100!

Today was a BIG DAY – 100 days post transplant. I thought up until last week that I would be released today, but because some remnants of disease are still present, things have changed a little.
It looks like I'll get to go home next Wednesday, but I will still have to come down here once a week for monitoring. I think the travel will be worth just getting to be home.

They will tinker with my medications and try to encourage my donor cells to be more aggressive. Time will tell.

July 30, 2004
Day 100

This day seemed a thousand miles away when I watched the technicians start my Bone Marrow Transplant. I was just trying to get through the day. But here we are, and I am so thankful.

I saw my doctor today and it's hard to tell 100%, but I see signs that point to a release sometime next week. Don't write it in stone – there are a lot of small things that have to happen, and Tuesday of next week is the day that we'll see just how my system has responded to a slight medication change that started yesterday. In some ways, I've done too well. I actually need for the donor cells to wake up and fight the last few CLL cells that are hanging around.

As usual, I will keep you posted.

August 3, 2004
Homeward Bound!

As much as Debbie and I have learned to love Houston, as many new friends as we've made, I am so excited to tell you that tomorrow my view of Houston will be from a rear view mirror! We're going home! Day 105 post-transplant and day 135 since we arrived, and suddenly – *home*!

It was all up in the air until this afternoon when my BMT team made their decision. I will still have to be in Houston once a week for the next little while, so I'm getting ready to rack up some serious air miles.

I'm not yet at 100%; I still have some wacky blood counts and Dr. Khouri is working with my meds to try to even them out. It's been a roller coaster day, but in a great way.

I've decided, based on your feedback, to keep the journal going. My journey is not through and I think the lessons that I've learned are not over.

I must thank you all again for your love, encouragement and prayers. I'm certain that my family would not have gotten through this without all of the above.

I'm sure that there will be some curves in the road ahead, but I'm not the driver. I'm fully confident in the skill of my Father to get me from here to there.

August 6, 2004
Sitting on My Porch

What a great feeling to turn into my driveway last night! It was one of those nights out here in the boondocks where you can see all the stars unhindered by any city lights. I just stood there with my mouth hanging open, looking at that incredible sight. It was a great view to come home to.

Deb, Chelsea and I drove the 855 miles in two days and everything worked out fine. After a great night's sleep, I spent about an hour this morning sitting on my porch with my whole family (including dogs) enjoying an unseasonably mild morning. A cool breeze, clear blue sky

170

– I could've stayed there all day. It was not like the usual August day.

I'm feeling great. I have to see my Nashville Oncologist today for blood work and to bring him up to speed on my treatment. Then I'll go back to Houston next week for the first of many follow-ups with the team at M.D. Anderson.

I'm so thankful for the prayers that you all have prayed for me. I'm safe at home and feeling better every day. You will never know how much the Bennetts appreciate your support. We will never forget your love and kindness.

August 10, 2004
A Lot of Catching up to Do.

It's been a few days now since we arrived back home in TN. It's been very good medicine for Debbie and me. We are starting to fall into the "home" rhythm and sure are enjoying the little things that we took for granted before. Our family really made the homecoming nice. Our yard was freshly mowed, and the house had endured one of my mother-in-law's top-to-bottom cleanings. Then we arrived and brought four months of "Houston supplies" to plop down in the garage!

Because of my immune system being at an all time low, all of our animals (a veritable zoo) have been banished to their outside abodes, a fact that they protest with an ear piercing volume each time they spot us outside. Our cats have tried to bribe us into relenting and making an exception in their case by bringing us "presents" and laying them at the door. I guess we are all dealing with the new realities in our own way!

As usual, I'm still struggling with my mind wanting to be back at 100% and my body actually being at 50%. I'm sure that this is all part of the process. I'm praying for patience. I was able to go to the studio and watch L5 record today. This is the album that we started before I went to Houston. Recording should be finished this week, and then final mixing will start. It's going to be a great album. I'd forgotten how powerful the songs are that we picked back in the winter.

Debbie and I leave for Houston on Wednesday night and will see the BMT team on Thursday. I hope to get the go ahead to start getting back on the road, but that's out of my hands. I can tell you that I'm so ready. When I was in Houston for the 100 days, I could accept the fact that I could not travel, but now that I'm home I'm having a hard time resisting the urge to push ahead. I know I can't, and every now and then my body sends me a nasty signal that I'm weaker than I realize.

The reason I'm up at 5 a.m. is because one of these reminders showed up at 3 a.m. It was a shock not only to my system physically, but a wake-up call to my mind as well. It was nothing serious, but it was unexpected. It was just another reminder that I've never been in control of this cancer rollercoaster. I'm just sitting in the front car as we slowly click, click, click up the long steep hill and then hang on for dear life as the curves and drops come without warning. That's pretty much how life is, isn't it? Times of anticipation followed by highs and lows but, at the end, exhilarating. Maybe that's what Jesus meant when He said He came to give us abundant life! One of my life lessons during the past year has been to remember that He is the Designer, I am the design; and even though I can't always see the path clear, He is never blinded to the straight way!

If you've never completely turned your life over to Jesus, I urge you to do so at this very moment. The dips and drops of life can never be successfully mastered without the Master. The media tell us daily that everything we need to succeed is inside of each of us. We just need the latest self-help book or video course to unleash the power. This is one of the devil's most seductive lies. I've lived long enough and been through enough trials to know that within ourselves we have nothing. Jesus is waiting for us to say the words. He longs to be our voice in the night, to shine light into even the darkest corners of the room. Don't listen to the vain philosophies of the present day. They are empty and powerless. Trust the truth of the Gospel! It will stand when everything else falls!

August 14, 2004
Update

I had hoped to get the OK to start back to work on a limited schedule yesterday at my first check-up, but it was not to be. Instead, on Wednesday night, shortly after we arrived in Houston, I started running a fever. Thursday morning it had reached the level that is a mandatory trip to the ER; but since my doctor's appointment was only an hour away, I decided against the ER. When my Dr saw my counts and the fact that I had a fever, he grounded me! I had to stay in Houston for another twenty-four hours. Friday morning, after a round of antibiotics, the fever was gone and Deb and I caught a 3 p.m. flight to Nashville.

When we landed and turned our cell phones on, both of our voice mailboxes were full. Between the time that we left Houston and landed in Nashville, a blood culture test had come back. It shows that I have a pretty nasty infection of the blood. A nurse will come to our home in Nashville to administer the medicine.

I hesitated about whether or not to share this news. In the end I thought, "Why would I not share it?" You Ropeholders have held me and mine up so faithfully to the Father. How could I not give you the opportunity to pray about this new development?

I don't want you to be discouraged with this news. I'm not. The team in Houston has told me from the start that anything can happen for many months and possibly years post transplant. We'll take them as they come. That's the entire reason that I have to be seen once a week. This way, nothing sneaks up on us.

I'm really fine, but your prayers are, as always, coveted.

August 17, 2004
Quick Update from Houston

Debbie and I are back at M.D. Anderson today for my weekly follow-up. They are still treating the blood infection with mega-doses of "goop." (I like to use medical jargon.) I'm feeling fine and am hoping my appointment in about an hour will give me good news.

I REALLY am ready to get back on the road, but am determined not to rush it. When I start traveling again I want to do it knowing that I crossed all the "t's" and dotted all the "i's."

August 26, 2004
Nearly Normal?

Today has been one of those days that almost feel normal. Since coming home I've had to resist the urge to jump back into the life that I lived before the transplant. This is both good and bad. I've felt fine today, and that gives me the feeling that I can hop back on the old "hamster wheel of life." I've enjoyed going to the office and checking the mail, and all the other things that I did in my old life, but every now and then I get a subtle reminder. Let's just say I'm not the Energizer Bunny. The strength that I feel is easily expended and I get the feeling of my "new life." Shortness of breath, overall fatigue, and then I get the urge to sit down and check my e-mail! It will all even out eventually. I have every reason to believe that my strength will return soon and there will be plenty of time for mowing, cleaning, and organizing. The transition between the two ways of life is tricky, but with God's help I'll get it together.

August 31, 2004
Cliché of the Day: Life Goes On

Yesterday was a real sad day at the Bennett house. Our thirteen-year-old Australian Shepherd, Maggie, died. For thirteen years she had stolen all of our hearts and she was a big part of our household. She had been declining for quite some time, but last weekend it was clear that the end was near. We all had our goodbyes, but she will leave a big hole in our lives. Someone said that that is why pets are just too hard. They attach themselves so much to us and then we have to give them up. True... but we feel that all the thirteen years of fun we had with her were more than worth the sadness we feel today. We have a million Maggie stories that still make us laugh.

On to today...

Deb and I flew to Houston this morning for my weekly check-up. Before we met with my doctor, we went to check up on some friends that we made during our time at M.D. Anderson. We got some very sad news about one of our friends. According to his doctors, his time is short.

175

He's a young man with a young family. To respect his privacy, I won't share his name. If you would just speak to the Father about "Roger's friend," it would be great. We are, of course, praying for a miracle; but in the event that he doesn't make it through, pray for his family that they will find the strength they need to go on with their lives.

Concerning my check-up, I seem to be doing fine. Next week I will have a pretty big battery of tests. This is a pretty important set of tests and I will keep you posted. These are just scheduled tests with the transplant. Nothing has gone wrong; they are just to check the progress of my new cells.

I made it through the last two weekends just fine on the road with L5. Until I am told differently by my medical staff, I will continue to travel with the group. I hope to see you all soon. Truthfully, the phrase should be, "we'll see each other from a distance." I'm still wearing the mask and am not supposed to have close contact with big crowds.

Thanks again for all your prayers.

September 3, 2004
Between Two Worlds

It's an odd feeling, being in this "recovery" stage, this "wait and see, then hurry up and wait some more" stage. At least in my situation, the body seems like it's playing April Fools jokes daily. I have felt great this week. Sleeping well, not pushing to complete anything. Just kind of hanging around and loving every minute of it. But then the e-mail bell dings and there in my inbox is my schedule of tests for next week in Houston. Three days of repeating tests that I took a month ago. I'm not whining or complaining; in fact, I'm looking forward to seeing my progress. It's just that it requires a different mindset than the one I'm in right now.

Right now, I'm slowly digging out from under a mountain of paperwork that greeted me when I got home. No big deal – I enjoy it. I'm packing to go out for another weekend with Legacy Five, and I obviously enjoy that. Then my reality meter pegs and I remember that there'll be no Labor Day party for me this year (no close contact with crowds), and Monday night I have to be on a plane to Houston. Tuesday morning it all starts over.

As I said, I'm not complaining. I'm thankful that I get to be in this "home" mode at least some of the time. A lot of my friends don't have that luxury. They would love to have to juggle home time with treatment time. It's just an odd feeling to have one foot in "home world" and one foot in "cancer city." But my point (and I do have one) is that Christians have a Savior that lives in BOTH worlds! Thank God! He is with us in the fun days of sitting under a shade tree in the front yard, and He is equally with us as we wait for the CAT scan or bone marrow exam to begin. He is not intimidated by our valleys. In fact, He has already been there! He has charted the course and is our glad escort through each trial we face.

Are you living in two realities? Do you feel that all hope is gone? I know it's easy for me to say from here in "home" world with the everyday sounds of my daughter watching TV in the other room and the sounds of my wife's garage sale coming from outside, but help is on the way! Our Lord is aware of our suffering, acquainted with our sorrows, and ready to send relief. Let me encourage you to continue to fight the fight. Keep the faith. There is a world that we can't imagine, a reality that will make our "light and momentary trials" seem like a million miles away! Don't give up! Don't despair!! He is faithful!

September 17, 2004
Update from Roger and Debbie

I am writing from the National Quartet Convention, and it has been quite a week for us all. Last night at the Singing News Fan Awards, Legacy Five was voted the Favorite Male Quartet of 2004. What an honor! Words can't quite describe the feeling for all of the group members and their families as that announcement was made! As a quartet wife, I could not have been more proud of all of our "boys."

Roger and I went to Houston about a week and a half ago, where he underwent a series of tests to restage his progress. We were hoping to hear that his doctor would cut down our weekly visits, but we got a different report. It seems that there is still disease in his bone marrow, and some nodes have increased in size since July. Basically, what this means is that the transplant is not working – yet. There are more steps to take to give it a "boost," however. Our next phase will be for Roger to undergo a type of chemo, not to tear down any more cells, but to boost them up. That will be a weekly treatment and, sandwiched in

178

between those, the doctor wants to collect more stem cells from Roger's dad to infuse them again. Hopefully, this will give his system the charge it needs to get the transplant working. We are trying to look at this as just a detour on this journey. The doctor tells us that this is not abnormal and that it can happen in many cases. We do covet your prayers as we embark on this new leg of the trip. This week at NQC has been good for us in that we have been freshly reminded of your love and prayers for our family, and we are so grateful for that. Rest assured that, while we were taken aback by this bit of news, we have not lost faith or hope. God is still in control, as always, and we are glad that He already has a plan in place. As a dear friend of ours has told us more than once, "God does not read the test results!"

September 21, 2004
Almost through, and then a surprise!

I had a feeling all day that some sort of twist was on its way. The day was Tuesday, September 14, and we were in the doctor's office waiting for him to give the results of all the tests I had taken the week before. I don't call it a negative thought that I had, but more of a prompting of the Holy Spirit to strengthen my whole armor of God. Whatever the origin, the feeling was valid.

According to Dr. Khouri, I still have disease in my bone marrow and my blood and several of my nodes, both in my chest and abdomen, have actually increased in size. This tells us that the cancer is still on the move. The main reason for this is that my new cells are not fighting hard enough, and the answer will come in the form of a "Booster Shot," so to speak.

My dad will again come to Houston to give us some of those wonderful stem cells of his. After a few treatments for me, they will be injected into my system. When this happens, I'll have to be in Houston for another week instead of one day.

So, yet again, I call on you Ropeholders to lift me up to our Father. Please pray that I don't miss an opportunity to lift Him up in my life. During my weakness, my prayer is that His strength will be shown to be perfect.

I know that too many of you will be in shock about this news. I know this because I was; but I'm not discouraged or cast down. God works the night shift, and I'm listening for His whisper in this midnight hour.

He lives, and we are in His Grip!

September 26, 2004
Catching Up.

Hello all,

I just wanted to give you all an update. My schedule remains the same as the previous post. I go to Houston every week to have treatment in preparation for the "booster shot" of stem cells that I'll receive. I'm feeling a little weaker as time goes by, and I battle fatigue almost constantly. This only has to do with the physical part of me. In the spiritual part of my life, I still trust God's hand and am believing in a victory through this fight.

I've been able to travel with L5 for the past few weekends and it has done me a world of good. However, I may have to be off the road for a few days while they administer this new treatment.

I love you all.

September 30, 2004
It's Not Real Until It's Tested

Not to be trivial or flippant, but did you ever notice how much of what happens in our "Church world" goes relatively unnoticed by the rest of the world? During our cantatas and other planned entertainment, most of the attendees are "churched" people. The "unchurched," for lack of a better word pretty much ignore us. They have much glitzier entertainment for the price of a movie ticket than they'll ever get from all the "seeker sensitive" rallies in all the churches in the world.

No, it's at times of great stress that suddenly a keen interest in our faith manifests itself. The catastrophic events, like 9-11 and, more recently, the hurricanes that pounded through Florida, are always followed by an increase in church attendance. I totally understand this feeling – I became much more eternity-minded the very day I was diagnosed with cancer in August of 1995. There I was, a Christian since the age of nine, and I had never had my faith tested. I knew all the right words and phrases, but could my faith stand the pressure? Since my faith is placed in the finished work of Jesus, and through no goodness or performance of my own, I'm happy to report that I firmly rest in His grip. Nine years later, through good days or bad (as one old timer puts it, "Feast one day; feathers the next"), I'm still learning about the absolute surety of God's Word.

In the motorcycle-building show that I've become addicted to, one of the big deals when constructing the bike is to put the gas tank to a pressure test. They put it through more pressure than it will ever receive in the real world; but if it's gonna fail, they want it to fail in the shop where no one gets hurt. I look at the examples in the Bible in much the same way. I don't know how much grace you're gonna need today, but here's what I do know: it was more than enough to sustain Moses as he lead millions of sometimes ungrateful Children of Israel through the desert for forty years, so I'm sure that somehow the world won't stop turning if I don't make it to the dry cleaners in time for the cut-off!

Faith in a risen Christ was enough to sustain the early church through endless days of secret meetings with the sentence of death upon them if they were discovered. So, if someone got my parking place or my pew at church, I think it would be safe for me to just get over it! See how perspective changes everything? God's grace is not on the endangered species list and it is in no danger of running out or not being up to the test. I know it may seem like the weight of the world is on your shoulders and your circumstances might point toward a terrible future, but I have been forced to pressure test God's faithfulness toward me and He has never failed. I've still got cancer, but me having a perfect, healthy body was never a part of the equation. God has blessed me daily; every morning new mercies are mine. I'm gonna use this body as long as it holds out. I hope to have many more years of reliable service from it, but when the day comes to trade up, well, you should see the warranty info on the new model I'm getting!

October 3, 2004
In the Hospital Again

Last week's check-up showed that I was experiencing a mild case Graft vs. Host disease. As I said this, can be a good thing; but I was again taken off the road for safety's sake. I'm glad I listened. On Friday night I started running a high fever. It reached the point at which I had to be taken to the ER. As it turns out, I have another infection that required me to be admitted. It looks like my system is responding and I'll be released on Monday morning – just in time to get on the plane to go back to Houston for my weekly visit. During these past two days, I've been reminded why I don't like hospitals!

It is just another time when God's timing proves to be better than ours. If I'd had my say, I would have been on an interstate somewhere with almost 103 degrees of fever – a real big red flag, but especially so for a BMT patient.

Anyway, I just wanted you to hear it from me rather than rumors that go around. I hope you are having a great fall!

October 4, 2004
Home and Then Gone Again

After spending the weekend in the hospital, I was released this morning at about 9:30. We are about to step out the door to head to the airport to fly to Houston. Sounds exciting, huh? My fever broke yesterday, and I'm anxious to see the results of my tests this week in Houston.

I know so many of you are praying, and I don't have the words to thank you. My family has drawn strength from your love. When I feel discouraged, I'm reminded of how blessed we are to have so many Ropeholders who are standing in the gap for us.

October 10, 2004
Clipped Wings Yet Again

It's been a few days since an update, but time has just not allowed. Here is what's going on.

I've missed this ten-day trip with L5 and, while it's been tough for me to sit home, it's a good thing that I wasn't on the road in the last few days. When I arrived home from Houston, I started feeling sick again. Long story short, that night I found myself again in the ER. The following day it was another MRI for Roger! (Fun times!) I have no results yet. I expect to hear something on Monday.

Speaking of Monday, that's when I go back to Houston. My life pretty much revolves around either in the hospital here or in Houston. But it could be much worse. I'm very blessed.

I'm doing a lot of writing right now, and the Lord seems to be trying to teach me a lot of lessons. I hope that I can share some of the thoughts with you soon. In the meantime, Debbie has agreed to help keep you posted when I can't.

October 17, 2004
In the hospital again.

On Wednesday of last week, after flying home from Houston, I got very sick very quickly, ended up in the ER, and was admitted to the Hospital. I was held there until Saturday, the sixteenth. I was released about 3 p.m. Almost as soon as I got home, the fever hit the level of "ER now." To summarize, after about nine hours of freedom I'm now back in very familiar surroundings.

The reason that I'm here is fever. A few nights ago, it climbed to 104.5. It's very disturbing, and we're not real sure why it's doing it. Debbie will probably keep you posted over the next few days.

Thanks in advance for your prayers.

October 18, 2004
"The New Normal"

I've spent most of the last week in the hospital or in the ER here in Nashville. Last night was the first night that I had slept in my own bed in quite some time. About 11 p.m., I started going downhill quick. My fever wasn't as high, but I had chills and flu symptoms. Deb was on the phone with my medical team here and in Houston. The decision was made for me to get on a plane ASAP and get to the M.D. Anderson ER by this evening. I'm not gonna lead you down the garden path – we are concerned. Here is bottom line: my counts look pretty good. Nothing in my counts shows that I should feel like this. That is the part that concerns us.

So here we go again. I've looked back at some of your comments over the months that I've kept this journal, and I feel so blessed that my family and I have had your friendship from day one. I don't have time today to tell you in the way that I'd like how much of blessing you've been to the Bennetts.

The truth is, I'm not doing as well as I'd hoped to be doing at this time. My doctors are not discouraged, and that is good for me; but I'm growing a little weary with the personal impact this is having on me. It's real hard to keep everything on a normal basis, but now there is this unspoken thing in every conversation; every small personal detail is impacted by my disease. I honestly think everyone in my family is holding up well, but I'm slipping a little. I'm just really ready to be back to normal, but I'm also beginning to realize that what I called "normal" is a distant memory. So now, God is encouraging me to get better and see what the "new normal" will be for the Bennetts.

October 23, 2004
More Waiting

After arriving in Houston, I was admitted to the hospital – after spending fifteen hours in the ER waiting for a bed. I was immediately started on round-the-clock antibiotics. My fever went away and they started the mandatory tests. Some we have results for and some we don't. My counts continue to drop. It looks like tomorrow (Sunday the 24th) I'll be given platelets and blood for the first time in this whole process. In some ways I feel a little better, but in others I feel worse. I guess it's all part of the fight.

I was released from the hospital on Thursday after being fever-free for enough time, and we were told I might have to be in the Houston area for a week or two. Those of you who know me know that I've never been forced to live my life with a schedule that is so vague – "A week or two? I've got things to do, is it one week or two?" But that is not how sickness works. Suddenly, the great equalizer forces all of us to conform to its schedule. Truly, I'm fine with this change in scheduling. I won't lie to you: I prefer the old way because it is so familiar to me. But in my weakness I'm now seeing that I can push myself as hard as I want, but my body can only handle so much. So, here we go again – more stuff to learn!

October 26, 2004
Lessons in an Elevator

We are at M.D. Anderson Clinic, in between having labs drawn and waiting to see the doctor. I decided to go down to the smoothie bar and get smoothies for Roger and myself (one of the drawbacks to being here so often is that I know all the "good" places to go!). We are blessed with many friends here at the clinic, and one of them is a Patient Affairs Director who offers us a nice lounge to relax in when we need it, so I parked Roger in there and headed off to the elevators leading to the cafeteria.

As I was waiting to get on the elevator, a man and his wife arrived, waiting also. He was obviously the patient – no hair, hooked up to chemo, etc. – and yet, he had a smile on his face, and held the elevator door for his wife and me to enter first. I smiled back, said my "good mornings," then stared at the buttons, as we do… I noticed his chemo was being delivered via a portable pump that he was carrying over his shoulder. Then I heard him say to his wife, "Man, this is so much nicer than that big backpack I was carrying before." She replied, "Yes, it isn't nearly as big and heavy."

Just a couple of sentences, and yet, it made a profound impact on me. I began thinking how much different the perspectives of most people were here than in the "outside world" past the cancer clinic. These are people who, for the most part, have figured out that the little things in life are worth being grateful for. These are lessons that have become more real to me as this journey continues: thankfulness for a more convenient method of chemo delivery; appreciation of a quiet place to wait for two hours in between appointments (as opposed to being upset at having to wait for two hours in the first place!); excitement over a "day off" between scheduled visits; a sunny day to lift the spirits; and the list goes on and on.

My prayer is that I won't lose sight of how important it is to be grateful for the small things in life. It makes the bigger issues so much easier to deal with.

Truly thankful for good friends,
Debbie

October 27, 2004
A New Road

Deb and I were sitting in the waiting room waiting for the doctor to come in with his report. For some reason, I was very agitated and nervous. I can't explain it, but I had a sense that something big was on the way. I was right. Here's the deal: my cancer has changed into a deadly form of leukemia called AML. I will go into the hospital next week to start another round of chemo. This time it will be much stronger. Then, after about a month of that treatment, I'll have another stem cell transplant. I've been up against bad odds before, but this time the odds are stacked high against me. I have a 30% chance of survival. That's the cold, hard truth. However, the chances of my dad being a perfect match were less than 1%, and that happened! I've decided that anything can happen, and I'll just continue to trust and let God handle the details.

Obviously, we are all in shock and trying to process this new diagnosis. Debbie, Chelsea, and Jordan are yet again so encouraging, and for that I'm thankful. I will keep you all posted as I can; Deb will do the posting when I can't.

I have been on a tangent lately to simplify my life. Long before I got this news, I've been weeding out the non-essentials. So, in that spirit, I'll face this new valley. I will simply trust God and leave the outcome to Him.

Some through the waters,
Some through the flood,
Some through the fire,
But all through the Blood;
Some through great sorrow,
But God gives a song,
In the night season and all the day long.

November 8, 2004
More Prayers Needed

I am writing this after spending the night with Roger in his hospital room. The first thing I want to do is to request prayer for him. He is in severe pain right now. The second thing I will do is back up and give you a timeline of what has been happening.

We arrived in Houston last Sunday night and saw the doctors on Monday. At that time, they had decided to watch his counts, which seemed to be holding fairly steady, and postpone the chemo to instead prepare for the second bone marrow transplant more quickly. Roger had some pretty good days there, and Monday we were feeling some sense of respite because he would not be immediately admitted into the hospital. Chelsea had flown down with him (I drove a very packed vehicle down) and she stayed with us until Saturday. We all stayed up late on Tuesday, waiting on election results. On Wednesday morning, Roger woke up with pain and started developing a fever, which led us to the ER on Wednesday afternoon, and admission into the hospital on Wednesday night, where he has been since.

The fevers have been fluctuating, going quite high at times, and the pain has become worse. Some pain meds cut it, but they have terrible side effects for him, such as hallucinations; but, when they change the meds, the new ones aren't as effective. Last night was the worst I have seen his pain. I feel very helpless at this point, and all I can do for him is give him water and rub his back.

The doctor came in this morning, and they have decided to go ahead and start the chemo today. Apparently, the pain and fever are coming from the disease, which is becoming extremely aggressive, so they have no choice but to begin treatment. The idea in postponing it was to give his body a rest, but that is not possible now. The doctor told us this morning that this new chemo plan will be really tough on him, but it should alleviate the pain as the disease is arrested.

The main reason I am writing this and being so straightforward with the information is that I feel that you can be more specific with your prayers. He so much needs pain relief right now. His body needs strength to handle this chemo regimen. I need the wisdom to know how to help him. His dad needs prayers for strength and calm, as he is by himself in Arkansas. Our children need prayers for peace and strength as they try to go about their own lives without us there, and deal with all of this long-distance. All of our family needs prayers as they wonder how to help, too.

Thank you for allowing us the outlet to ask for all of these things. We are truly blessed with good friends and prayer warriors. We know that all things work together for good to those who love God and are called according to His purpose, and we lean on that promise.

Safely In His Grip,
Debbie

November 9, 2004
A Better Day

God is still answering prayers, and thank God for all of the prayers you have sent up! After having a really tough couple of days, Roger is feeling much less pain today, and his fever has remained down, as well. You can see the difference in the way he feels just by looking at him – even the nurse commented on that. (Of course, he felt like shaving today for the first time in a week, so that may have made some impression on her!)

One day after his first chemo treatment, his counts are beginning to head in the direction they need to go. He is low on platelets and clotting factors, so some blood products are needed before they can put in another central venous catheter in his chest tomorrow. It sounds scary, but it's so much easier than being stuck for IVs and blood draws constantly.

There are no words to describe how uplifting your comments and prayers have been to us. Just reading the messages you send to us on the website is comforting, and there is a sense of well-being that comes with knowing that so many are praying for us. Again, I say, we are so blessed.

Current orders are for the chemo to continue through Friday, then to reevaluate from there. I still don't have a time table past that. He is having a few side-effects already, but they are not too bad. This is a tough regimen, so we expect that he may have a few bad days, but we have been surprised before!

Thanks for your concern for me, as well. I tried to donate platelets today, but my iron count is a little too low. That lets me know I need to get a little more rest, and make sure I don't wear out. I have been spending the last couple of nights at the hospital.

One more prayer request: I have plans to fly home Saturday to see Jordan in his leading role in his senior play and for his eighteenth birthday party (his birthday is Thursday). Pray for Roger as I leave him for the weekend. He receives excellent care here, but I think he misses me a little when I am not here!

In Christ's love,
Debbie

November 12, 2004
Still Improving

Thank you for all of the uplifting comments you have posted. It is quite comforting to sit and read them all.

Roger is having a much better day today. Side effects from the treatments have been minimal. He was finally able to have the central line put in his chest, and his counts are still going in the right direction from the chemo. Of course, the chemo makes a lot of good counts go down too, so he is more at risk for infections and bleeding. Rest assured, we are all treating him with kid gloves!

As I prepare to fly home for the weekend, I am leaving Roger in good hands. His dad drove down from Arkansas to stay with him, and the two are spending time catching up on all of the happenings around Strawberry, AR.

Roger MAY get to be released from the hospital tomorrow, still pending lab values, but it is probable. You know he is looking forward to that! His dad is a good cook, so maybe he can coax Roger's appetite back. The food at M.D. Anderson is good, but anything gets less appealing after a few days.

I spent the afternoon getting things ready for his return to the apartment. It sure will be good to have him back there!

On another note, Jordan's play went well last night (opening night and also his birthday). I am really looking forward to seeing it on Saturday. Fortunately, the media department at the high school will be filming the play, so Roger will get to see it on tape.

Thank you for your faithfulness in praying and loving us. We can certainly feel it at all times!

Very blessed,
Debbie

November 17, 2004
Begin Again

Here's a short update. My dad is in Houston and going through the testing and blood work required for the next transplant. This all seems so familiar. I guess because this is the second time all this has happened. I'm so thankful that my dad is so up for all of this. What a guy he is. I'm so proud of him. I got my schedule today as well. I'll be in and out of the clinic for all the pre-testing for the next few days, and then on November 30 I'll be admitted into the hospital to start my second transplant.

As Debbie told you in an earlier post, this cancer has become more aggressive and so this transplant will have to be more aggressive as well. God has held us so tightly during this entire ordeal and He has continued to pour His grace out upon me and my family.

Legacy Five are doing very well. They continue to maintain a full schedule and have taken a load off my mind concerning me missing so many concerts. I love them all and thank God for their friendship and support.

Scott Fowler has stepped up to the plate in a way that he and I could have never dreamed. He continues to do both his job and mine with a great attitude, and without complaint. Please pray that God will continue to pour out an extra measure of strength and grace to this great man.

I'll be in touch. I hope all is well with you. Remember, you are precious in His sight!

November 18, 2004
Moving Along

I am sitting here typing this afternoon while Roger is receiving platelets. His dad is sitting with him in the Transfusion Unit, and he is allowed only one visitor at a time, so I thought I would sneak over and make a post. Things are progressing toward the second transplant, and Roger has been out of the hospital since Saturday, so that is good news.

We received approval from the insurance company for the second transplant! (Apparently, since this one is the full-blown thing, and not considered "experimental," it went through okay.) Of course, God's timing was perfect: since I had asked Roger's dad to come down last weekend to stay with him, he was already down here when the approval came through, and was able to start the pre-testing immediately. I have spent the last couple of days shuttling the two "boys" between appointments and testing, and have a few more days of that to come, but it is working out just fine. So far, things look fine and we have been given an admission date of November 30 for Roger's transplant. Actually, he will receive a week or so of chemo before the transplant, as before, so I will update you with the actual transplant date later. This admission date, however, will allow him to spend Thanksgiving at the apartment with family. His dad will still be here, and my parents and our kids are coming down, as well. We should have a great visit.

Roger continues to battle low counts and fatigue, but that is not unexpected from the last round of chemo, coupled with the seriousness of the disease. He is a real trooper, though, and rarely complains. The only problem I am having with him currently is getting him to take one of his medicines – a liquid anti-viral, which he says is the worst thing he's ever tasted. It reminds me of that commercial where the kid is hiding from the mom when it is medicine time. I need to think back to how I tricked Chelsea and Jordan into taking "yucky" medicine when they were little!

We are all doing fine, as far as having everything we need, etc. So many have asked what they can do to help, and again, I will say, that prayers are the main thing. We are enjoying the cards that so many of you have sent our way! I just wish we could write a thank-you note to each one of you, but I hope you do understand that that is just not possible. Know that you are all in our prayers of thanksgiving to God.

Speaking of Thanksgiving, we have so many blessings to be thankful for this year. I hope that your family can count many blessings, as well.

Jordan says to say thank you to all of his well-wishers regarding his play and his birthday. I was so proud of him when I got to go to the play last weekend. He had several friends over on Sunday afternoon for a get-together, too. I had a great weekend just being at home with him and Chelsea. Chelsea, as you may know, has taken a semester off of college to help out in the mail order office, and will probably take another off. I don't know what I would do without my two responsible, giving, loving, kids. (I can't call them children anymore, now that my baby has turned eighteen!) They have really pitched in and gone the extra mile through all of this.

Well, I had better go and check on the patient. I know he is more than ready to get back to the apartment and into his bed. Please pray for his physical strength, especially in the next few days, when his testing will be more strenuous.

We love you all,
Debbie

November 25, 2004
Thanksgiving

Happy Thanksgiving to all!

I woke up this morning to the most amazing aromas. Debbie and her mom, Louise, had concocted one of their signature Thanksgiving meals and I had an appetite! This is a good combination. You would have been proud of me – for the first time in quite a few weeks, I ate like the "old" Roger.

As we held hands around the table, I took a quick inventory of my blessings in the room. My wife of twenty-three years (soon). My two kids who have made the transition from fun and happy little kids to two fun and happy young adults who are the joys of our lives. Deb's mom and dad, Bob and Louise Westbrook, have treated me like one of their own kids for nearly twenty-four years and my life has been richer.

I then thought about my family at home in Arkansas. My working on the road for all these years has limited my time with them, but I love them so much. My cousins, granddad, and a slew of uncles and aunts are never very far from my thoughts. So, when I bowed my head today, the emotions of thanksgiving were very close to the surface as we prayed.

Another blessing we had was that it was a beautiful day in Houston, and I got to go for a drive for a couple of hours that DID NOT involve going to the hospital! These thankful thoughts come on a day that we set aside to be thankful, but this sickness that is a constant presence in my life has taught me to be thankful for the blessings great and small every day! Every day! Each morning His mercies are new! Lord, help me to be thankful every day!

November 30, 2004
New schedule again, and identity theft.

Well, it looks my transplant will be pushed farther into December, but my team has decided that the extra rest will help all concerned. So here at almost the last minute, the plan is tweaked a little more. Don't be discouraged – it's all under control, and the extra time will let the Christmas presents arrive from my internet stores. Since I can't be out and about much, I've become quite the cyber-shopper superhero known as "Captain Bluetooth." I can show you how to save a bunch of time and sanity! Don't even ask about my security measures. I pity the criminal who would try to steal my identity! I've got some out-of-work Navy Seals standing by to get the Bennetts' credit card that has been compromised. Sure, they're each seventy-eight years old and have to communicate with blinks and grunts, but I would not want to be around when my crack team gets buckled into their 1969 El Camino, their oxygen tanks rattling in the back and their walkers and rascals lashed tightly to the roof by the CB antenna, and tears out of headquarters at a top speed of 45 mph. (If you happen to get stuck behind this impressive bunch, be careful – they stop at all Krispy Kreme stores.)

Anyway, departing from that 2:00 a.m. bout of creativity just now... I just wanted let you know that my transplant has been moved back by a couple of weeks. Debbie and I will keep you posted.

By the way, we had a great "chuck-it" meal today. We stirred some primo leftover Turkey into a bowl filled with some of the most valuable Thanksgiving side dishes. It turned out perfect and cost us about $1.00 for one can from the outside (Kroger). By the way, you know what a chuck it meal is, I'm sure – find the leftovers, chuck them in a baker's dish with bread crumbs, and it is special!

Thanks again for your concern. Rest easy; I'm resting easy, and certainly NOT overdoing my bounds. I'm content now in four rooms.

Again, we love you and yours for all the kindness you've shown us. You all were in my thoughts in a special way on Thanksgiving.

December 5, 2004
Quick Update

Monday will hopefully start the last round of tests before the transplant. My dad arrived this afternoon, and tomorrow the ball starts rolling again. God is certainly using this part of the process to teach me patience. Every day that nothing major happens, I think, "I could've been on the road tonight," or "I wonder what the last flight out is... I could meet L5 in wherever." Well, just about that time, one of my symptoms decides to make its lovely self known; the next minute I'm back in the wheelchair or back on pain medicine and I'm reminded that this is for real. Honestly, as any M.D. Anderson alumnus will attest, you learn to take plenty to read and be prepared to chill out for a while. You can usually find Debbie at one of the tables where one of the industrial 2000-piece puzzles are just waiting for the TRULY patient (not me!). Anyhow, I'm grateful that in the hours of waiting I'm not going any more nuts than I already am.

I'll be in touch as the transplant schedule comes into focus.

December 10, 2004
A Surprise Visit

We always try, these days, to find the silver lining to the clouds, and it really does help make days brighter. We are, yet again, on hold as to when the new transplant procedure will begin. This week, the doctor told Roger that he will have to undergo a liver biopsy this coming Tuesday, due to some elevated levels that have them concerned. Please be in prayer for him Tuesday morning during this procedure. They tell us it is pretty standard and "easy," but they will be going in through his jugular vein to do it. They also say that sounds a lot worse than it is. The results will tell us more about his ability to endure the next treatments and transplant. Anyway, we are still in a holding pattern.

However, that does leave us with a few extra days on our hands, so we decided to jump on a plane and head home for the weekend, and were able to surprise a few friends in the process. We came home Wednesday night and have surely been enjoying the time with family. That's where the "silver lining" part comes in: if we were still on schedule, we couldn't have had this extra time in Tennessee, something we had totally not expected.

God's ways and timing may not be our own, but He always shows us that His plans are better than ours anyway!

When we return to Houston on Sunday night, we jump back into the routine of doctors' appointments, tests, etc., while waiting on the hospital admission date to approach (whenever that may be). It is easy sometimes to feel frustrated, but again, we are learning many lessons in patience.

Roger's test results are improving in many areas, showing that his body is responding to the treatments that he has already had. We are very grateful for that!

I'd also like to add how extremely grateful we are to you all for your prayers and support. I may say that in each post, but it will never be enough. Because of the financial support you have provided, we have been able to make these trips and keep two households afloat. We are also thankful to Southwest and their Rapid Rewards program for the free tickets that we used to come home this weekend!

We hope you are having a blessed Christmas season and remembering the real reason for the season. He is alive! He is living in our hearts and pouring out His blessings on us continuously!

December 14, 2004
Jugular Update

It's all behind me now! I know it's not so bad and I will not dread it in the future, BUT it is pretty sore. My neck feels like I took a glancing blow from the bat of a steroid enhanced major league baseball player. But enough about me. (Well, maybe a little more.) Things seem to be fine with the liver. It's chugging along, doing its thing just fine, so full steam ahead.

Dad will fly down tomorrow and start his shots on Friday. These shots will build the number of stem cells for harvesting on next Tuesday, the 21st of December. My outpatient treatments are supposed to start on the next day. December 22 will be Day -12 for me. On Day -6 I will be admitted to start chemo, and on Day Zero I get my tank filled up with the Billy Doug Bennett premium blend, well-aged stem cells. Then it's up to them to scour my body like those little scrubbing bubbles that you use to clean your bathroom and forcefully evict every deadbeat, drain on society, living off MY good cells, cancer cells. Did you like that medical description of a stem cell transplant? Some medical student will print that out and soon the major medical schools of our land will be teaching the Roger Bennett Method of Stem Cell Transplantation. Ahhh, my legacy: scrubbing bubbles of stem cells.

Your prayers are working. I have had more energy in the last two weeks than I've had in months. I've felt great. Thanks for being so faithful. I wish I could answer all the e-mails, but I can't. I do, however, read them all, and am blessed. I wish I could talk with you on the phone; I can't. If we only spent five minutes per call, I couldn't do it! The day would be gone. So, yet again, I'll try to tell you how blessed our family is to have friends like you. The cynical person will say that these words are meant to keep me on your good side, but the person who really listens will hopefully know that in the most humble, sincere way I can, I thank you all for your friendship. I can't wait to get back on the road to play and sing for you and to share some of the things God is teaching me through this time.

One last thing. I've never seen as many prayer lists and prayer groups as I have recently. I know they've always been there, but my perspective has changed and I'm awed at the commitment to prayer by you people.

This is not just for me, but for people all across the world. I believe that we as the church have, in the past, left our most powerful weapon unused and rusting on the shelf. The Word says that the effectual, earnest prayer availeth much. *"Availeth much."* That is beautiful King James English that means in our twenty-first century language, "works to our advantage in a great quantity." I think most folks going about their lives miss that point. I know I did. It's like the old saying, "The only people who don't believe in miracles are the ones who've never needed one!" I am now convinced of the power of prayer – not only on my behalf, but on the behalf of the whole world. When I hear someone say, "I'm praying for you," in my heart I think, "Well, I need to get out of the way and let God have room to work!"

What an awesome God we serve, that He, the Creator, is concerned enough for His creation to move Heaven and earth to show us His love; that He loved us enough to send His son Jesus to rescue us from ourselves; that He cared enough about our daily lives that He sent a comforter in the Holy Spirit to soothe us and remind us of that land that is waiting for us. Thank God! I'm about to make myself shout for joy.

Keep believing, singing, and praying!

December 21, 2004
Christmas in America

Since my forced sabbatical, I've learned to deal with downtime in several different ways: reading, meditating on my blessings and, when I feel like slumming, I watch a lot of TV. I guess it would be fair to say that I'm pretty much "up" on current events and, to some extent, pop culture. Much pop culture that I see only serves to take me out of a Godly attitude and move me into the attitude of, "How stupid can we become and still survive?"

The reason for this post are the sickening debates that I hear daily about the word "Christmas" versus the word "holiday;" the banning of nativity scenes on public property; the word "Jesus" being removed from our children's "holiday songs" at school; and the overall removal of anything resembling Jesus in our Christmas celebrations.

I heard someone say on TV the other day, "If you did not already know the story of Jesus, based on the way we celebrate Christmas today, you would have no idea that He was ever born at all." Pretty strong words, but true. I'm so ashamed that the majority of people in this country who claim to believe that Christmas is about the birth of Christ, have been quieted by those who object to Jesus. (Some just don't care either way.)

This is not a post meant to stir you up to be belligerent with your faith. On the contrary, I want to encourage you to live your faith in a more grace-filled way than you ever have before. I do have a couple of suggestions:

1. Don't fall into the "Happy Holidays" trap. True, there are other holidays that we must respect; but ask yourself a question: would you be offended if a Jewish friend were to say to you "Happy Hanukkah?" Of course not. You would smile and return the greeting; and there's where you add, "And a Merry Christmas to you!" We live in a country where our freedom of both religion and expression provides us with the right to joyfully live our faith. The ACLU and all the lawyers from coast to coast can't change that unless we allow it. Don't be naïve – there are small groups who seriously want to see us shoved back into the dark ages when the mention of our faith in Christ was by law relegated to our homes only. They won't win, but we must be aware of their tricks.

2. Don't become filled with anger and become in the eyes of the world exactly what they always thought Christians were anyway: people full of hate who are determined to rid the earth of all who disagree with them. The Word says we will be known by our love. Don't misunderstand, I'm not telling you to smile and be run over. Quite the contrary – smile and never waiver! Never give in! Never stop living a spirit-filled life in the midst of a lost world that is *itself* full of hate. We MUST be the ones who point others to the source of joy: our Lord Jesus.

It's a great time to be a Christian. The world is hungry for the message of the manger, the story about a baby who was born to save the world, yet was sleeping in the hay that night. Those are the most humble beginnings of a story that was to become the greatest ever told.

So use this blessed time of year to shout from the housetops, "Jesus saves, and He loved the world so much that He came to die for our sins!"

I think that's a pretty good message not only for this time of year, but for every time of the year!

December 24, 2004
Christmas Eve

The Bennetts are getting to witness history in the making tonight in Houston. According to Frank Billingsley (the weatherman on Channel 2) and his weatherdog, Radar (our favorite), this is the first time since records were kept that Houston has had a white Christmas Eve. We are warm and cozy and say "Let it snow!"

I'll bring you up to date on all the medical stuff next week. I want to just enjoy these holy days. Chelsea and Jordan will be here on December 26. My dad will stay until the next day, so we'll all be together for a little while. It will almost seem normal!

It seems appropriate that, tonight as we celebrate the first Christmas present given to man in the form of Jesus, Debbie and I take another opportunity to tell you what a support you all have been to us. In every circumstance, no matter how serious the setback, you Ropeholders have never failed to pray and to love us. Being on the receiving end of this vast amount of prayer has been the most humbling experience of my life. Regardless of the outcome, I will never be the same.

So enjoy your family and be sure to take time to remember that this holiday is not about snow, presents, eggnog, or turkey. It's not even about old St. Nick. These are all just side items and are fine – if kept in perspective. The baby shivering in the night in Bethlehem, who would change the world forever, is indeed the source of our joy of Christmas!

JOY TO THE WORLD!

January 01, 2005
Happy New Year!

2005 is barely two hours old, and I'm starting it off right: I can't sleep. So I decided to wish you all a happy, healthy 2005.

May you in every situation learn to trust God with your whole heart.

May you spend more time with your family and less time at work.

May your stress levels go down and your contentment level go up.

May the scriptures find fertile soil in your heart.

More than anything, may the joy of Jesus be so evident in your life that others will want it in their lives as well.

In His Grip!
Roger

January 4, 2005
A New Year's Update

Well, as promised, here is an update from Roger's doctor visit today. We picked up Doug, Roger's dad, at the airport yesterday, and they both saw the doctor today, following lab tests. Both seem to be recovering from the bad colds they had, but Roger is a little behind his dad. Anyway, Dr. Khouri felt that it was safe to proceed with the stem cell collection. That means that Doug had a couple more tests to run, then this weekend, he will again receive the injections that cause the stem cells to over-produce. If all goes as planned, the collection will take place the first to mid-part of next week. Then, Roger will be scheduled for admission, and begin his pre-transplant chemo. (I am guessing his admission may be a couple of weeks from today.) That means, though, that he will have to undergo ALL of his tests again (bone marrow biopsy, CT scan, MRI, PET scan, etc.), as the FDA requires that they all be completed within thirty days of the actual transplant, and the delays have caused that deadline to pass.

HOWEVER, this waiting again presents its own set of "silver linings" to the clouds. Dr. Khouri agreed that it would be a great boost for Roger to be able to go out this weekend with Legacy Five! As you probably know, this Friday night in Marietta, GA, is the actual five year anniversary date of Legacy Five's beginning, and it will mean a lot to him to be there. He is very excited about it. Not only that, but he will continue to travel with the group for the entire weekend, before flying back to Houston to resume tests, etc.

As much as I would LOVE to be with him, I will be staying in Houston with Roger's dad, playing nurse, and administering the injections that are necessary. So I will have to trust him to behave himself and stay away from crowds at close range!

We look forward to all the exciting changes that are coming in 2005 (including transplants, high school graduations, getting back to TN, etc.), and we are ever mindful that you are lifting our family up in prayer. That means more than we can express. Happy New Year to all of you, and may God Bless You!

Debbie

January 7, 2005
Back in the Saddle Again

I just got off the phone with Roger following the concert in Marietta, GA, and he sounded like his old self – energetic and loving what he is doing. Chelsea drove to Georgia today to be at the concert and she said it was great, too. I know they both enjoyed the evening!

Greater Vision was with Legacy Five tonight, so Roger got to be with them, too, as well as many other friends. I can see that this weekend is going to be even better for him than I expected! And, may I add, I am so proud of all of my L5 boys – 5 years of ministry, and they get better all the time. (I know I am prejudiced, but I also speak the truth!) We are blessed to have all of these men and their families as our friends.

Thanks for all the extra prayers this weekend. We are proof that they are working.

I begin giving the injections to Roger's dad in the morning. You might want to pray extra hard for him! I was practicing on an orange the other night, but Doug told me I might should have been practicing on a watermelon – he has the same sense of humor his son does. He knows to be nice to me, though, since I hold the needle.

Well, bedtime is calling. I hope you all have a great weekend. The Bennetts can't help but have a wonderful one!

In His Grip,
Debbie

January 13, 2005
Marching On

It has been another hectic week, but we are happy to report that all is well. Roger had a great weekend on the road and, as I suspected, it made him more than ready to get through with all of the medical stuff, and get back to work.

His dad and I survived the weekend of shots, and I believe he is none the worse for wear! I discovered yet another skill that I never thought I would have. Life is pretty amazing at times.

I picked Roger up at the airport on Monday, and drove him straight to the clinic for tests, which took over six hours, so he was pretty tired by the time he got back to the apartment. Then, Tuesday, his dad began pheresis to collect his stem cells. We were pretty confident that it would be a one-day procedure this time, but when we arrived back at the clinic Wednesday morning, we were told that another collection was required. He is really a trooper – this is not an easy thing for a 72-year-old man, but he is very glad to do it. We go back this morning to see if they have enough yet or not.

Roger is scheduled for more tests today and tomorrow, but the CT scan is over with, and that is his least favorite. (I can't imagine why he doesn't like drinking those lovely Barium shakes!)

Well, smells like the coffee is ready, and I hear stirring sounds from the guest bedroom, so I will close for now. Keep praying – it is sure working!

Marching on,
Debbie

January 14, 2005
My Hope for You

I hope that you are experiencing blessings in your life right now. Remember if you are not, and it seems things are the darkest they've ever been for you, God is not taken by surprise or asleep. Keep trusting and keep praying. Resist the temptation to falter in your faith. Just one month ago, I was given the worst news yet concerning my cancer. But today, only a few weeks later, my heart is so light and filled with joy! There may be more bad news ahead but my Father has made a way through for me and he'll do the same for you. He loves you so much! (And so do I.)

January 18, 2005
Here We Go Again

My bone marrow results show that the disease is still active and progressing. The scans show, however, that the nodes have not changed much, if any, since the last test. This is good news as it indicates that the disease is not in an advanced stage. I feel great – better every day, in fact. Dr. Khouri says this is a good thing. The stronger and better I feel, it will help me get through the transplant.

I'm excited to get going and get this behind me again. Debbie and I will keep you posted as the process moves forward. To those of you who saw Legacy Five these last two weekends, thanks for being so supportive. It was very good medicine for me. I think that it was a very good reminder to me of what I love to do and am called to do, and a very good incentive for me to get this over with so I can get back to it.

January 25, 2005
Here We Go!

We are on our way to the hospital for Roger to be admitted – finally! We saw his doctor this morning and were told, yet again, that this will probably be a more trying time for him. He has a form of chronic Graft vs. Host disease that could possibly cause some serious side effects when the new cells are introduced. However, we don't dwell on "possibly." We know for certain that God is still in control and He already knows what we will face and what the outcome will be.

One thing we are grateful for is that Roger's doctor, Dr. Khouri, is scheduled to be on inpatient rounds (which is not always the case), so he will know all the particulars of Roger's disease, etc. We also got a call from our dear friend, Reverend Glenda McDonald, who is the chaplain on the BMT floor, who said that Roger has been confirmed on the eleventh floor – the BMT floor, and NOT the isolation floor! They even told him he could bring his fan with him (he can't sleep well without it), so things are looking up before we even get there!

I will post more later, as will Roger. I have some insights I'd like to share when I have more time.

Until then,
Debbie

January 27, 2005
Morning Reflections

I am sitting in the hospital room on day two of Roger's chemo treatments, watching him get some much-needed rest. The alarm just went off on his IV pump, indicating that his chemo is finished for the day. While I am sitting by the window, watching the rain come down, it gives me time to reflect on this past week.

Life can be a roller coaster sometimes, as we all know. This has been one of those weeks for me. We started the week off able to be in Tomball, TX, with Legacy Five and enjoy the talent and ministry of those wonderful men. (Believe it or not, I don't get to see them very often.)

On the way home, while still riding a "high" from the concert, Roger began running a fever and it continued through the night. Monday, he felt better, and we were able to spend a few hours enjoying Chelsea before we had to send her off on a plane to Tennessee. As any parent knows, it doesn't matter how old your child is, it is still hard to say goodbye, even for a while. It is times like these when I feel very inadequate as a parent, knowing that I have given up some of my children's youths to be in Houston for Roger's treatments. I have to keep reminding myself that I know this is the path God showed us to take all those years ago, and He has kept His hand on my kids, even when we were unable to be with them. By the time we got back to the apartment, I was feeling better. Then Jordan called that evening, and we spent about an hour on the phone with him, parenting long-distance, soothing some of his senior year stress – another plunge down the roller coaster hill.

Tuesday morning, we were scheduled to see Roger's doctor in preparation for his admission on Tuesday evening. As expected, we were told of some possible side effects, etc., and left feeling a little bit apprehensive. Then, when we got home, we got a couple of phone calls from friends who were looking out for us at M.D. Anderson, and things began to look up again. The hospital room was in place, along with a few creature comforts, and we were again reminded of how blessed we are.

Jordan called, also, and worked his schedule out so that he can come down this weekend, so that makes two weekends in a row that we get one-on-one time with one of our kids. Definitely an uphill ride, now!

Roger has had a couple of good days so far. His counts are going down, as expected, and that makes him weaker; but he is keeping up his walks around the floor and is still able to eat. Those are very good things.

Someone has said that they think we are "courageous." I can assure you that without Christ, you would see a very different Roger and Debbie Bennett. HE is our source of strength, our hope, our confidence! I was driving in my car a few years ago, when I heard a man interviewed on talk radio – if I could remember who it was, I would certainly want to give him credit for this saying. It was so profound, I grabbed whatever I could find and wrote it down while still driving (NO, kids, I DO NOT recommend this!). I have kept it in my wallet since. What he said was this: "Courage is not the absence of fear. Courage is the realization that there is something more important than fear."

Wow.

What that said to me was that, no matter how hard things seem at the moment, you keep going, because you know that there is worth in the struggle. Hard medical treatments? The more important "something" is the end result: health. Difficulties with a spouse or a child? We keep going because the more important "something" is a valuable relationship. Just taking a moment to think of the ultimate outcome can be a significant factor in anyone's ability to be "courageous." And ultimately, as Christians, we can draw on Philippians 4:13 – we are able to do all things when we have Christ as our strength (a Debbie paraphrase, not meant as an actual translation!).

Just a few morning reflections. I hope your day is going well. I know mine will!

In His Grip,
Debbie

January 28, 2005
So Far, So Good

First, thanks to Debbie for posting the last couple of days. She's great (as you can tell). I've got three chemo treatments behind me with just a few side effects. Tomorrow the treatment will be the first time I've had a particular kind of chemo. It's different in that I have to eat quite a bit of ice before, during, and after the treatment. This drug is very hard on the membranes inside the mouth, and the ice will help avoid sores and burning.

Yet again, I'm reminded of the faithfulness of God. The idea that we can glory in our weaknesses because of His strength is liberating. I'm so blessed to have the medical care that I'm receiving and the friends who have rallied to my – our – side. However, the most important component in this valley is the grace and faithfulness of God. There are many unknowns in this time of my life, but the bedrock statement that I count on is this: "I can do all things through Christ who strengthens me." That never changes. In Christ alone...!

January 31, 2005
Day 0 (again)

Well, after three months of waiting and wanting to move ahead with the transplant, it's over! Finally. Today at 11:35 a.m., the technician started infusing my dad's cells into me, and before noon I was finished. This transplant is a little different from the first one. The chemo was quite a bit harder, so I got pretty sick yesterday and today, but I'm feeling much better this afternoon. I have so much to be thankful for, and I certainly am.

So the countdown begins. The last time I was much more concerned about timing, but this time I am more concerned with this working. So when they say jump, I'll ask "How high?" I can't wait to get back on the road with L5 and again be able to personally tell you how much your prayers and support have meant to the Bennetts. We are so blessed with friends like you.

Debbie prayed for me today just before the transplant. Her sweet words to the Lord brought tears to my eyes. It felt like every word she said split Heaven wide open. Thanks, Deb.

February 8, 2005
Day 7, and Authentic Christianity

My counts are way down. The white blood cell count is very low, and platelets very, very low. This is exactly what the doctors want. I am a little bit ahead of schedule in many ways and we are so thankful. The downside to this is I'm extremely tired and my walking has taken a back seat during the last few days. I'm being honest when I say that this transplant has been significantly harder to

215

endure than my last one. Yet I still feel strong and am very hopeful about the outcome of transplant.

I'm at day seven, and in a perfect world that would mean ninety-three more to go until my release from M.D. Anderson. Sounds like a long time, but at least I can see some light at the end of the tunnel. (I hope it's not a train.)

I've been doing quite a lot of thinking lately concerning *authentic* Christianity – like whether or not what our hearts do (actions) line up with our mouth says. I was watching a morning news show today and the report was on how many husbands cheat on their wives. Evidently it's becoming sort of an outbreak across our nation. They sent an undercover reporter in to a bar to see how quickly a married man would approach her. Sure enough, in about three minutes, we were treated (through a hidden camera) to seeing a middle-aged man bust out his Romeo skills. The reporter noticed his wedding ring and asked him about it. Very brazenly he laughed and said, "It comes off real easy." And with that he slipped the ring that his wife had given him as a symbol their commitment, put it in his pocket and continued his "what happens in Vegas, stays in Vegas" routine.

You say, "Roger what has this to do with authentic Christianity?" I'm glad you asked! There have been countless times that I would've brought shame to the Lord if it hadn't been for one small thing. Guess what it was. No, not my wedding band – I'm still in love with the girl that walked down the aisle to begin our life together almost twenty-four years ago. Rather than keeping you guessing, let me give you the situation.

I was out running errands and one of my stops was the scene of a major mistake by the owner of the business. The owner got very aggressive, my temper flared, and I was going to go on through the drive through, park, and go into the establishment and finish our little spat. Then I remembered I had on a Christian message T-shirt. I was stumped... I even looked around in the car to see if I had any other shirt to put on. The only thing that stopped me was the "message" shirt I had on. If I had found a different shirt to put on, the argument would have escalated. Then the Lord spoke to me: "Is your Christianity so trivial that you can take it off like a T-shirt? Put on a plain shirt and let the guy have it? Is My sacrifice and calling so meaningless to you that you can shed it like a shirt only to put it back on when you're in the mood to be associated with Me?"

I was so caught in my sin. I would have felt better to give that guy what I thought he deserved, if only I hadn't worn that "I Believe" T-shirt. Pitiful conduct. As I drove home, I begged God's forgiveness. I asked Him to help me realize that being a Christian is much more than a garment to be taken on and off; it is the power of the Gospel, a treasure stored in jars of clay.

That's what being an *authentic* Christian is all about. *Live* the Gospel, don't just read about it. *Be* the hands and feet of Christ, not for recognition, but because He changed your life and you want to be more like Him and less like you.

I believe the harvest is plentiful and the time for revival is at hand. Lord, help us to be really authentic messengers of your Gospel.

February 12, 2005
Day 12, and the battle between the drugs and Roger's peanut brain

One reason that all the old sayings stay around forever, and are considered by some to be cliché, is because they're true! The one in specific for me today is, "My, how time flies." I'll say. Looking at my bulletin here in my hospital room that says Day 12, I can't believe it. I've sat here many a lonely night, staring at the board and thinking, "*MOVE! LET ANOTHER DAY HAVE ITS TURN!*" Then out of nowhere my doctors are saying things like, "Wow, your counts have really moved up quite a bit. We might be looking at releasing you in a week to ten days!" I said, "From your lips to God's ears!" Then, early this morning after a real tough night of reaction to pain pills, the last thing I expected to hear was, "We may release you next Monday or Tuesday!" After the clouds parted and I was able to speak, the doctor said, "Obviously, if you keep having problems like last night, we could not let you go home." But he continued, "I think last night was a fluke." Good to know! So that's it – I may be released early next week to start building my strength back up, to rest and let the Lord to His work! I'm happy to share with you this latest bit of good news.

All right – about last night. Yesterday I started having really high fever (for me). It shot up to 103.8 and just hovered there. Well, the fever and the headache proved to be a double threat, and they started me on drips and pills in big doses to get ahead of my body. It was a game of cat and mouse. (I was losing.) Somehow, I ended up down some hall all alone. Debbie had gone to the apartment just a few minutes before. The sweet nurse kept questioning me, and I knew my medical records, my room number, the whole bit. But in my mind I was waiting for Chelsea and Jordan's luggage to be sent up to our suite of rooms that I had just bought! (There are no suites like this at MDA.) She finally convinced me to follow her back to my room. It was a real strange feeling because, as I was making my case to her, it fell apart right before my eyes. I would say, "You're right, I know." This took a while to wear off, about six hours before it started making sense to my heart. My rational mind would say, "You know you are just reacting to the pills;" but my impulsive part, my heart, said, "Can't you tell them how you feel? This is embarrassing for me and for you!" I finally prevailed through the medicine wearing off and the Lord allowing me to relax in Him.

To sum up, God still cares for us and I think sometimes He is amused by us. I feel that, during those special days when we are at our funniest, God pulls up a chair and asks anyone close to join Him. He says, "Come quickly, the Bennett boy is about to give us one of his best!"

I'm sure I'll never hear the end of it.

February 13, 2005
Another Hurdle Jumped

The doctors have cleared Roger for release tomorrow, barring any unforeseen circumstances, so I have been carting things from his room for two days now. Tonight, I brought his keyboard back to the apartment, and I think the security guards wondered what in the world I was doing hauling that thing around at 10:00 p.m.!

I just wanted to say to my Valentine: Thank you for showing me and telling me EVERY day that you love me. I love you, too, more than I can say.

Together, we are
In His Grip,
Debbie

February 14, 2005
Freedom!

I'm at our apartment, lying in my bed and typing on the computer – no IVs, no vital sign collection; just peace and quiet all around! Thank You, Lord.

Now starts the fight with the "unknowns." There will be small tweaks up and down with my medication to give Dad's stem cells the greater chance for success.

I feel better already. I start my daily appointments tomorrow, but at least I'll be able to be outside just a little bit each day.

February 17, 2005
Hospital, Home, Hospital, Home – pause – Repeat.

I have so much for which to be thankful that any complaint seems the height of ingratitude. I thought about it a lot today. Debbie and I have been dealing with the loss of one of our friends we made early last year at the beginning of both our transplants. Our friend was a strong, strong lady who had an incredible husband. He rarely had left the hospital during the last ten months. I walked past Bev's room each day that I walked and was just amazed by her strength and determination.

I wasn't feeling well that Saturday so I didn't walk. On Sunday, Deb went with me to walk. As we passed Bev's room, we noticed her door standing open, and the cleaners were inside. Deb said, "I'll bet that they had to take Bev to ICU again last night." This was almost a routine thing: the doctors would put out whatever fire they could at the time, Bev would somehow rally, and in a few more days the fight to the death would start again. But this time that wasn't to be the case. Bev passed away on Saturday; she made her last trip. Her husband, Bob, was so faithful in her care. He slept in her room every night. He was very involved in her treatment and he was hard to get around if he thought that something needed to be happening but wasn't. I guess now Bob will go back to the life he led just ten months ago. We hope to see him again someday. Bob, if you read this, just know that we are glad that God sent you our way. We know that our paths crossed for a reason. We will meet you someday in a land where we will never grow old, get sick, or have to be separated ever again.

Today we saw another friend, Ashley, who has beaten the odds. The doctors literally call her "The Miracle." She is a beautiful young lady who continues to amaze the Bennetts. The day we met her, she had gotten bad news. She and her mom were on the way for a very important test, and there as we prayed for her healing and were asking God to kill the cancer, I didn't know what to believe. It was one of those times when we are asked to believe in something more that our eyes can see. If our eyes could have seen what God wanted to do in Ashley's life, we would have been stunned to see the beautiful young lady in front of us today. Thank God for you, Ashley. Tell your gramps that Debbie and I send our love and prayers his way, as well. We want to see that herd of miniatures he has.

See how God works? This post started out to be a little grumble about not getting to get back to my life soon enough. Then, in just a few minutes' time, I was comforted by His joy. I'm sure that Satan felt confident that Bev would soon be in his domain – then, at the brink, God sent His best envoy to lead sweet, strong Bev to her new home! What a Savior!

Given the chance, it's easier to fall prey to the mindset of "if you can't beat them, join them." I can only tell you that the best way to go may not be the easiest of the two

221

choices you've got. Yes, you may have to do quite a bit of work to stay to the heart of God. Yes, it may be better in the short term to turn away from the hard choice and relax. But that way of slouching through life would only end up as your demise! If you choose to walk by faith, not by sight, turning instead to the right, following His plan and feeling His presence and listening for that whisper in the night, it will be a life well spent that leaves a trail of lives touched forever, because you weren't afraid to get your hands dirty. And then, at the time for this life to be over, it is in no way an ending. There is a place that can't be described by mere words. As the old song says, it is "a fair haven of rest for the weary; How beautiful Heaven must be."

I hope for your life that the lists of hard choices will be long and well rewarded.

February 22, 2005
Counts cooperating

I'm still in the grind of spending four to six hours in the hospital daily. We are looking forward to the time that the medical team will see fit to see me only every other day. I'm not complaining, because at this point all of my counts are rebounding big time. I'm scheduled for a bone marrow aspiration around the first of March. This will tell the tale, so to speak. The hope is that I'll be totally engrafted with my dad's donor cells. That would be very good news indeed.

I haven't mentioned it, but I am a cue ball again! Here again, a silver lining – washrag and Sea Breeze vs. shampoo and hair dryer. I can sleep a little later now!

There are quite a few differences between this transplant and the first one. Everything is showing more signs of major DNA changes. My skin has that dry crocodile look in a few places. If you've ever seen Mayor McCheese on the McDonald's commercial – that's how I feel. Big ole bubble head with a skinny body. Real attractive. Of course, I've still got Deb fooled. She goes on and on about how much she likes my new hairstyle. Today in the hospital, she got so excited. She found a bunch of snow-white sprigs coming in on my bubble head. She's thrilled. She's one of those people who likes gray hair on a man. I'm blessed that either she loves me a lot, or is a spectacular actress. Either way, it makes me feel better.

I'm still having a hard time building up energy. The medical team I see assures me that this is normal. Evidently, with the harsher drugs involved in this transplant, I can expect to have these days. I'm having to slow myself down and just wait until they release me before I can get back on the road. In this case, time is creeping by.

OK, we've watched Radar (the weatherdog) on the news, and we can now officially turn in for the night. Oh, that reminds me – you should see me in my "sleeping cap!" It keeps heat from escaping my bubble head, and on certain cold nights I have to use it to sleep. Very stylish.

February 27, 2005
Ups and Downs

It has been one of those weeks – one step forward, two steps back, but nothing that is unexpected in the course of a bone marrow transplant. The good news is that we finally got a couple of days "off." That means that we did not have to go to the clinic on Saturday and Sunday, but got to do the IVs and stuff at home. That is like a mini vacation. Roger's counts are still returning to normal, more quickly than we had expected.

The side effects this time around, however, have been more pronounced. Again, not unexpected, but definitely more wearing. Twice now, Roger has had episodes with his ankle and foot that have put him in such pain that he literally could not walk on it. They are guessing that gout is to blame, although no specific markers were present. That has given me more practice in wheelchair driving, though. I managed to get him in and out of elevators without taking his foot off! We decided not to go the route of the old pain meds that made him "goofy" (his words), but the ones that were tried did not even touch the pain. The drug of choice for relief was steroids, and a quick course of those did the trick. However, when he came off of them, the pain quickly returned, more severe than before, so he was put back on them, but in a lesser dose. This has led to another set of problems: on Friday, his blood sugar was at a critically high level. Now we have had to learn how to do glucose monitoring and give insulin injections as well. We are hoping that this is "temporary diabetes" and will resolve itself as meds are tapered off. The concern is, though, that both of his parents had/have diabetes, so there is a family history there. Yesterday, I was able to get to Target and do some major grocery shopping that included lots of low-carb and sugar-free foods. I am a little limited in that he still cannot have fresh fruits and vegetables, so my culinary abilities are challenged.

I have to say again, Roger is a very good patient. If he keeps on being this good, I may get him a glucose monitor that sticks him somewhere besides his fingers! Actually, that is what I would have bought myself; but we were given this type at the clinic, and it is fine for now.

Although Roger has felt pretty lousy the last couple of days, we are hopeful that this week will bring some changes. He is scheduled this week for a battery of tests that will be thirty days post-transplant, and they should give us an "inside view" of what is going on.

Just keep us in your prayers, as you are so faithful to do. Believe me, we feel those prayers, and they sustain us! We remain grateful, and IN HIS GRIP.

Debbie

March 3, 2005
Looking Up

More long days, more tests, but, finally, some good news. We got the preliminary report from Roger's bone marrow biopsy today, and things look pretty good. It will be a few days before the rest of the report comes in. The major number we were looking at was the "blasts" – in layman's terms, the bad cells. Normal bone marrow should be blast-free. Pre-transplant, Roger had 56% in his marrow. Today's report showed 1%, and that is considered in the normal range – praise God!

He still has an MRI (he had one yesterday, but only on his ankle, and we don't have that report yet) to go, as well as a PET scan and a CT scan. That one is his least favorite, and wouldn't you know they scheduled it on his birthday, March 10? Happy Birthday, Roger! I wonder if the barium comes in birthday cake flavor?

Yesterday, we planned on our usual five or six hour day, then we would return for the MRI last night; but we ended up being there for fourteen hours straight. Needless to say, we were totally worn out by the time we got home. It turns out that he needed extra meds due to some side-effects. They have now added mega-dose steroids to what he already was taking, so now he is concerned about getting the "balloon head" (his words again). Of course, I told him not to worry about it; it will go away when the steroids stop, but it is inevitable that it will happen. Steroids are scary to me.

Good news, though – his pain is better again. The bad news is that his sugar is too high again, so he needs more testing and insulin shots. Today was the first day he could actually walk into the clinic, though – no wheelchair, so we are happy about that.

Well, that's the news from the Texas Bennetts. (It's OK – I am actually a native, since I was born in Texas and lived here the first 4 years of my life. And I guess we can truly say that Roger is a genuine Transplanted Texan too!) Hope you are having a great day. If not, MAKE IT ONE!

Looking up (in more ways than one),
Debbie

March 4, 2005
Some Really Good News

First, I want to thank Debbie for taking up my slack in posting this week. The week has been a rough one for me. There have been big swings in how I have felt from one day to the next, but we made it to Friday. That was "results day" for my bone marrow test. I believe Deb shared how my counts were rebounding very well. So today Dr. Khouri came to see me to tell me that there are NO CLL cells in my marrow, and NO AML in my cells either!

I sprang up like a shot out of the bed to receive my high fives around the room. I can't tell you what feeling

226

went through us all. Then there was some small print. It seems that my dad's cells are awake and working hard, but when I asked, "Will this continue to improve, or at some point in the future could the upward momentum we have now slow down?" The answer is, of course, that we don't know. But this is still very, very good news!

I wanted you Ropeholders to know right away, because I think that the power of your prayers moved Heaven. We've grown to depend on your faithfulness.

Thank You, God, for Your goodness.

Let this news increase your faith – not that we'll never be sick, but that this has again proven His presence in our life.

March 8, 2005
Hectic Days, but Good Days

Everyone around here is still doing great since our good news the other day.

I'm in the middle of a few setbacks, small ones so far. The diabetes is really a chore to deal with, as are the various pains that come along with training the new cells to keep on trucking.

I'll be in an MRI tube tomorrow at 6 a.m., and then typical four hour stay in the hospital for IV meds.

I feel great and feel stronger all the time.

March 11, 2005
A Happy Birthday

Well, it's the day after Roger's birthday, and we did have a very nice day. I stayed up late the night before and made sausage balls to take into the clinic. I also made a diabetic birthday cake. (Note: this particular recipe would be great for setting fence posts or re-mortaring brick.) Luckily, when we got to our appointment for his IV meds, the nurses had decorated his room with a "Happy Birthday" banner, balloons, and had a sugar-free candy bar on his pillow. Later they came in to sing to him and gave him a cake (this one was delicious!). They are so sweet!

As we suspected, the barium for the CT scan did not come in birthday cake flavor; but, thanks to Maurice Templeton, he now knows to ask for a "special" mixture that involves Diet Sprite, and he says it is a lot better.

With the blessing of Michael, a great part of our daily team, we went out to dinner (at an off-time, Michael!) with our good friend Lisa, who is also one of Roger's nurses. It was actually quite comical, because she was still in her scrubs, and Roger was hooked up to an Intermate pump of medicine and had his mask on. I guess people thought he must really be something to get to come out with his own nurse! The Intermate pump it is an ingenious device that works on vacuum principle, and because of its design it is referred to as a "baby bottle." I have to get up every night during the night to unhook it, flush lines, etc., and I never thought that at my age, I would be getting up in the middle of the night to tend to a baby bottle again! Just goes to show, we never know what to expect!

We are very excited that it seems that we WILL be at Deer Park, TX, this Sunday night (barring any unexpected circumstances). Roger will not be able to mix and mingle, but he is very much looking forward to being on stage with the rest of the group! Meanwhile, I am baking cookies that have happily redeemed my credibility as a cook.

Until then, we remain
IN HIS GRIP,
Debbie

March 16, 2005
A Surprising Visit

Well, because I'm getting stronger, I'm down to three days a week in the hospital. Today is one of those days. Usually it is a long, uneventful day. Not today! More good news was on the way. My chief BMA doctor, Issa Khouri, walked into my room and started giving me a ton of results. The one that stuck in my mind was this: "Your bone marrow is clear of cancer, and the bad chromosome that indicates aggressive AML is gone as well."

My face nearly split in two! Thank God for His blessing. I'm still in for a fight with Graft vs. Host disease, along with various infections and viruses. But we are so thrilled with today's news.

I should still be here for about two more months, but news like today gives me strength to go on.

March 21, 2005
Midnight by Midnight

I love the phrase in the Bible that says, "Morning by morning His mercies are new." Inexhaustible grace.

I've found it to be true in the night – midnight by midnight, if you will. I think we all need to be reminded that God neither slumbers nor does He sleep. He is on the job.

Have you had a time in your life recently where, during the daytime, you were able to maintain a strong face? You've fooled everyone in your circle. Even your closest friends and family have no idea that you are in a spiritual fight to finish. But in the night, when you are alone, the facade crumbles and life is real – and real bad. What do you do then? Give up? Give in? Escape in any way possible?

All of these responses have been tried by millions of people before you and will continue to be tried until Jesus comes. They are all spiritual Band-Aids – a temporary fix at best.

I never thought that I would be able to give advice on this subject, and I'm certainly no expert, but here is what I'm learning. God's plan for our lives very rarely includes a file for you to read before starting the test. Oh, we do have the ultimate battle plan in His word; just nothing that tells you how to navigate the mine fields you face today. Here's where it gets a little hard. Trust, believe, lean, obey... and last, but never least, wait. Wait. Yep. Wait. The answer is probably not what you want to hear tonight. I'm sure that there are emergencies that seem unwilling to wait, but casting your cares on Him doesn't really work if, as soon as you cast them, you pick them right back up. Wait. Trust. Believe, lean, and trust.

In my experience with cancer, I've become extremely aware of the blessing of waiting. Waiting is not natural for me. I much prefer to get to the root of the problem and fix it. I've learned that it can't always be fixed, but it will never ever be fixed if I run ahead of God, looking back over my shoulder to see if He is keeping up with me. It's like saying, "I trust You, Lord. Here I go; try to keep up!"

The blessings that I've received by giving my problems 100% to Him are as countless as the stars. And you know what? One hundred percent of the time, His answers are always better than mine.

So give up trying to shape a victory with your weak ability. Put the problem down and wait for your Father to pick it up. Then you'll be able to see the path that He is taking. You might even catch a glimpse with your spirit eyes of the true scope of His loving plan for you.

Take a spiritual load off. Have a seat and start listening for the still, small voice.

Midnight by midnight, His mercies are new!

March 27, 2005
Why the Cross, why the Tomb?

In the current environment of political correctness at any cost, the idea of a "bloody Gospel" offends many people. A majority of Americans describe themselves as spiritual, even believers; yet the same number reject the idea of a blood sacrifice for the sins of the world. Why? I believe there are many different reasons, but I think they all stem from the overall problem with sin. Sin is out of style, if you will; yet it was sin that took a Savior to the cross. Not His sin, but *mine*. A death like no other yielded a victory unlike any other.

The cross is offensive not just to many of our generation, but it was equally (maybe even more) repugnant to the generation of Jesus' day. Crucifixion was a death reserved for the lowest of the low. A person of stature never ended up on a cross. Certainly not a King or a Savior. No, this was reason enough for the intellects of the day to reject the death of Jesus as anything more than a solution to the problem of this troublemaker from Galilee. Yet the greatest mind of the day, the Apostle Paul, continued to "glory in the cross." What was foolishness to everyone else was precious to Paul. The very symbol of a horrible death was now the very embodiment of Salvation. I'm glad for that and I, too, glory in the old, rugged cross. But it doesn't end there! Having endured the nightmare of the cross, feeling the absolute weight of the world on His shoulders, experiencing even the forsaking of His Father, Jesus' work was only half complete. The tomb was waiting.

It was not remarkable for a man to be killed on the cross. Across the Roman empire, literally thousands of people died on crosses every year. No, the method of death was not original. It didn't start with Jesus, and it would not end with Him. What is unique, and what causes my heart to beat faster, is the knowledge that Jesus was the *first* and last to leave the tomb under His own power! Death was rendered powerless against the power of God. This man, Jesus, the Lamb of the world, was now the complete fulfillment of the good news of the Gospel! Death defeated – life the victor! The precious blood had been spilled out for the salvation of all.

I know you are all very busy. I've talked to people tonight who are getting ready for sunrise services and all kinds of special services for Easter 2005. I think it's great, and I wish I were physically able to participate. But I want to remind you not to get so caught up with the demands on your time that you forget the reason that we celebrate this day in the first place. The cross was temporary and, thank God, so was the tomb! He is Risen! Let those words be the foundation of everything you do, today and every day of your life! Through the sacrifice of Christ we, too, defeat death! We too become victors!

I know a little about blood, having been through two bone marrow transplants. They tell me that my donor cells are doing well, and I'm thrilled with that. But, on a much larger scale, I had a transplant when I was nine years old that is never in danger of failing. I exchanged my eternity for His eternity when I made Him Lord of my life. My sin was traded for His perfection! My weakness for His strength; my sadness for His joy. I was undeserving, yet given a place at His table. What grace has been extended.

Why the cross, why the tomb? No one had ever defeated these two horrible things. They should have been the end of the story of Jesus. Should have been, but...

He is risen, He is risen indeed!

April 11, 2005
George Younce Makes the Last Move.

George Younce, 1930-2005

Have you ever been in a situation in life that would be best described as surreal? You know the facts, but the facts don't line up with your heart.

That's how I've felt all day. I got the message this morning on the way to the hospital that George Younce, the world's greatest bass singer, the man who, with Glen Payne, gave me my start way back in 1979, had passed away. "It can't be true," I thought. George has pulled through so many critical times in his life that I was sure he'd pull through this one. It was not to be. At 3:30 a.m., George stood in the very presence of his Lord Jesus. I can just see the event with my spirit eyes. Here was a man who'd sung about Heaven for years, and now he can sing about it from a firsthand perspective! I like to think that his buddy and partner of so many years, Glen Payne, was waiting in line to meet George and tell him where to meet him for the "all-eternity" singing.

One night, about two months ago, I was feeling a little sad. It was late and I couldn't sleep, so I fired up my iPod and started listening to some old Cathedral tapes. Many were recorded in the 1970s, before my time with them. I got very emotional. Not just one emotion, but many. I laughed for a long time. Then, as George would say, my eyes started leaking. Just a trickle at first, but as I listened the tears flowed like a river. Glen Payne has been gone since 1999, and my thoughts were obviously on George and the struggles he was having. Suddenly, I got the idea to make him a CD of what I was listening to and send it to him. I put about twenty songs of the very best of George and enclosed a note that basically said, "If you ever wonder why so many people say that you are the best bass to ever sing, put this CD in and all will be made clear!" The next day, on the way to the hospital, I had a voicemail of George laughing and thanking me for the CD. He said, "You know, I wasn't half bad was I?" That was followed by his trademark belly laugh. When I returned the call, we talked for a while. I didn't know that it would be the last conversation that I would have with him, but if I had to pick one that would be it.

Words can't say how much Debbie and I love the entire Younce family. I can't imagine the pain and loss they are feeling right now. So, again, I come before you faithful Ropeholders and ask you to bombard Heaven in their behalf. Pray that God will send His sweet spirit in a special way to comfort George's incredible wife of nearly fifty years, Clara, along with Gina, Dana, Lisa, Tara, and George Lane. These will be tough days, but I know the Younces well enough to know that there will be laughter with the tears. George was a unique individual, and one of the true greats in any form of music. Everyone who knew him knew that, just under his massive talent for singing, there was a massive talent for joy, jokes and laughter. Those are my favorite memories of George.

The first time I heard him sing up close was at my first rehearsal at Glen and Van Payne's house in Stow, OH, just before my first road trip with the Cathedrals. My jaw dropped when Younce went down to a low A-flat and just sat there on it. Perfect tone, pitch, everything! I had a hard time not being a fan just then – I had to act like that was something I saw every day! When we left that night on our way to Winston-Salem, NC, George started telling stories on the bus. My jaw was still aching from rehearsal, and now my sides were hurting from laughter. He had us rolling in the floor.

So, George, my small tribute to you tonight is this. Thanks for being the best. Thanks for showing the young singers a work ethic that we could strive for, and thanks for giving me my career nearly twenty-six years ago. If it weren't for a George and a Glen, you might not know a Roger Bennett.

Tonight George is truly In His Grip!

May 3, 2005
Weekend Update

I am sure that many of you are anxious for an update of how the weekend went. We have been so busy since getting back "home" to Houston that I am just now sitting down to the computer. Roger is trying to get some sleep while waiting on IVs to finish up (then it will be time for the next one...), so I thought I'd type while I am waiting to tend to all of those medicines.

What a roller coaster weekend! We left Thursday to fly to Fresno, CA, with luggage and a cooler full of medicine. That in itself was quite interesting, because one of the planes we were on was so small that they actually had to strap the cooler in a seat! It wouldn't fit under a seat or in the overhead bin, and we could not risk checking it. I was just glad there was not a full plane so it had a seat to sit in!

Fresno was a great experience, and it was good medicine for Roger to be back with the group. He said he felt "rusty," but I thought that Legacy Five did a great job. I realize that I am biased, but I truly admire those guys and their love for God – they just happen to sing well, too! We enjoyed some great fellowship with them, and got to eat some great food. Then, on Friday afternoon, one of the members of the medical team called and told us they had found an "obscure and rare" infection in one of Roger's tests. We have NO IDEA where this one came from, since it is normally only found in Africa or underdeveloped third world countries (none of which we have been to). Less than 0.5% of the cases are found in the US. Of course, we always knew Roger was special, but does he have to keep proving it? Anyway, because of the sensitivity and rarity of the medicine required, we had to leave Fresno early on Saturday morning and fly back to Houston to get it.

Having done that, however, we decided to catch a flight Sunday and go back to San Diego to meet L5 again for their concert at Shadow Mountain Church in El Cajon, CA. We were so blessed by being there. Dr. Jeremiah and all of the people there were so gracious and welcoming. After the concert, we slept really fast and caught an early flight back to Houston on Monday morning, landing Monday afternoon and going straight to the clinic for scheduled treatment. There we learned that yet another infection had been identified and began treatments for that. We are back to the "baby bottle" medicine that keeps us up changing it at night!

Tomorrow is another clinic day. We hope to learn more about what is going on then. The good news is that the blood counts are still holding fairly well. These new infections might put a delay in our going back to TN, but then again they might not. We see Roger's doctor on Friday, so maybe we will have a better idea of a timeline then. Thursday is the big test – another bone marrow biopsy – to see how the transplant is holding. We are at day 91 today of our 100. It really has seemed to fly by these last couple of weeks.

Two of my brothers are driving down from TN tomorrow to take a U-Haul full of "stuff" back for us. We will keep the necessities here with us until we head home for good.

Well, Roger just called me to come in, so I will close for now. Rest well and remain as we are: in His Grip!

May 9, 2005
Just a quick update

Happy belated Mother's Day to all the moms out there. My two precious kids did their part to call and wish me a happy day yesterday. This was my second Mother's Day in Houston, and it was a very stormy one; but today it is sunny, humid and hot. Today we are back to the routine again, and Roger begins a week of more testing.

He is still battling the infections, and today we found out that he has a flu virus on top of it all. No wonder he has felt bad all weekend. We have added more pills to the arsenal. He is also battling pain in his ankle again.

He has two CT scans and an MRI scheduled in the next couple of days; there is also a PET scan in the near future.

Even though it is Day 98 today, we are not looking at being released on Day 100. The doctor suggested an extra three weeks or so, depending on how the infections respond. (We WILL be at L5's Celebration 2005, unless something drastic occurs, though!) Two of my brothers were down over the weekend to take a load of stuff home for us. We do have to relocate apartments this Friday, since this one has been re-leased; but this way we won't have as much to move.

We will update as we get test results in. For now, just continue your prayers – we do appreciate them more than we can say!

May 21, 2005
Here's the latest

As we hoped, all the day ninety tests (which include a bone marrow test, CT scan, PET scan, MRI, and of course a complete blood work up) showed no cancer activity at all! I have another MRI scheduled for next week. This one is of the brain (shouldn't take long).

Now, concerning the dreaded side effects – these continue to give me problems. I have three separate issues right now. All three are infections in different parts of my system. I won't bore you with their medical names and details, but please pray that they will be resolved soon. Debbie and I will be going to Tennessee next weekend for our son's high school graduation and L5's homecoming. We are so excited about both events. Jordan has worked hard, and we are so glad that we'll be able to share this milestone with him. We've missed so many things down through the years in both Jordan and Chelsea's life that the ones we do get to attend are extra special.

Back to the boring stuff – the feeling I get from our medical team is that if it were not for the side effect issues, we would already have been home. Thank God that the cancer part of the process is looking good, so we'll just leave the timing stuff to our Father. His plans are much better than mine!

This part of the transplant is a little scary, actually. There are so many cases where the transplant goes well, and then the "little things" like infections do the real damage. During the past few weeks I've especially had to lean on the Lord. This is the time when every little ache or pain feels like cancer. You cancer patients know what I'm talking about. You try not to be a hypochondriac, but you find yourself in the middle of the night staring at the ceiling, wondering what that ache you feel is all about.

Then you remember that jalapeño pepper that you just had to have at dinner...!

Anyway, I'm so thankful and grateful to God for His loving kindness. I hope I can always keep an eternal attitude during this trial, and the next one, and the next one. Trials won't be over until we cross over to our real home, so until then I'll just keep trusting. He is never taken by surprise by our trials. God never says, "I didn't see THAT coming!"

May 27, 2005
Dog-Tired, but Home!

Debbie, Chelsea and I just got home a few minutes ago and are severely whipped! Our day started early with me having a two-hour blood transfusion. Noon found me out like a light in an MRI tube. That is my favorite way to get an MRI, by the way! Then we headed to the airport to wait for a late plane. I've always heard that "all's well that ends well." I see that it's true in this instance.

So now it's off to sleep for a few hours. Then tomorrow's Jordan's big day. Graduation! And Deb and I get to be there. Thank You, Lord, for this blessing. If that wasn't enough, after graduation we *hot foot** it to the Gaylord Opryland Hotel to begin Legacy Five's Second Annual Homecoming. I've been told that well over 3,000 people will be checking in tomorrow just to be a part of Celebration 2005. What another great blessing that my family and I will get to attend and participate. God is good!

So that's it. I get to be nearly normal this weekend. (I can hear you who know me well: "Normal?")

Have a great Memorial Day weekend!

hot foot - to travel at a high rate of speed, generally in a vehicle; but occasionally used in this manner: "Wal-Mart is having a sale on motor oil, let's *hot foot* it *ovar.***"

***ovar** – "over there." Generally pronounced this way in the more civilized areas of the South, and Arkansas.

June 1, 2005
Dog-Tired but Home II

This seems like an every day event right now: I'm tired but can't sleep. So I write to you all.

Legacy Five's homecoming (Celebration 2005) was a complete success. We had such a wonderful, blessed time – laughter, tears, and a ton of great Southern Gospel music.

You'll have to forgive me and understand when I say that my favorite event of the weekend wasn't at Opryland. It was the graduation of our son Jordan. He and his buddy, Ryan, played guitar and sang during the ceremony. Jordan didn't warn us, and Deb and I bawled like newborns.

I'm still having a few problems with my counts. I'll be in the hospital for about six hours tomorrow trying to get them all moving in the right direction. As usual, you have overwhelmed Debbie and me with your awesome support, love and, most importantly, prayers. I'm trying to return the favor, but I don't feel that I can do for you what you have for me. I'll keep trying.

June 13, 2005
Day 133, and Homeward Bound!

Hallelujah! Our visit to the clinic this morning went great, and they told us we can go home to Tennessee!

There aren't enough words to express how excited we are. There are still some wobbly counts, but no infections are showing up, so the rest can be treated with medication. This means taking IV fluids home, but that is very much routine for us; it is not even an issue. We will see Roger's oncologist in TN a couple of times a week for lab tests, etc., but that is okay, too. We will be coming back to Houston a couple of times a month as it stands right now but, if all goes well, that won't last too long either. Then we'll stretch it out to once per month, once every couple of months, and so on.

We were discussing at lunch that we don't remember how to be "normal" any more. I am sure there will be adjustments all around, not only for us but for Chelsea and Jordan, too. Those are just a few more hurdles to jump, but they are surely welcome ones.

So the rest of the today and tomorrow will be spent tying up loose ends here in Houston, loading up for the trip home, distributing leftover food and supplies, closing out mail boxes, refilling prescriptions, saying goodbyes, and whatever else we think of. Hopefully, we will be on the road by tomorrow afternoon, and reach TN on Wednesday. Thank you in advance for your prayers for our safe journey.

June 16, 2005
Home – Beginning or Ending?

As I sit here in my favorite place in the world (my porch), I have some time to think about the last few days. Because of the incredible demands of our schedule in the last few days, I've not been able to put my feelings down. Today, however, is a perfect day to reflect. From my vantage point on the porch, I can see one of my neighbors' herd of cows. They are jockeying for a shady spot in the line of trees at the end of their pasture. Straight ahead, I'm observing a battle *royale* between about a half-dozen blackbirds and one blue jay. So far, the jay is winning big time. It's a loud, frantic fight; but I get the feeling it's more for entertainment than anything. Finally, the closest drama to me is Chelsea's cat, Leia, washing her hands and trying to decide whether or not to allow our smallest Cocker to exist in her space. Quite an exciting afternoon, but just what I've been craving. But even with my great view of the surroundings, I really can't tell how any of the dramas I'm watching will turn out. Will the cows come to an understanding and call it off? Will the Jay finally give up and fly to another branch? Will Leia relent, put her jealousy aside, and allow Ladybug a place on the porch as well? I don't have enough info right now to say. Only time will tell.

That's kind of how I feel about being at home right now. After an 800 mile car ride, no rest for several days, and a few other problems, I can tell you that it will take Debbie and me a while to get settled mentally. My thoughts are, "Is this an ending or a beginning in my life?" Maybe it is both. I hope that it is the end of medical problems for awhile, and a chance to experience some joyful days, both personally and musically, in my life. Or will it be the opposite – a short break from struggling only to begin again? That's the way it was last time. There was

243

a time in my life when these thoughts would have been a "day-killer" for me, but not now. It's not because I'm so much stronger; it's that I've had to trust a plan that is bigger than me and, in trusting the plan, I've become better at trusting the Planner. He's proven faithful.

So today, even with the view that I have, I can't tell you how all this will end. I don't have enough information for that; but I do have enough information to kick back on my porch and watch the beautiful creation around me, leaving the plan in the hands of the Planner!

By the way – the cows worked it out, the jay left, and the dog and cat have begun a roadmap to peace.

July 5, 2005
Fireworks and Check-ups.

We are getting ready to be out the door to the clinic for my latest check-up. This is always a little stressful for us, but not something we can't handle with the Lord on our side.

Last night when we arrived in our hotel room, Deb and I were absolutely worn out and wanted nothing more than to cuddle up in the bed and sleep for ten hours.

Let me back up a little bit. I admit that yesterday I'd been griping about missing the fireworks show on the Fourth. We got on the plane too early, and got to Houston too late. Bummer.

So, we were sitting around watching the news when Debbie said, "Did you hear that?" I sure did! I ran to the window and there, perfectly framed by the incredible Houston skyline, was the beginning of their awesome Independence Day fireworks display. It was like Christmas for us. We ran to douse all the lights in the room, and then just stood in front of the huge window in our eleventh floor room. We had the best view in the joint!

We really enjoyed it, and it helped us put the check-up thoughts behind us for a while. So, even though this morning we are rushing around to get to our appointments on time, we're happy!

July 19, 2005
Back to Reality

Well, we made it back from the Alaskan Cruise, having had a wonderful time. We were able to take a few family members along, and I think everyone had a great time. My dad turned eighty-three while he was with us on the cruise, and he got to go fishing in Ketchikan, AK. (He caught a King Salmon, which bit my brother on the finger – apparently they have teeth!) While this cruise is a very relaxing one, it proved to be a bit taxing on Roger, physically. He did get to rest but, under my orders, he will be resting more.

We are in Houston for another round of tests and doctor visits. We arrived tonight ahead of Hurricane Emily, and tomorrow Roger will have a bone marrow biopsy, and then will see his doctor on Thursday. We are always anxious for those test results to come back, but we pray for patience while waiting.

Things are still unfolding back at the Bennett house as we try to get back into a routine there after basically a year and a half of absence. We are still unpacking from two moves, added to unpacking from the cruise, and trips to Houston. But, as we all know, it will all still be there when I get back!

Chelsea had her twenty-first birthday yesterday (!) and is planning to go back to school in the fall. I am so thankful for her taking this past year off, running our mail order office and keeping the house standing. Jordan is gearing up for a week-long road trip with five of his buddies. They leave Saturday. So, if you see a minivan with no air conditioning, loaded with six teenage boys, I'd steer clear if I were you! (Seriously, you might want to pray for all of us for that week.) We are blessed that his friends are great kids, just like he is.

It's late, and the tests begin early in the morning, so I will close for now. Thank you, as always, for your continued prayers and support.

July 25, 2005
Still Resting

It's late, as usual, but I am still hanging in there. I promised to post results of my tests last week, so here they are: the bone marrow biopsy still shows that I am in remission! Praise the Lord for that great news! I still do have some little bugs floating around, and I am coughing, etc., etc.; so they are tweaking my medications and watching me again. I fly back to Houston tomorrow for follow-up visits. Chelsea is going with me this time, as Debbie is knee-deep in a project at home.

I continue to be amazed at the frailty of the human body. While rejoicing in the good news that I am still cancer-free, I stumble around trying to gain strength and control over the rest of my body. Debbie, Scott, and the doctor have put me on more rest. I took last weekend off and, truthfully, it is day-to-day as to whether I have the strength to go out. I am assured that it will happen, and I anxiously await that day. This is just another way God reminds me that I need to lean on Him. He is, after all, the true source of strength – not just for me, but for all of us.

So, for now, I will wait patiently, rest when I am told, and try to learn the lessons He has set before me.

July 29, 2005

The good news is that my cancer is still in remission (it has been three months). The bad news is I'm still dealing with some major treatment-related side-effects. Thus, I've been grounded. This time I have to agree, though; I know that my present condition would not allow me back on the bus. But, again, it's a day-to-day thing and could turn around for the good very soon. That's what I believe will happen.

God remains constant, loving and on the job.

August 12, 2005
A Great Check-up!

Well, the latest check-up was a winner! My counts were better than they've been in months. There are still just a few small things to deal with, but nothing big right now. My family and I are enjoying a weekend together. Then, next weekend if all goes well, I'll rejoin Legacy Five for the first time in forever.

God is so good. It has been a long road, but it feels good to at least know that I'll be back on the road in just a few days.

August 21, 2005
A Quiet Sunday Morning

I have a few hours before I leave for Houston for my regular check up and decided to bring you all up to date. My writing has suffered lately, but I think a more normal schedule is just around the corner for me. I've missed posting to you.

OK, here's the latest. As some of you may have heard, I had a strange set back this week. I woke up on Thursday morning with a high fever and it would only climb higher during the day. When it reached the danger zone about 2 p.m., Debbie called our team at M.D. Anderson and asked them what to do. I was supposed to leave that night for my first weekend back with Legacy Five, so I was crushed that this new sickness looked like it was going to delay my going on the road again. It did.

The team suggested that I see my oncologist here in Nashville, Dr. Dana Thompson. My fever was at its highest (103) when we called to see if we could see him asap. He said, "come in right away."

As you know from reading this journal, they never tell you that you are out of the woods with a BMT and fever is a grade A red flag for something nasty going on in your system. Bottom line...they don't play when it comes to fever. Dr. T. wanted to admit me right away, but I talked him into letting me go home and try to sleep through the night. So we made a deal if my fever came up again I would go straight to the ER and they would admit me for the weekend. I agreed and went home and straight to bed.

Now the good news. By the time I got home that afternoon my fever had dropped to 96.3 and would stay there all weekend long. So I've been able to rest here at home and try to build up strength. Thank God! The fever has yet to return.

When I get to Houston, I expect to be run through the paces but that's fine, I'm very patient. I don't want to do anything foolish at this stage of the game to jeopardize the outcome.

If all goes well I plan to join Legacy Five for next week's concerts. I'm hoping that this little episode has been a "blip" on the screen and nothing to worry about.

Of course Satan has swooped in to put in his 2 cents worth, attacking my confidence and trying to steal my peace. I don't know if he has a tail or not, but if he does, it was tucked when my Father evicted him from the room. I had no power to fight but the Spirit of the Lord booted him out of my house as if to say, "My child needs his rest...OUT!

I'm thankful to be His child!

In His Grip!
Roger

September 6, 2005
A Quick Update

There should be words enough for my family and I to thank you all for your prayers, but there aren't. We'll just leave it at we could not have made it this far without all your prayers.

The reason you haven't heard from me lately is that I've been a little sick with those pesky side effects and trying to get back out on the road. The good news is that I'm doing better and I have made it back on the road! More good news, my son Jordan is traveling with Legacy Five for the next year playing bass guitar (and doing a great job, I might add, all fatherly prejudice aside!).

Debbie and I are in Houston today for checkups....more good news, my counts are doing well. I'm maintaining all the right levels. There are still lingering problems and to be honest (as I've tried always to do) I don't feel so great. My energy is under attack and that keeps me from being motivated to do the things that I have to do. Pray for a change in that area.

We drove right by the Astrodome in Houston today and saw a tiny piece of the thousands of refugees from Katrina. Our prayers are so important for these people as is our money. Pray that God will lead you in how you can best help in this tragedy.

Well, our airplane is about to board and I want to be on it!

We love you and remain tightly in His grip.
Roger and Debbie

September 19, 2005
Health and NQC Update

First to the health...I've made it through the two weeks that the Dr. gave me between visits. A few non-life-threatening side effects came into play. Mostly just intense pain that was resistant to meds. But as usual, God gave me grace for the moment and I made it through every commitment that we had. Just by way of testimony, let me stop here and give a heartfelt plug for the National Quartet Convention. It is indeed the biggest and the best multi-day Southern Gospel event in the nation. Both artists and groups are lifted up and blessed but the most important one to lift up is Jesus and I'm proud to say that He is the center of the NQC! In addition to the usual great singing and fellowship, each year the <u>Singing News Magazine</u> has their fan awards presentation. 1000's of subscribers vote for their favorites in each category. This year we were so proud that Frank Seamans was voted favorite Horizon Individual and I was voted favorite pianist. Thanks to all the readers of the Singing News for your love and support.

Deb and I leave for Houston tomorrow after an afternoon of tenor auditions. I see my doctor on Tuesday and have some treatments scheduled for Tuesday evening. Then hopefully we'll fly home early Wednesday. The cancer may not get me, but the schedule may! Ha.

I have much to share with you and starting next post I'll start sharing some "heaven nudging" that I'm feeling in my heart.

Still depending on your prayers!
Roger

September 21, 2005
Safely Home

Well, for all of you who knew we were in Houston this week, we wanted to let you know we are now safely home. Actually, there were no motel rooms to be found in Houston, so we had to stay in Galveston - right on the beach! There was certainly a lot of activity as we drove back to Houston this morning to catch a flight, as the evacuations had begun in earnest. Let's do remember to pray for all of those who are preparing for Hurricane Rita's possible landfall in that area, as well as those who had come to the area as evacuees following Katrina, who are now being moved again. It was strange seeing all of the people who were being housed at the Astrodome when we arrived, then knowing that they were all moved out last night.

Roger's checkup was uneventful this week. Still fiddling with a few counts, but that is really the norm for now. Change this medicine, up this dosage, try this new prescription, stand on your left foot and jump up and down, etc., etc...... No, really, his doctor is very good at keeping on top of all the symptoms and side effects that he experiences, and we are still assured that things are going as expected. It just doesn't always feel too comforting to know that this is the norm for the time being, but we do know that God is still in control, and He gives the strength and grace that we always need.

Roger and Jordan are off again tomorrow evening, so keep them and the rest of "the boys" in your prayers.

I enjoyed meeting each of you that I was able to last week at NQC. You are all truly being used by God as encouragers!

So, I remain In His Grip,
Debbie

October 01, 2005
Heaven Nudgings #1

I mentioned a couple of postings ago that I wanted to share some info with you that wasn't health related. Some "nudgings" that I've been feeling lately and wanted to see if they relate to you at all.

The attack on all things Christian has just about worn me down. As you can imagine with my only activity for most of the day being sitting down, I get to watch a lot of TV. Not ONE day goes by without several vicious outbursts from the other side about how terrible Christianity has been for the world. Comics strip all of the reverence and awe away from the name of our Savior in the most blasphemous way. Many weak-willed politicians cower at the very thought of admitting that they are believers. Frankly I've had it. As for me, I'm gonna stop being a silent witness while the world bashes away unchallenged by some Christians. I know that sounds harsh but hear me out. Believers in Christ are the last to receive the tolerance that the world wants to give everyone else. I mean Everyone else. I watched with horror not too long ago as an ACLU lawyer argued a case in favor of releasing a known sex offender back into a neighborhood with innocent children, while her comrades at the ACLU were suing a teacher who had a Bible lying on his desk. He didn't read it during hours, never mentioned it, but brought to read over his lunch break. He was fired.

All of this came together for me during the Katrina/Rita crises. I watched heroes by the hundreds rushing down to help, but the only reporting I got was how all of this catastrophe was President Bush's fault. That while he was watching his oil profits from Haliburton and maybe even reading his Bible, he did like a modern day Nero and "fiddled" while New Orleans sank. Now a month later this has been totally disputed. We were late getting in some places which he as the leader takes responsibility for. But the viciousness and disrespectful ways the enemies attacked him took much of the emphasis OFF of the people who really needed the help. I was proud to see our president hold up under the strain. *"The truth shall set them free!"*

Now, how is this a heaven nudging you say? Simply this: We've let our behavior be programmed by the world. We are supposed to grin and bear it while our way of life is threatened. Here's my nudging. Don't lose your love or empathy toward your enemy, but strengthen your spine and speak out in a firm but friendly voice whatever it is you are wanting to defend. I have done it a couple of times recently and it actually went quite well. No blows, no shouting, just two people disagreeing agreeably.

Take this for what it's worth. If it strikes a chord with you ....try it. If you know that you could never do it...don't. But whatever you do, do it in the love of Jesus. Speak kindness to those who despise us...you'll drive them out of their mind!

Love to you all....I go back for a checkup next Tuesday and will be in touch ASAP after I get results back.

In His Grip!
Roger

October 14, 2005
Hanging In There

The past few days have been spent just lying around, trying to gain strength. After the last L5 tour, I went to Indiana to retrieve Roger and bring him home to rest while the rest of the group went to Mackinac Island for a conference. Our original plans were for me to join Roger and go to the island with him, but he was really worn out, and badly needed the rest. He developed a pretty bad cold or something, and the doctor put him on some more antibiotics and anti-flu drugs, which seem to have helped tremendously.

So, after some beautiful days here at home, Roger is off tonight for the weekend with Legacy Five, and looking forward to it. We have an extra week off from check-ups in Houston, since his doctor will be out of town for the normal two-week check-up. The last check-up was basically the same as the ones before - tweak a few meds, get some infusions, then go on our merry way. The next one (Oct. 25) will include a follow-up bone marrow biopsy.

On the one hand, that is a stressful test, since the results are pretty conclusive as to the state of the disease; on the other hand, it may be one of Roger's favorite tests, since it is done under conscious sedation, and the drugs are very "happy" ones... (I, however, dread it since he has told some really big tales to the staff while coming out from under the sedation....don't ask!).

Thank you for continuing to pray for our strength. I would have thought things would have settled down by now, but ongoing issues tend to be very wearing on the body and mind. I would also ask you to pray for the family of a fellow transplant patient who has received some very bad news regarding his time left. I won't mention his name, but God will know. Your prayers keep us going, so we stay

In His Grip
Debbie

October 26, 2005
The Long Haul

Well, with most of the results in, I'm holding my own. I hate to keep posting this phrase but I'm still having quite a few small side effects. The good news is the blood work is normal, and 1/2 of the bone marrow test is normal. The actual biopsy of the bone itself won't be back for a couple of days. I'll let you know how it turns out.

As far as my road schedule, I'm still under quite a few restrictions but so far have not missed many dates. Some nights if I run out of steam on the first half of the concert I will have to sit the 2nd half out. I don't like it but that's the reality. In addition, my wife has several spies that are on my own bus. If they send a red flag to her it's homeward bound for RB! I guess that's ok, they all have my best interests at heart and I know better than to go up against such a great congregation of witnesses.

On the emotional front, I've been feeling a little helpless lately. I've had a few friends get very bad news in the last few weeks and I feel so hurt for them. I know this is on the physical plane but it's hard to stay positive about their chances when it's clear that time is short. I talked to a sweet man the other day. I only knew him as Grandpa Springer. He was a big Cathedral fan and was grandpa to another bone marrow patient (4 transplants), Ashley. Anyway, his time was short but the day I talked with him we had a great chat. He was a wonderful Christian man and was "heaven sure" but the last thing I said to him was "don't give up." In 3 days his body did give up but I don't believe his faith ever did!

Which brings me to my last update point: my spiritual health. On our first recording called "Strong in the Strength," Deb and I wrote the title song. I want to leave that chorus as my spiritual update.

> Strong in the strength of someone else,
> Trusting a hand that never has failed.
> Living a life of spiritual wealth,
> Strong in the strength of someone else,
> Strong in the strength of someone else!

In case it's not clear, Jesus is my strength and in my weakness His strength is perfect!

In His Grip!
Roger

November 08, 2005
Test Results and Trophies

I got good news a couple of days ago regarding the bone marrow test. It came back all clear! Debbie and I again want to thank you for your prayers and love during this long fight.

There is no change on the "side-effect" front. I'm still very weak and struggle with the issues involved with recovery. I just have to get it through my head that I'm a slow responder I guess. My spirit is willing... you know the rest of the quote.

I'm still amazed at God's faithfulness to me. When I have small faith, His strength is mighty. There have been times during the last 10 plus years when I had given up on myself, but He never did.

To be honest about the situation, we are in the midst of some heavy lifting right now. Some days our spirits are low. Several of our friends have lost their battle with cancer and with each passing, a small chink will appear in our armor. Needing renewal yet unable to renew ourselves, we once again fall before the Father exhausted and sad, and once again He gives us peace beyond our understanding.

I know that these words may seem like trite little phrases strung together to form a sort of hayseed theology. Some might even say that we are delusional, grasping at any spiritual straw we can to make sense of the cancer. I don't condemn or judge if you feel that way, but I will say this in no uncertain terms: God is real, and God is good. We live in a bad world; a world that is ruled by the prince of the power of the air (Satan). He is the author of lies and confusion. He subtly appeals to our intellect to insert doubt of the existence of God. But God remains and shall forever. Your reasoning will never reconcile the unseen. So many well-meaning people refuse to acknowledge anything they can't see or touch. This will lead to a lifetime of frustration and bitterness.

The Kingdom of Heaven is invisible to our mortal eyes, but it exists. The cross of Calvary has long ago crumbled to dust but its effects still reverberate around the world! Christ died for our sins. In our place He endured an agonizing death. But His resurrection on the 3rd day sealed the fate of all who would but believe! Thank you Father for your love manifested toward us by your Son Jesus. We are forgiven, forever, amen!

It sort of puts our "light and momentary troubles" in perspective when viewed through the lens of what God sees in us. We are His trophies of grace!

In His Grip!
Roger

November 24, 2005
Happy Thanksgiving!

The Bennett House - 2:00 am. Thanksgiving morning.

Well, all the chopping and dicing are finished. All the food is just waiting to be cooked and/or plated. I didn't do much this year as far as cooking is concerned. I wanted to. I've been watching the Food Network for the last month and thought I was all "Emerilled Up".

It was not to be. But I had an alternate plan. The same alternate plan I've used for 24 years... Debbie! I married way above my head and that includes the kitchen! So, as I sit here writing to you Ropeholders, I can smell the results of her work. We are sharing the cooking this year, friends and family are bringing "categories:" meat, sides, and desserts. About 2 PM tomorrow, my belt is coming off, the phone is going to be muted and our annual Thanksgiving celebration will start.

If memory serves, this will be my first Thanksgiving at home in a while.

So, in addition to being thankful for the food I'll eat tomorrow, my heart will be full of thanksgiving for the faces around my table.

My Dad is with me this year! Before he goes home we will have had at least a week together that had nothing to do with my medical condition. Thanks for that Lord.

Of course, Debbie, Chelsea and Jordan will be with me as well. How could I ask for more? But there is more.

We will have friends with us tomorrow that are not mere friends. They and their brood are as much a part of our family as any blood relative. What a blessing.

And then what Thanksgiving would be complete without in-laws? Yet again, I hit a home run in that department too. We'll have my old bat mother-in-law and father-in-law, Louise and Bob Westbrook, along with brothers-in-law, Bobby and Tony.

I'm already making plans to be in Arkansas for Christmas to see all my folks that I can't be with tomorrow so if y'all are reading this, look out 'cause in a few weeks, we'll be honking in the front yard!

I look back at the "novel" I've written for you tonight, and it wasn't supposed to be that way! I was just going to wish all of you from all of Legacy Five, the most blessed Thanksgiving ever. But I started thinking about my own blessings and there you have it.

I guess to close I'll just say, I've found that business, money, and strength all can fail. I'd much rather be sitting at my table tomorrow, on the road to recovery physically and feel fully alive in my spirit because of all the blessings my Father in Heaven has bestowed so abundantly to me!

So from all of Legacy Five...we are thankful to all of you as well. You are our life-line and we love you!

In His Grip!
Roger

November 29, 2005
Another Setback

Well, Roger and I flew down to Houston last night for his check-up today, suspecting that the doctor would not be too pleased with his condition. A few more little issues have cropped up, and after discussing them all with his doctor, and finding some positive virus cultures, he is now back in the hospital. This is not too traumatic; actually, it is for the best. Dr. Khouri wants to repeat quite a few tests, and with the state of Roger's suppressed immune system, he thought it would be best to just admit him, and have all the tests run in a concentrated area, rather than us having to run here and there for each one.

So, I am headed back to the hospital now, after a shopping run for hospital-worthy pajamas and sugar-free snacks (among the many issues, his blood sugar was sky-high, due to the steroids he has been on again).

We are not panicked, but would appreciate your prayers. Hopefully, we will have some test results by early next week. Gotta run!

Firmly In His Grip, and glad to be there!
Debbie

December 02, 2005
An Unexpected Detour

This is a hard post for me to write, from the standpoint that I am not sure I can explain things coherently. First, let me say that Roger and I both know that we are in God's hands, so we do not worry about the details too much.

This morning, we found out that Roger's AML (the cancer/leukemia that necessitated the second transplant) has returned.

While not exactly unexpected news (the "minor issues" he has been facing the past couple of weeks were symptomatic of a recurrence), it nonetheless is a blow when you hear the doctor say the words.

Many snippets of songs have been running through our minds - some we have penned, and others that have been a blessing to us. What a comfort!

Roger is still in the hospital, and will remain there for the next few days. We are still waiting on more test results and doctors' visits that will give us more information. We don't have a plan of attack yet, but it looks like chemotherapy will be the first line of defense. Another concern is that Roger has lost his voice, due to either a mass on his vocal chords, or an enlarged lymph node that is pressing on the chords. Again, we don't know definitively. There is some discomfort involved, but I do admire how he is hanging in there. We are both at peace with the diagnosis, but there are a few moments of fear and uncertainty that crop up now and then.

We will keep all of you posted as we gain more information, but we would love to have your prayers: for us as we are in Houston; for Chelsea in Tennessee; for Jordan as he is on the road with Legacy Five, then back in Tennessee; for our extended families; and for the doctors and nurses as they treat Roger.

We are still right where we need to be:
In His Grip,
Roger and Debbie

December 09, 2005
Out of the Hospital

After 9 days, Roger is now out of the hospital. It is good to be in an apartment, where we can cook something besides hospital food, and sleep in a real bed.

While in the hospital, Roger received 5 days of intensive chemotherapy, and the enlarged nodes seem to be responding very well to it. After a day or so of the chemo, the node on his vocal chords had reduced in size to where his voice began coming back, and is now back to a more normal level, aside from being very weak. His counts have pretty much bottomed out, but that is to be expected with this chemo regime. He had to receive blood before leaving the hospital, and is expected to need platelets over the weekend, but that also is not unexpected. The doctors have requested that we "hang around" Houston for a month or so, but it is all up in the air as far as schedules go. We will keep you posted as we find out what we are to do. Every doctor that saw Roger in the hospital was very encouraged with his progress. We just don't know the long-range plans yet. It does look like we will be in Houston for another Christmas, and our 4th anniversary in a row! (For those who have asked, I am not renting a mailbox here for just a month.)

Thank you so much for your prayers. After the first couple of days post-diagnosis, we have felt a real peace about all of this. No matter the outcome (and we do have a positive outlook), we know that God already knows how it will turn out, and His plans are for our good, so we have left it all in His hands. That frees us from having to worry about it, so we can just be the best witness we can be for Him.

We love you all, and hope that you, too, remain
In His Grip,
Debbie

December 16, 2005
A Brief Update

Just a quick note to say that Roger was re-admitted to the hospital in the wee hours of this morning, but is doing very well after a couple of transfusions, and some IV medications.

He was running a high fever, and with such low counts, it is standard practice to admit and treat aggressively. If all continues to go well, he should be discharged on Sunday to go to the apartment in Houston. I will keep you posted. Thanks for the prayers!

Debbie

December 20, 2005
Back at the Apartment Again

After a day's delay in getting released, and then spending hours waiting on the "go ahead" yesterday, we finally made it out of the hospital and back to the apartment in Houston about 7:30 last night. It was so good to be out once again!

We are now getting ready to be back at the clinic for appointments at 7:15 this morning (apparently REST is not a part of the recovery process!).

Things are still pretty tentative, as far as counts and infections go. We had hoped to possibly slip away for a couple of days to go home for Christmas, but that doesn't seem likely. It's okay, though. Chelsea and Jordan will come down a couple of days after Christmas, so they can spend Christmas Day with grandparents, aunts, uncles, and cousins. We all know that Christmas is about more than a date on the calendar anyway!

Again, we will keep you posted as we are able. Specific prayers for Roger right now would be for his fever to stay down; his infections to clear; his strength to come back (he is still very weak); and to be able to begin to put on some of the weight he has lost (I've offered a transplant, but they aren't going for it).

We hope your Christmas is joyous, and that you experience His love and peace throughout the season. All of you have been such a special gift to our family, and so we remain safely,

In His Grip,
Debbie

December 29, 2005
Merry Christmas (late)

Sorry for the long silence from me. My life has been very much up and down lately and as always very busy running to and fro!

Now that my cancer has recurred, we are moving at a hectic pace to stay in front of the disease. This post will bring you up to date on what we are facing.

The AML recurred a few weeks ago and I underwent immediate chemo which again God used to save me. I stabilized and my AML physician, Dr. Michael Keating started working on a plan of attack.

The plan is still being decided on and many people are involved to make sure that I qualify for the treatment. We should know any day.

My condition... depends on when you ask. Some days I feel almost back to my old self, others I feel like death eating a cracker (old folks' phrase at home). I've been taken off the road on a day by day basis. Hopefully I'll be back in the saddle very soon.

I've remained hopeful and optimistic throughout and still am. God is holding me tightly and my friends are calling me and treating me just like normal. In other words they cut me no slack! Just what I need.

We had a wonderful Christmas with our little family here in Houston. Our kids are still here and we are just chillin' (yeah I'm staying young with my vocab).

I hope that your Christmas was wonderful. I hope we all never fail to see the wonder of the manger!

In His Grip!
Roger

PS. I'm completely bald again! For your entertainment, I will post a picture soon!

January 04, 2006
A Belated Happy New Year

I hope you all had a safe and joyous Christmas and New Year. The Bennetts had our usual unusual time together. Seems like every time the Holidays roll around, I have to have a "flare up." We are at home for a few more days then back to Houston. We don't know if we'll be there 4 days or 4 months. Everything is so fluid right now, that it's safe to say that we don't have a clue what to expect.

Yet isn't that the way all of life is? We are plugging along making plans, setting goals, running the rat race. We think we've got a handle on things. Then one day we find a lump that wasn't there before and in the matter of hours our plans, goals, and striving are put to the side. The only constant now is Jesus. The only dependable advocate, the only One who really knows how we feel. I'm so thankful for His presence.

We'll keep you posted with any new updates. Please know that the Bennetts love you and don't take for granted your prayers. We pray for you as well. We hope that as you serve God in 2006, it will be the greatest and most productive time in your life.

He saves! Let's get the word out.

In His Grip!
Roger

January 13, 2006
All the Way

Today as I sit in Houston recovering from my latest round of chemo, my mind is drawn to the old hymn "All the Way My Savior Leads Me." For some reason the Lord brought it to my mind. As usual I try to find out how it relates to me. After reading the lyrics again (several times) today, it's hard for me to find a word that doesn't apply to me.

I started a long journey over 10 years ago when I found that first lump on my neck. I must confess that Debbie and I have been in the deepest valley of our life in the last 2 years. Lately it's just become such a grind. There is not a single day that passes that we don't have to deal with something related to cancer. I don't know what we would have done if Jesus stayed with us up to the 8th year and then said, "OK, you are on your own now Bennetts, I've given you 8 years but I'm bored and gonna move on." What a terrible thought and, thankfully, a complete fiction. In His word He promised His presence until the end of the age. He said that He would stick closer than a brother and I have experienced that this is true. I've had a bunch of bad days. Depression and despair are frequent stalkers in our lives. But even with constant bombardment by the enemy, the constant protection of our Savior is the remedy for these attacks. Not part of the way – All the Way! Even if the road leads through the valley of the shadow of death, He will not desert us. He is always there to lift us up and encourage us to finish the race well. Thank God! T he excitement that comes from feeling His presence in the midst of the storm puts a smile on the faces of the storm-tossed.

All the way He leads. Here is an especially good verse.

All the way my Savior leads me,
Cheers each winding path I tread;
Gives me grace for every trial,
Feeds me with the living Bread.
Though my weary steps may falter,
And my soul athirst may be,
Gushing from the Rock before me,
Lo! A spring of joy I see;
Gushing from the Rock before me,
Lo! A spring of joy I see.

Loneliness and uncertainty can drain the joy from your life and paralyze your progress. When that happens... nip it in the bud! Remember that you have a constant companion who loves you more than you'll ever know. Not a part time protector... All the way!

In His Grip!
Roger

January 25, 2006
A Small Break

I'm writing this from our home in Tennessee. My meetings with both sets of Doctors at MDA agreed that a break was needed and home would be the best place to be. My counts are slowly rebounding after the last chemo treatment. My AML has presented itself only on my head. There are times that I don't even know it's there but other times when it's actually pretty painful.

The new treatment trial that I had hoped to be included in was full. But a new vaccine clinical trial will begin in about 6 to 8 weeks and I'm on the list. The only drawback is that I have to be off of chemo for 4 weeks before the trial. This will be fine if the AML will co-operate and not flare up again. It's a big waiting game.

I feel ok right now. I haven't been out of the house for 3 days and that has helped. I'm missing a trip with Legacy Five and that has not helped. But I'm not down, I feel optimistic about all of it.

It's a time of testing and I hope to come through it refined as fine gold.

Other than all of the above, things are good at the Bennett house. I'll be in touch soon!

In His Grip!
Roger

February 03, 2006
A Happy Anniversary

It has been a few days since our last post. We have been enjoying some "home-time" here in Tennessee. This is actually the longest stretch of time we have been home in almost 2 years!

January 31 was Roger's one-year anniversary of his 2nd bone marrow transplant. We never got that far past the first one, so it is one to be celebrated, even with the other things that have come up.

Here in TN, he had another dose of chemo a week ago, and as expected, his counts have dropped significantly, leaving him vulnerable to just about everything. He was thinking of going out on the road this weekend, but due to his low counts, and some impending illness on the bus, he WISELY took advice and stayed home. He is itching to get back out there, but he knows that when he is stronger, there will still be time for that.

We are still watching the signs to check the progression/regression of the disease, but as of today, the outward signs of it seem to be diminishing. He had a couple of shots yesterday to boost his blood counts and his immunity, so that should help, too.

As for the Bennett household, all is well. Chelsea and her cat have moved to an apartment about 35 miles away, to be nearer to school, and out of the traffic and commute. (Dad is still trying to come to grips with that!) Jordan is on the hunt for another job, and has applied to school in the fall to become a luthier (for those of you - like myself - who would not have recognized what that is, that is a fancy name for a guitar builder/repairer). This will be right up his alley, and we are excited for him, although the school is in Michigan, and will mean we are destined to become empty-nesters...

We hope it is a good day wherever you are. Here in TN, we are looking for some possible snow this weekend, and it would be a nice change of pace for us. We plan to light a fire, stay warm and dry, and remain

In His Grip,
Debbie

February 13, 2006
Still in Tennessee

We are still in TN, over 3 weeks now. Roger has been dealing with a few issues, one of which is an up-and-down fever that may land him back in the hospital for a while. He sees the doctor again today, so we will see how that goes.

Life is pretty sedate, as far as what he can do right now. It is never sedate as far as what the day may hold.

One day is a pretty good day, and another may be more challenging. However, it is still good to be home while going through it all.

Roger's dad is coming for a visit this week, and bringing a load of home-grown Arkansas firewood. That will make a nice setting for lots of fireside chats. Those two rival each other with their storytelling!

Thanks for your continuing prayers for strength and healing. They help us remember that we are always

In His Grip!
Debbie

February 14, 2006
A Valentine's Update

As expected from yesterday's symptoms, when we went to the doctor, he put Roger straight into the hospital here in Nashville. His fever was pretty high, and his counts were so low, that he needs to be treated with IV antibiotics for a few days. So, we are back in all-too familiar territory once again!

There is no cause for alarm, as the low counts which prevent his fighting off infections on his own, are expected following the latest chemo. It just has to be dealt with, or very serious consequences will be felt.

Doug (Roger's dad) has postponed his visit with us, as both he and Roger would rather visit at home than in the hospital.

Finally, I would like to wish a very happy Valentine's Day to all of you who are so faithful to read this journal, and keep us in your prayers. This is a day to celebrate love, and you show your love to us by your actions. More

271

importantly, you show Christ's love, and that is what we should strive for each and every day.

I would like to add a personal "Happy Valentine's Day" to my sweeties: Roger, Chelsea, and Jordan. I am so lucky to have you as my family, and you all make this trip a real joy! I am content, because I know that together we are

In His Grip
Debbie

February 22, 2006
Home Again, Home Again...

Just a quick update today. I brought Roger home from the hospital yesterday, after an eight day stay. We were both more than ready for his release! He had multiple transfusions of both whole blood and platelets while he was there, as well as continuous IV antibiotics. One of the culprits seemed to be a bacteria that likes to cluster around the line that has been in his arm since November, so that was removed. Hopefully, he won't need many immediate IV treatments or infusions. The line was nice for those, not having to get "stuck" every time, but it will be nice not to have to take the extra care with it.

As I said, this is quick. Since I have also spent the last 8 days at the hospital, my house needs some attention. Roger's dad is on his way here today, and he might appreciate not having to kick a path to his room!

Until next time, may we all remain

In His Grip,
Debbie

March 06, 2006
Reflections and Renewal

What a week it has been. It still seems so incredible that we lost our good friend, Anthony Burger. It was good to be able to visit with his family, and see them walking this journey with Christ. Roger and I have seen so many who do not have that calm assurance, and what a difference it makes in the way they handle tragedy. I do not know how they manage to make it through the day without Jesus. What a blessing to know that Anthony did have that assurance, and that he is home now with the One Who loved him most. Russ Taff, in speaking at the funeral, noted how the ship's staff marveled at the way a ship-full of Christians handled such a tragedy. As Romans 8:28 says, "All things work together for good," and while we certainly cannot think of a death being "good" in our earthly minds, we see the testimony of the saints being played out in front of hundreds on that ship who may not know Christ personally. Another piece of Anthony left behind to plant seeds...

On another subject now: Roger was able to go out on the road this weekend, for the first time since... I really can't remember! I was concerned that he would forget to take his medicine, that he would overdo it, etc., etc.; but from all reports he did very well. He called me each day a couple of times to "check in" and update me. He pretty much stayed on the bus the whole time, resting, until time for concerts; then he rested during intermission, as well. They will return to TN later this morning, and he has a doctor appointment this afternoon, so we will see how he fared physically. I know that, mentally, he got a real boost this weekend – not to mention spiritually!

I personally should have done a little more housework while I had the time, but I took advantage of the time to rest. Jordan and I also got to take Grant Howard to Chuck

E. Cheese's for his 8th birthday on Friday. It has been years since I was in that place!

Well, the day is calling, the cat wants his breakfast, and the dryer is buzzing. Back to the real world. May your walk today show everyone who may be watching that you are

In His Grip,
Debbie

March 14, 2006
Better Days

Well, Roger has now been on the road with Legacy Five for 2 weekends in a row. We saw the doctor here in Nashville today, and he is very pleased with the way his counts are beginning to recover. There was some concern last week with the rate they were recovering, so today's news was very welcome. Tomorrow, Roger will be having a CT scan to check out some other issues, so more of that good stuff to drink is in his future. Yum!

Roger is still having to rest a lot, since his fatigue level is very high, but he is thoroughly enjoying being back "in the saddle." We both still find it hard to believe we have been back home for so long, but it is a feeling we can surely live with. It has been great going to church with Chelsea and Jordan again. I am even digging into a few projects that have been sorely neglected (although there are some I may put off a whole lot longer).

Anyway, thanks for all the prayers and birthday wishes for Roger. He says the birthdays have a lot more meaning for him than they used to. Each one is truly a celebration, and a concrete reminder that we remain

In His Grip!
Debbie

March 23, 2006
Update Time!

Hey everyone,

I'm still in a holding pattern. God is graciously giving me strength for each new day. I really don't know much about the clinical trial that I'm supposed to take part in, but I assume it's on hold until my counts recover.

The good news is I'm able to travel some now. This weekend will be the fourth in a row that I've been able to participate in.

It's been great to be out with my buddies again and to see so many of you in the flesh! Keep us in your prayers. We're not out of the woods yet, but we're trusting God to bring us through them!

In His Grip!
Roger

(And a note from Debbie: We will be in Houston on Monday for a check-up with doctors there. Thanks in advance for the prayers. I will also be with Roger at Deer Park on Sunday night for the L5 concert. See some of you there!)

April 05, 2006
Roger's Latest

Hello to All,

Things have been going very well. I got a bug last weekend and have been battling fever again. Based on my counts the doctors think it's just a temporary thing. It sort of popped up out of nowhere, taking us by surprise.

I had a check up in Houston last week and Dr. Keating says that we are in a "watching phase," the disease is inactive right now so we'll just keep a close eye on it.

I've sure enjoyed being out with the quartet the past 4 weeks and am looking forward to a lot more time on the road.

I've been getting your e-mails of encouragement and I certainly thank you for each one. You keep lifting us up and the Father keeps blessing!

In His Grip!
Roger

April 11, 2006
Through the Storms

Over the weekend, we had severe storms and tornadoes in our area, but we rode them out with God's protection. We all had a little hail damage to vehicles, etc., but nothing compared to others in the area who lost both homes and lives. We continue to get reports on the news of more storm survivor stories, and they are truly incredible. Whole neighborhoods were simply wiped out in a matter of seconds. It was a very intense afternoon, but we did have some comic relief during the storm by trying to get all of us - including 3 cocker spaniels and 2 cats -

into the "safe" closet! But, again, God was watching over us and all of Legacy Five and our families are safe. We need to continue to remember those who are less fortunate than we are in our prayers.

Roger was home over the weekend, due to a lingering virus of his own, and then a new stomach bug was making its way around the L5 bus, so he was unable to join them. Hopefully, after a few days' recovery for all of them, they will be whole again when they set out after the Easter break. I think it would be mighty hard to keep Roger home again... he got used to being out these past few weekends, and he is so looking forward to the California/West Coast trip coming up. His blood counts are continuing to recover, and his doctors are pleased with those results. We think his last bout with fever was a viral thing, and from all indications, his body was making a valiant effort to fight the infection on its own, so that is wonderful news.

As we prepare to celebrate the risen Christ during this Easter season, we are mindful of the great sacrifice that He made so that we might have life. And what an abundant life He has bestowed upon us! We have so much to be thankful for. Our blessings just keep pouring in. Let us not lose sight of the true meaning of this blessed holiday, and may we always give thanks that we are

In His Grip,
Debbie

April 19, 2006
Released to Travel

Three sweet words! I'm going to get to go on an 11 day trip with the quartet. We'll start in Lebanon, PA and end up in San Diego, CA. Talk about a lot of miles! Pray for Gary our bus driver!

I'm feeling better. I'll meet Deb in Houston on the Monday after our concert in San Diego and have the once over at M.D. Anderson. We are praying for some more good news.

My platelets are lower than normal so I tend to bleed pretty easily. This is one of the areas I have to be real careful about.

But, here again, God is in control. I'm confident in Him loving me more than I love myself. So I'll rest in the peace He gives!

If you haven't tried it... you should.

May 03, 2006
Bone Marrow Test Results

This morning Debbie and I were waiting for some big news and we got it. My latest bone marrow test results were in and by all accounts, there is no AML in my marrow. Great news. I still need to see another doctor tomorrow as it seems as if I have some chronic graph vs. host disease that will require treatment.

As usual Deb and I thank you for the prayers and support during this long road. We will keep you posted when we know all the details.

I hope you will sleep as well as I will tonight!

In His Grip!
Roger

May 25, 2006
Gearing Up for the Weekend

Yes, I know it has been too long since we posted, but that is good news, as we have been very busy these days. Roger is feeling better, has been able to travel to all Legacy Five dates, and we are anticipating a great weekend at "Celbration" here in Nashville.

Roger has battled a cold and/or infection of some kind, but lab work continues to be good - improving, actually - so we keep going forward. Following Celebration this weekend, Legacy Five breaks for vacation, so that should give him more time to rest - or work on a couple of projects. We head back to Houston for another checkup the first week of June.

Have a safe and happy Memorial Day weekend, and don't forget to thank a veteran for your freedom!

In His Grip,
Debbie

June 10, 2006
Let Me Introduce Myself

Hello,

My name is Roger Bennett and I'm your friend with cancer. I figure that it's been so long since I've posted, a re-introduction might be in order.

Life suddenly got crowded again! That's my only excuse. You all have been so faithful to check this journal daily for the last few weeks with no new info and I thank you for it. I will do my best not to let so much time pass between future posts.

Debbie and I just returned from Houston 2 days ago and my counts continue to improve. My energy is up and I'm able to be on the road again on a full time basis. That's part of the reason for no new postings. Legacy Five's plate has been full. We just had a great weekend at our Homecoming at the Opryland Hotel on Memorial Day weekend. We recorded a live CD of 12 new songs and we've been editing furiously to meet a completion deadline.

This CD is gonna be great! It has some of the strongest material we've ever sung and I can't wait for you to hear it. You can go over to www.legacyfive.com to take a look at some photos from the weekend if you'd like.

The Lord continues to strengthen me and I remain totally optimistic about the future. I win either way, but I'm sure enjoying being able to travel again and to start writing again. I hope you'll check this page often so I can share some of the good things God continues to teach me.

Stronger everyday and still in His Grip!
Roger

June 28, 2006
Status Quo

June is almost gone. It seems like it just got here! Legacy Five was on vacation most of the month, and we spent our vacation on Little Pond Lane. We thought about planning a trip somewhere, then realized that home was where we most wanted to be. It was great remembering what it was like to be in TN during the summer months. We got some yard work done, and put flowers on the front porch, so when it's not too hot to sit out there, we enjoy the fragrance they give off. We did make a Father's Day trip to Arkansas to visit Roger's dad and grandpa. We think it's the first Father's Day he has physically spent with his dad in over a quarter of a century! We enjoyed going to church with him, and taking him out for a lunch afterwards before heading back home.

Things are "status quo" with Roger's health right now (hence the title of this post)... .meaning no changes that we are aware of. I guess there will always be some things that crop up, and we will always wonder what they mean, but for now, we are just hanging in there, and trusting God to take care of the details.

We are just a little over a week away from the Alaska cruise, and are eagerly waiting on that. Please pray that Roger's health maintains, and that he can enjoy his time in Alaska. Last year, although he was present on the cruise, was challenging for him, since he was still in recovery mode. I have booked a photographic trip for him and Chelsea in Juneau, so the two shutterbugs should have a great time, doing what they both enjoy so much.

Roger and Scott F. have spent this week in the studio finishing up detail work on the new video, so today will be spent resting and breathing a sigh of relief that the work is done. (We still don't have the release date yet, so don't ask!)

Thank you for your continuing prayers. We know that they are what has sustained us through many days, months, and years. God is good ALL THE TIME, and so faithful to keep us

In His Grip,
Debbie

July 02, 2006
Another "Step Back"

Well, Roger just can't let a little excitement pass us by.
Seems he was feeling better today, so he decided to tend to
some housekeeping issues on the porch (while I was in the
house, let me add), and, long story short, we ended up in
the ER getting a temporary cast put on his ankle, which is
broken in 2 places.

We won't know the full extent of the injury until we
talk to the orthopedic doctor tomorrow (at least, I have to
call him tomorrow, then we will see from there). At first,
the ER doctor thought it would require surgery, but
perhaps not.

Thanks in advance for your prayers. We are still
hoping to make the Alaska trip later this week. I promise
to post more as soon as I have more info. Without going
into detail (sorry for this, Roger...), I am thankful that God
keeps even those who do not use good judgment

In His Grip!
Debbie

July 06, 2006
A Little More Info

We saw the ortho doctor today, and now Roger has a
real cast on his leg. (Yes, it's the left one, so his "pedal
foot" isn't affected.) Good news: no surgery required. Not
as good news: no Alaska cruise for him. Seems there is
some concern over the foot not being elevated during the
long flight to the West coast, and if swelling, or blood clots
should occur, it could cause some real problems. So, we
all decided that staying home with what the doctor calls

"aggressive elevation" would be wiser, though not as much fun. His balance isn't that great on dry land right now, and adding a little ship movement might not help much!

However, even though I won the debate over whether we should go to the ER or not last Sunday, and a few more since then, Roger has won the one over whether Chelsea and I should go ahead and go on the cruise. (We are.) I have very mixed feelings over leaving him to his own devices - we all know where that can lead him - but since he is not as able to climb on things he shouldn't be climbing on, he may do alright. And, his dad is coming to be with him while I am away. So please pray for all of us. I admit to needing a little R & R, but it may take some coaxing to get my mind out of Tennessee.

His cast will stay on at least 6 weeks. It is a non-weight-bearing cast, which means he will have to be on a walker or crutches all that time. (It's scaring our cat to death!) Then, if the healing goes well, they will switch him to a boot cast.

Needless to say, Roger is not too happy about missing the cruise, but as we have learned over the years, we just roll with the flow and make the best out of what we are given. It sure makes it easier when we know we are safely

In His Grip!
Debbie

July 22, 2006
Back in the Saddle Again

Well, Roger is back on the road again this weekend, and he was mighty anxious to get out there! The group only has a 2-day weekend, so it will be a good one for him to get his feet wet (no, that would not be appropriate!)...

Just an update in a nutshell as to what has been going on: Chelsea and I went on the Alaska cruise, while Roger and his dad stayed in Tennessee. As far as the cruise went, it was wonderful, as usual, but I don't think I'd go without Roger again. That was just strange. However, Chelsea and I did spend a lot of good time together, and I played caddy for all of her camera equipment. It was fun, and I learned a thing or two about photography.

Roger and his dad had a good week at home. Doug brought up a couple of famous Cave City, AR watermelons (you don't know what you're missing!) and carted him around on a few errands and studio appointments. Roger did get a lot of L5 work done while he was sitting still!

This week, we had appointments in Houston with both clinics, and they were pleased with the counts, etc. We don't have to go back for two months this time. That's always great news! When we got back from Houston, we had another appointment with the orthopedist. They had to cut off the original cast and put a new one on, due to the first one being too loose now. X-rays showed that things are still about the same as when he first broke it, but that is fine, since no one expects bones to heal up in two weeks. This cast will be on for about 4 more weeks, at which point he might be put in a boot cast if the healing is on schedule.

So, all in all, things are rolling along at the Bennett household. I would ask a personal favor and request prayer for my dad, Robert Westbrook, though. He was admitted to the hospital this week, awaiting surgery in a few days, and is in a good bit of pain. I will be going down there to sit with him a few hours each day so my mom can get some rest. My brothers are sharing that responsibility as well.

Thanks for your faithfulness, your prayers, and your friendship. We have a great network in our community of believers, and we are held tightly

In His Grip,
Debbie

August 08, 2006
Sorry, and Thanks to Debbie.

Boy, do I feel like a lump. Debbie told me today how long it has been since I posted, and I couldn't believe it. So, to all of you, I say I'm sorry; and to Debbie, I say thanks for keeping you updated.

It's been a really strange time for me lately. When I did a really dumb thing and broke my leg in 2 places, I had no idea how it would make a change in my day to day living. I'd never had a broken bone before and wasn't prepared for the level of helplessness that I would face. My mode of transportation is either crutches, walker, or wheelchair. It embarrasses me every time someone in the group has to wheel me into a restaurant or other public place. Not because there's anything wrong with the chair or the other equipment, it's just that it's a constant reminder of my ignorance when I climbed up on that porch and then found myself flat on my back in the yard!

Summer has been going well for Legacy Five. We've been really busy and having some really great concerts. It's a lot of fun singing the songs from our new live recording. It should be released in a couple of weeks.

As far as my serious health questions, I'm due for another "staging" check-up in September in Houston. I'm feeling very well and am simply leaving it in God's hands. The doctors feel that my remission will not be a durable one, that I'll have to fight another battle sooner or later with the disease. I can't live my life in a state of limbo, waiting for the other shoe to fall, so to speak. Constantly holding my breath wondering and worrying what the next check will bring. At times like this my emotional strength is not up to the task. So I depend on my Heavenly Father's strength. He's proven faithful at every crossroads, and even if I don't get the news that I expect, He has grace and joy for me in the toughest of times.

I've learned that my sweetest time of the day is when I'm having my prayer time. The events that seemed so important a couple of hours prior seem hardly worth the worry while relaxing in His presence, making my petitions known, or maybe just listening for His leading. That's the time that I finally understand the phrase, "the things of this earth will grow strangely dim in the light of His glory and grace."

Thank you for all of your prayers for Debbie's dad and her family. Her dad spent 11 days in the hospital and had surgery, but is now back home regaining his strength.

So now you're up to date, both physically and spiritually. I promise that my postings will again become frequent. As usual, my entire family is depending on your prayers.

In His Grip!
Roger

August 16, 2006
To Be Like Jesus: The Confessions of a People Pleaser

When it's my turn to say grace before the meal, I usually end by saying, "and Lord, help us to be more like You." Words quickly spoken, while the smell of Deb's home cooking fills the room. Many times I say it out of habit and don't even think about the radical statement I just made.

"Make us more like You, Lord"? If we mean that, we are opening our lives up to a radical change. Good change, great change! But radical nonetheless. Jesus wouldn't invent an excuse not to stand up in the face of sin. He wouldn't do like I've done occasionally (to my shame) and kept quiet in a situation when some Christian should have spoken up. I tucked my tail and concentrated heavily on my meal. I'm sure to an innocent bystander I looked as if I'd never seen mashed potatoes before!

My social life would certainly change. I wouldn't be consistently hanging out with people just like me. People that never say, "That doesn't sound right – prove it!" To be more like Jesus, I would search out uncomfortable (at first) situations where I would be the only Christian in the house, then just sit back and wait for the Lord to swing the door wide. I would stand up in love but with conviction.

If I came across obvious wrongdoing (thieves in the temple or some modern day disrespect to Jesus), I would follow His example and not stand for it. Not for the politically correct or the faint of heart.

Instead, the *people pleaser* in me rears its ugly head and tries to smooth things over. I know we are supposed to be peacemakers as well, but I've missed a lot of witnessing chances simply because I didn't want to rock the boat.

Unfortunately, the fix to this spiritual shortcoming will involve times of awkwardness and possibly uncomfortable conversations. But it can be fixed. You've heard the old saying that "every journey begins with one step"? I think that's a great way to change our behavior from "people pleaser" to "people reacher."

Let's start right now, let's take the first step... *more like Him and less like us!*

In His Grip!
Roger

August 24, 2006
The Battle Continues

My journey with cancer has been filled with peaks and valleys. I've learned to try to find something positive in each of these places. It seems that it's time for me to learn from another valley.

My cancer has relapsed. I found this out at my check up this week in Houston. I've already had a chemo treatment and the doctors think that everything is still early and we're not worried.

Debbie and I are home now. I'm packing, getting ready to leave out on the road this weekend. As usual with this form of treatment, my "crash" will come in about a week. This is normal. It's one of the most irritating parts of the ordeal for me. I was just getting strong enough to actually visit face to face with folks again. Now I have to go back into cocoon mode.

As always, we covet your prayers. Pray that I will be aware of the lessons God has for me through this new valley.

Be of good cheer, we are in His Grip!
Roger

September 05, 2006
A Treatment Update

Wow, thank you for your many comments! We surely know that we have lots of prayers coming our way, and for that we cannot say "thank you" enough.

The Labor Day Celebration was a great success, and we had a wonderful time of spiritual recharging while we were there. So many people approached me, asking what they could do for us, and truly, the most important thing we need is your prayers. We couldn't get through any of this without them. And we do feel them!

As expected, Roger's latest round of chemo has all but wiped his counts out. He had a shot on Friday before the Celebration to boost his cell count, and it did help, but today his platelets were so low that we had to go to the hospital for an infusion. Now that that is done, he will rest at home, and get to feeling stronger again. That is his main problem right now - the weakness and fatigue. But, trooper that he is, he soldiers on. He is aware of his limitations, though, and does not take risks, so don't worry about that.

We are spending the next few days relaxing at home... and being on the lookout for a new litter of kittens due any day. Seems Chelsea couldn't resist rescuing this adorable kitten at her apartment complex, and when she brought her to us, we got a little more than we bargained for. Not ones to back away from a challenge, though, we will nurture the little babies and then find them a good home. We are never short of excitement around the Bennett house!

I am off to bed now, where I will sleep soundly

In His Grip,
Debbie

September 11, 2006
Off to the NQC!

Just a quick update. Roger and Jordan left today for the week in Louisville, KY, at the National Quartet Convention. First, we made a stop at the doctor's office for lab work. Platelets are still low, but the good news is that his white count and neutrophils (the things that fight infections) are good enough that if you see him around without a mask, it is OK! You might want to get out of the way, however, if he is able to get a scooter. He is a man on a mission when he is on one of those things. No, really, I hope he will be able to get one. That place is huge, he is still in a walking boot, and his strength gives out pretty easily.

I listened to L5 onstage tonight, and I was proud of what I heard. In case you don't have the live feed in your area, you can log onto www.solidgospel105.com (that's our local access) and listen to the live performances all week! These guys do a good job of keeping everyone clued in on what is going on, with interviews, and lots more. OK, enough of the plug.

I am heading to Louisville myself on Wednesday. Meanwhile, I am still on "kitten watch" - I think this cat is going to hang onto her litter until they are fully grown! I don't see how she can get much bigger... Chelsea will come back to Little Pond Lane for the end of the week while we are gone, and take over.

Now, all banter aside, please pray for Roger's strength and health this week. We head to Houston next week for appointments and tests. We will update you as we are able.

In His Grip,
Debbie

September 17, 2006
Can't Sleep, Thought I'd Say Hi

Hey everyone,

I survived NQC this week and was able to complete all of my duties! Thanks to all of you that specifically prayed for me last week.

As you may have heard, the kittens arrived while we were gone. Seven healthy, pretty, little kitties, and one tired mama kitty. Pearl (the mom) is just a baby herself, but she's using the instincts that God pre-programmed her with to be a natural.

I never thought of myself as a cat person. We all love dogs. Well, I'm proof that you can be both.

Sleep has eluded me so far tonight. I went to bed at 7:45 p.m., wasted and expecting to be asleep within minutes. I've yet to bat an eye.

Today is a busy day and the start of an important week for me. I see the orthopedist to see how my leg is healing at 1:00, and then at 5:00 we fly to Houston for some planning on how to deal with this latest relapse. It doesn't seem to be responding to chemo. I'll let you know something as soon as I know anything.

Love you all. I've been thinking tonight about the reliability of God's Word. It literally brings joy to a tired body and mind to know that we have a Father who loves us so much that He gave His Son for our sins. I couldn't have done that. But The Son was willing in His great love to save us.

That may be why I can't sleep tonight. I can't shut my mind down on this wonderful truth!

Tired, awake, but still In His Grip
Roger

September 20, 2006
A New Valley, Same Enemy

Well, the news was not what we'd hoped it would be. My cancer is much more aggressive and will require a third transplant ASAP.

This time the news was quick and to the point. I'm in a situation that is tough to survive if not treated quickly and accurately. Exactly the opposite news we wanted.

However, let me tell you some great news!

1. A donor has been located, and is an 11 out of 12 match.
2. We have approval from the all-important insurance company.
3. I'm healthy as a horse in every other respect.
4. If things go well, I could be finished with this ordeal by early March 2007.
5. The new chemo is much more "non-toxic" than before.
6. Both Doctors are using the "C" word: cure!!!
7. I'm totally optimistic about the outcome.

The biggest bummer is that I'll be separated from my friends and family in Arkansas and Tennessee for a few months. Plus, I'll be off the road until my counts take hold and start moving up. I really dread this part.

My hope is still built on the solid rock of Christ. He is going before me to prepare the way and make it straight for me.

Please pray for Debbie that she'll be able to find new strength to go through this with me again. Pray that I'll find all of the lessons and truths that God has for me again. I am so hopeful and full of faith, because God has proven many times in my life that He is faithful and able to sustain me through any trial.

So, now I ask for our Ropeholders to help me again. Your prayers and love have been the hands and feet of

Jesus throughout my fight with cancer. I will keep you posted at every turn.

Tomorrow is outpatient surgery for me. I'm not looking forward to it, for I'm a scaredy-cat about some of this stuff! Ha!

New valley, same enemy; but guess what, Enemy: Same God!!!

In His Grip!
Roger Bennett

September 27, 2006
Cats in the Box, or the Story of a Good Parent

Well, I'm sure you loyal readers of my journal are waiting for the latest word...

About our cats! Sorry, I couldn't resist. I'm sitting where I always sit in my den. Pearl, our mama cat, has decided that the very best place for her new family of seven is behind our TV and stereo. She is doing great, but sometimes she has to get out to do the essentials: eat, stretch, and you know the rest. Then it's back to the baby box. That is where she spends almost all day, every day. Tonight I'm working at the computer and Pearl has left the box just for a minute. She passes me with a glance and disappears into another room. Just then, one of the babies cried: not a loud wail, just a forlorn little mewing. Almost as soon as I heard the baby, I heard another sound. Mama was hightailing it back to the box! In she goes, and the crying stops. S he didn't get a break, but she did what all good parents do – what's best for the baby.

All of this, of course, can be a parable for the way God works, and it should be. I've said God has His ear tuned to the cry of His children, and I'm so glad. But I also see it as a model of good earthly parents. I know it was in my case. Mom and Dad had their own lives to live and a paycheck to make, but I never cried for long when I needed them. In the night, I would sometimes wake up scared or sick; and not just one would show up in my room, but both. It just seemed normal to me, and that's the way Deb and I have tried to raise ours.

My mom would come in from work before my dad. I'd have finished my homework and be watching TV on the one channel we could pick up. I'd hear the door open and she'd say "I'm home." Then I'd hear the sound of the top of a Pepsi bottle being opened (with a real bottle opener – twist tops had not even been thought of then). Then, after being up since 3:45 a.m., she'd bring the Pepsi in to me and set it on a coaster on the coffee table and give me a hug. The Pepsi was for me, her brat kid.

Now I think back on that, and as a grown-up I know that she was tired and wanted to rest; but she still spent some time with me and then went and fixed supper for me and my dad. Now I have a sense of what that means. I don't want my kids to think about anything negative that Deb and I go through. I don't think any parent would. But because we raised them to pray, I know that their prayers mingle with those of all of you other ropeholders.

What I'm I trying to say tonight, I guess, is this: spend your life as you have to, try to follow God's plan, but don't get too far from the "baby box." They'll always need you.

I thank You, God, that You are the ultimate parent and are never too far from Your babies.

We feel your Grip!
Roger

October 06, 2006
Moving Fast

Well, things are moving fast. Deb and I went to Houston to consult with our doctors, and as soon as we got on the plane, my fever started a steady rise.

I had packed my thermometer in checked baggage, but we knew this was not good. Upon landing in Houston, we got the complete story: my fever had reached a lifetime high of a little over 104.0 F.

Deb didn't pass go or collect $200.00; straight to the M.D. Anderson ER we went. They admitted me at 3 AM on Tuesday and I was there until Wednesday evening about 6 PM. All the tests pointed toward the fact that my cancer is now much more aggressive than before. So as soon as my fever dropped, the busy beavers in BMT started moving everything forward by at least a week.

Unexpected, but we've dealt with this before.

Our secret, a forward pass to God! We can change nothing within ourselves so I'll just again take my hands off the wheel and leave it to Him.

As soon as I have concrete dates and a Houston address, you'll be the first to know!

Still trusting, still optimistic, still fighting, and still,

In His Grip!
Roger

October 23, 2006
My Latest

Sorry for your not hearing from me in a while. I have some dates and info for you.

I start all the tests tomorrow at 7 a.m. Then, day-to-day, the tests continue for the foreseeable future. I'll be admitted into the hospital on November 10 (My Mom's birthday) and that will be "Day minus 6." "Day Zero" (transplant day) will be November 16. I've been pretty sick during the last few days. I've had 5 days of treatment and have responded well. I feel much better. Thank God for His sustaining grace. He has many times been quiet, but never silent. My hope is built on the Solid Rock of Jesus.

People say, "Three transplants!? No way." I might have said that at some point, but my real power doesn't lie within the transplant. It's in the combination that God has put together. I refuse to put God into a box. If I'm going to trust Him, there's no expiration date. I'm gonna trust Him with my whole heart and my whole life. He will be the one to make the schedule of my life and I've seen enough of His trustworthiness that I feel sure I can continue to trust Him with the trivial details of my life. The very fact that He is an engaged, hands-on, and present Father should be all we need to say, "Lord, with Your Grace, I'll trust You with it all! Even until the end of the age. "

So with faith I will say I am

In His Grip!
Roger

October 28, 2006
The Best Made Plans of Mice and Men Often Go Awry.

I never thought I'd start a post by quoting Steinbeck, but during the last 48 hours, every plan I made was met with a resounding NO!

Check this out....

Saturday (today) was to be our first of 3 days of home rest here in Houston. I was so looking forward to it. The weather is beautiful and I wanted to think and see anything but the hospital for 3 days.

Not so fast, Bennett! Yesterday morning I came in for a simple blood draw and a vital sign check. Still, so far so good; then the thermometer had its say: 102.4, I believe, is what it read. The staff at M.D. Anderson don't mess around with fever. So I was immediately taken to the ER, where Deb and I stayed for nine hours, being treated, taking more tests, and waiting for a room. They admitted me at about 8 p.m. last night.

"Ok," I thought, "I can get over the fever tonight and still be out in the fresh air over the weekend." Not so fast, Bennett. I was at least 2 units low on blood (which I'm getting as I type). I don't know what the price for a unit of whole blood is, but I feel sure it must cost more than filling up my gas guzzling, global warming SUV. And!!!!, You can't get a Zero candy bar and Dr. Pepper in the mini mart on a protective environment floor. (Note to self: have Debbie smuggle up Zero bars and Diet Dr. Pepper) (She's too pretty to go to jail!)

Anyway, you have to become flexible, because the doctors are paid not to do shoddy work. I still want to go home, but there it is.

I'm doing well and am extremely optimistic about the outcome of these many days of fighting.

So now that we are here in Houston full-time, I'll be able to keep up my posting schedule a lot better. When I can't, the best writer/editor that I know will be putting in her 2 cents' worth! What would I do without my Debbie?

I hope you all have a great weekend. I can make a money-back guarantee about one activity you might be able to attend.

Surf over to www.legacyfive.com/concert_schedule and see if the fellows are singing in your area. I promise you will not be disappointed. In the unlikely event that you don't like the concert, ask Scott Fowler for a refund! (Good luck! Ha.) Love to all, be of good cheer! Jesus has overcome the world, and we who know Him are

In His Grip!
Roger

November 07, 2006
Counting Down

We have had quite an eventful few days. Seems like Roger has needed platelets and/or blood almost every day lately - we just can't keep his counts up. T herefore, he is very tired and sleeps whenever possible, but the powers that be over at the clinic like to disrupt that cycle with multiple appointments! It is all a part of the process, though, just getting ready for the "big day." We have had some LONG, LONG days leading up to it, I must say. Friday and Saturday were spent with complications, making it necessary for us to be over there for hours and hours; and Friday in particular was a pretty painful day for Roger. They were exchanging his CVC (a semi-permanent line implanted as an IV of sorts, to put it simply), and it got lodged in his neck, against a collar bone, and a rib (there are 3 separate lines). Without sedation, they had to go in and reposition it - again, with no small amount of trouble and pain. Then, Saturday, he had another round of pre-transplant chemo, and needed blood and platelets. We ended up being in the treatment area from 8 a.m. until after midnight. Needless to say, we were sleeping in on Sunday morning. We are grateful that our church has a live internet stream of the Sunday services, and since we slept through that, they have it available for later viewing, as well. OK, so now you know we were backsliding Sunday!

We have had the pleasure of meeting new people this week, and some of our friends in the area brought us a huge meal yesterday of good ole Texas brisket with all the trimmings (thank you Willie and Sandy Wilson!). They always bring plenty to freeze for later, so we will be eating well for a while.

Meanwhile, our dear friends the Templetons are in town for Maurice's check-up, so we will have a nice dinner with them tomorrow. We are trying to do all that Roger feels like doing before his looooong confinement, without tiring him out too much. We have been stockpiling books and computer programs for his entertainment while in the hospital.

Thanks for keeping us in your prayers. On the days when we feel we just don't have the strength to do this again, we get a gentle push from above, and we feel those prayers coming our way. You all are so faithful to remember us and we don't take that for granted - ever. Those prayers are ways to remind us that we are securely

In His Grip!
Debbie

November 10, 2006
A Big Day

Well, today is the day Roger goes into the hospital. We expect it to be sometime tonight, since they wait for discharges to be completed. Meanwhile, we head back over at 7 a.m. today for another platelet infusion. I am going to have to get back to the blood donor room and begin donating platelets again. It just takes a while, and I have not had the time yet.

I can't say we haven't dreaded this day to some extent. Knowing what you face can sometimes make the process more difficult than it was the first time. Please pray specifically today that Roger will NOT be on Floor 12. While we get the greatest of care there, it is the Protective Environment, and it is extremely confining. We are hoping for Floor 11, where there is a measure of (relative) freedom – i.e., fewer masks, gloves, and shoe covers; and the ability to walk around the nurse's station when he feels able; etc., etc .Otherwise, he is confined to his room for the 3+ weeks that he is in there. At least, we hope if he IS on Floor 12, that he will get a room with a window!

Gotta run, time for a shower and then it's off to the clinic again. It will be a busy day, getting packed and filling out papers.

Feeling kind of nervous, but still firmly

In His Grip,
Debbie

November 12, 2006
Settled in for the Duration

Our prayers were answered: Roger got to be in a room on Floor 11 - WITH a window! So far, things are progressing well. He has had two rounds of chemo, a couple of blood infusions, platelets, medications, etc., and is tolerating it all well. He will have a few more days of chemo, and the stem cell transplant itself will take place either next Saturday or Sunday, depending on the timing of the arrival of the donor cells. Please pray for his donor during this crucial week. What a selfless act he is performing, giving the gift of life to a totally anonymous person. We could make several comparisons there as to what our whole Christian existence is about...

We just finished having church via internet, and it was, as usual, a great sermon. I have to confess that I was rushing, trying to get here, get hooked up online, etc., and I was not in the proper frame of mind to go to church. I am thankful that God is able to get around my attitude and still bless me in spite of it. I will try to be more patient with my circumstances, and quit trying to orchestrate them so much. It works out much better when I allow God to be in charge!

Until next time, we are still happily

In His Grip,
Debbie

November 14, 2006
News from the Front Lines

Hey Folks,

First I want to think Debbie for keeping you up to date. I love to read her posts and many times when I'm not up to it, she stands in the gap for me. Thanks Dobra (don't ask).

The title of tonight's post is really a double subject. True, I'm on the front lines personally getting ready for my transplant. By the way, I start my fourth day of chemo tomorrow and have yet to be sick. Thank God for His blessings. I had a staff member walk into my room this afternoon. I was sitting in a chair working on a computer problem, and he looked at me and said, "When the patient gets back, can you have him call me?" I said, "You're looking at the patient!" It made my day. I feel fine and am grateful to be held tightly in my Father's hand.

Now, on to the other front line story. As I've mentioned before, when in the hospital, the TV pretty much is locked down on the History Channel. I can't get enough. During my last transplant it was the Food Network, but this time it's the History Channel, hands down. If you've watched it at all, you know that many of the documentaries are about various wars down through the centuries. My interest lies in the WW2 era. I know so many people who served and endured hardships too gruesome to print here.

I'm always struck by the youthful faces carrying their gear, marching into literally the most dangerous event of their young lives. I can't help but get misty eyed when I think about all the brave young men and women who gave all in defense of our way of life. From the Revolutionary War to WW1 & WW2, to Korea and Vietnam, Bosnia, and both Gulf Wars, so many answered the call of their country.

302

My Dad's only brother was a Junior - Joseph Emerson Bennett, Jr., to be exact. He was drafted in WW2. He was trained in England for heavy armament duty. By all accounts, he was very good at it. But when it came time for him to get into the fighting, some superior decided that Jr. Bennett was needed more at the front lines. He was to fight in hand-to-hand combat. In the last letter his parents received, he told them that he wouldn't be coming home and that he loved them very much. Prophetic words. He was killed a few weeks later in the Battle of the Bulge. A kid 20 years old (my son's age), cut down in the most terrible way. As you can imagine, it devastated our family. My Dad has his photo on the wall at home, and I never pass it that I don't say thanks in my heart to the uncle I never knew for defending a nephew that he would never know.

War is horrible no matter when it occurs in History. The weapons are just more advanced, but the young men and women are the same as generations before them. They knew that death was inches away, but they fought on. I'm sure many had the same premonition as Uncle Jr., that they too would not be coming home; yet they fought on.

We are in a war no less deadly than previous ones. But this time we are not fighting an army that you can see. We are fighting a foe that gleefully sends out men, women, even little boys and girls to blow up as many people as they can. They have been trained since early childhood that martyrdom is the ultimate wish. The thought of "homegrown" terrorists should bring a chill to the heart of each person that treasures freedom. Lord help us.

Before I close, let me tell you my latest lesson learned about the front lines. Christians are in a conflict much more dangerous than any physical conflict. We are fighting for souls. Satan has pulled out his most effective lie so far: Political Correctness. It is quickly destroying not

303

only our language, but it is effectively keeping Christians' mouths closed lest they be labeled a hatemonger. Elton John made headlines this week by saying that, if it were up to him, all religion would be banned! He elaborated, "Religion produces hateful people."

He's right about many so-called religions, but he's dead wrong about the redeemed Body of Christ around this world. Religion has been used as justification for untold deaths since the beginning of time. I shudder when I see misguided people do the most terrible things in the name of God. But there is a Church that will never be stopped. This is the Church that Christ built by defeating death and offering ALL people a way of escape from our sins. The Church I'm talking about consists of the ones who quietly go about the work of caring for the "least of these." This Church around the world, who live with persecution every day, yet still meet together to worship the Lord and share Salvation's plan against the penalty of death. That's the Church that you rarely see on TV. It's not good TV to show a man who loads his truck to overflowing and heads to the poorest area he knows to share not only physical blessings, but also the Words of life that our Savior secured for us. That's boring TV, according to the producers. But they are ever on the lookout for a pastor falling away from his calling. They are plugged in when someone in the church steals money, and attentive to a myriad of other burn outs. Now THAT's great TV.

My encouragement to you is to realize that we are on the enemy's ground. We are most assuredly on the spiritual front lines. But the Lord reminds me that we are not of this world and He will stay with us even until the end of the age. The battle cry should be, "Wake Up!" The time for slumber is over. We've got the message of life, not death, and we need to take God's Message as seriously as our enemies do their religion of hateful murder. But instead of plotting to kill and maim whenever possible, our plan is much better: Jesus loves you so much that He died for you, that you should not perish! Now that's something to take with us in our daily battle on the front lines for the salvation of the world.

In His Grip!
Roger

November 14, 2006
Schedule Update

Not to take away from Roger's newest post by posting another entry, but I just wanted to let all of you prayer warriors out there know that Roger's transplant will take place on Thursday (November 16); or, if the cells are later getting here that day, it will be done on Friday the 17th. Originally, I had told you it would be Saturday, so I wanted to give you the correct date.

He is still hanging in there. His nurse Katie told him that "boring is good," so he is trying to comply!

One more big day of chemo, and then the big day. We appreciate your prayers.

In His Grip,
Debbie

November 16, 2006
The Transplant is Happening as I Type

Here we go! At 11:30 a.m. CST, the donor cells started their lifesaving slip drip into my body.

I decided to write you a few times through the transplant, to give you a play by play, so to speak. I'm doing great so far. No reaction yet. The doctors expect that the rough days are ahead, but I'm of good cheer and calmness. Thanks to God for Grace... That Grace for the moment. It never is late – sometimes not even early -- but He always shows up to give comfort.

That is why, live or die, I've lived my life,

In His Grip
Roger (transplant boy) Bennett

November 16, 2006
Transplant Complete

I didn't get a chance to write during the transplant again. It was over in about an hour and a half. No adverse reactions yet, I'm just wiped out and am gonna give in to a nap attack. I start radiation tomorrow and we move into a new phase in the transplant: fighting rejection, trying to make sure we don't cause any more damage to other organs, and a million other things that can come up. So thanks for your prayers. Deb and I want you to know we need every one!

Sleepy but still In His Grip,
Roger

November 19, 2006
A Sunday Update

I have been sitting in Roger's room for about seven and a half hours today, and he has been awake for maybe half an hour. For some reason, he just can't wake up today. He didn't sleep last night, though, so I know he needed it. I was worried that he might not sleep again tonight, but he has been so soundly asleep all day that I think he might just sleep the night away as well.

Things are going as expected, which doesn't really tell much, except that all of the ups and downs are "expected." The morning after the transplant, he was running a very high fever and had a tremendous headache, so he did not go down to receive radiation. They will try that again on Tuesday.

He has had to receive many infusions of blood and platelets, but that also is not unexpected. For those of you who have asked how to donate in his name, I cannot really tell you anything, except to check with your local blood donation center. I know the ins and outs here at M.D. Anderson, but that is as far as my expertise goes!

Also, for those of you who have asked about the technicalities, I will be happy to share what I can with you in a later post. It is too long for today's post, as I am having to edit myself as I go. I am typing in rubber gloves, and I am not doing a very good job at it! Roger is again in contact isolation due to a virus they found in him, and I have to wear gloves and gown when I am in his room.

Thank you again and again for your prayers. The transplant itself is rather uneventful, but the days after can be quite interesting, to say the least. It's pretty boring, but they like that kind of thing out their patients!!

Until next time, we are still In His Grip,
Debbie

November 23, 2006
Happy Thanksgiving

Happy Thanksgiving from M.D. Anderson! Today is a day of reflection - both the good and the bad - but, by the time you list it all, you have to realize that the good far outweighs any bad that may be on the list. We are very blessed. Sure, we'd prefer to be at home around the table loaded with a big feast, and it's the first Thanksgiving that we have ever been away from Chelsea and Jordan; but we are in a place where there is good care, and that is most important at this time.

This week has been one of lots of ups and downs. Roger has been in a lot of pain, particularly with severe headaches, and his blood pressure has been extremely elevated. He is also now on a heart monitor because of irregular heart rhythms, and his blood sugar has been very high as well. All of this, we have been assured, can be handled by adjusting medications (at any one time there are probably between 15-20 bags of stuff hanging on his IV pole), so they work at that. They are so good to do what they can to help. Meanwhile, it is hard to sit and watch while I know I can't do anything to help... and even harder for Roger to be patient while he feels so bad. But, this too shall pass. The doctor figures it will be another week or so before his counts start to recover. They have to reach a certain point before he can get out of the hospital. We are glad, too, that even though he is still on contact isolation, he did not have to leave the 11th floor, or his room. People entering and leaving have to do the gown, glove, mask thing - a pain, but not so bad all in all.

This Thanksgiving Day is sunny and warm/hot in Houston, not the weather I prefer for this time of year! However, this morning as I was making sweet potato biscuits (his mom's recipe) to take to him, I was listening to a great radio station here in Houston that plays only

Christmas music all season long, and it put me in the mood! (I think it is www.sunny99.com if you'd like to listen via internet.)

All in all, things are going along... up and down, but still going. We have so much to be thankful for. Our blessings are too many to count. So, I hope that whatever your circumstances this day, and the rest of the holiday season, that you, too, are able to count your blessings, and realize that God will never release us from His care. We are SO blessed to be

In His Grip!
Debbie

November 24, 2006
Ditto Debbie!

This will be one of the shortest posts from me. You can tell by the previous post that God blessed me when Debbie in a weak moment said yes to me.

After two of the most grueling days in my life, I've enjoyed two of the best so far. I've felt like a new man. Thanks to you ropeholders out there who refuse to stop praying for our family! You are very precious to all of us.

In His Grip!
RB

December 02, 2006
Checkin' In From RB

If you don't see a post for a few days, especially during this time of the transplant, it could be that I'm not able to write and Deb is doing what she is supposed to be doing and that is help keep me alive, or things are going so well that we decided to post later.

This time it's somewhere in between.

At the beginning of the week, I started having breathing problems and some heart related episodes. No heart attack -- but the beats per minute were just out of normal range. I remember very little about those two days and nights. As far the old misery factor goes... I lost that round.

But here's where it turns the corner. I can almost tell you when you rope holders grab the rope and start bombarding Heaven on our behalf. It seems that my body hears God's orders and, at an instant, the Comforter has come.

So I seem to be over the hard part concerning the actual in-patient stuff. More good news, if everything goes as expected, I'll be released from here in the hospital, to Debbie's custody at the apartment to recover. They tell me it's very critical that I do what they say during this period, so physical therapy begins on Tuesday. We will be in touch.

IHG,
Roger

December 04, 2006
A Change of Scenery

YES!! We are at the apartment this afternoon. Roger was released today from the hospital after 24 days. Now, we go to the schedule of back-and-forth to the clinic for treatments daily. But that is a good problem to have.

We came in, plugged in the Christmas tree, ate a sub sandwich, and he went to lie down in a bed that has nice soft sheets, and no motor that pumps up the mattress every time you move (well, actually, we learned how to turn that motor off early on). So, while he is napping, I am posting, and getting ready to go back up to the hospital pharmacy to pick up LOTS of medicines. They all know me there, though, so they won't be surprised at the big bags I will be carrying off.

For now, though, we are so grateful to be back in the apartment together. God sends His blessings on all of us who are

In His Grip!
Debbie

December 11, 2006
Still Improving

One week after being released from the hospital, and Roger is still working hard to recover. His counts look very good, the doctors and nurses are impressed with them all, and the waiting game continues. He is experiencing lots of fatigue and weakness, but when we think of all that his body has been through, and in the concentrated amount of time it has taken, it's not surprising.

I know he would love to be back to his "normal" self (whatever that means to him!), but we have to remember it is just 25 days post-transplant, and we still have a way to go. He will have his first follow-up test this Friday (bone marrow aspiration - painful, but he doesn't mind since he gets to be sedated!), and that may tell us a few things; but I doubt it will be too conclusive, since his AML disease has not been present in his marrow in almost two years - it has presented in other, more unusual ways. But anyway, they know what they are looking for and, again, they seem pleased with the progress.

We have a few exciting things coming up. First, our 25th anniversary is this coming Sunday, so I need to plan a menu and find a good holiday movie to watch here at the apartment. Then, on Monday, Roger's dad, Doug, and his friend, Jane, are coming for a visit for a few days before Christmas. Chelsea and Jordan will come down Christmas night and stay a few days. I confess to being a little disappointed that we won't be home for Christmas again this year, but we are totally in agreement that Christmas is not about a day or place, but about the actual reason for the season, and we can celebrate Christ anywhere we are!

So, though we may not post for a few days, please realize that if there is any news to report, we will do so immediately. Otherwise, we are busy with treatments, tests, and holiday time, so please do not worry. We are firm believers in letting our prayer requests be known when we need them.

Time for bed, and sleep before tomorrow's clinic visit. Roger has already beat me there; he was pretty tired and slightly feverish tonight. Thanks for checking on us, praying for us, and knowing we are firmly

In His Grip,
Debbie

December 21, 2006
Back in the Hospital

Just a quick update, as I don't have much information to go on yet. Yesterday, after feeling unwell for a couple of days, Roger's doctor re-admitted him to the hospital for testing and treatment. Today he will have an upper GI scope, and a colonoscopy as soon as they can get it scheduled.

This, of course, puts another monkey wrench in the "plans" (which I long ago figured out were useless to make!) – Roger's dad was here for a visit, leaving today, and we had "planned" to celebrate Christmas with him last night. We all decided we were big boys and girls, and we would be able to live over not getting to unwrap gifts together. Pray for Doug's safety as he drives back to Arkansas today.

I must run. I will update when I have more information. May God keep you all

In His Grip,
Debbie

December 24, 2006
Still in the Hospital

As I wrote earlier, Roger was admitted to the hospital on Wednesday this week, due to some complications that the doctors wanted to check out. As of the doctor's visit today, we expect that he will still be in for a few more days, including Christmas.

The biopsies that were taken on Thursday are not back yet, but we think he has "Graft vs. Host Disease," which is where the donor cells attack different parts of the host's

(Roger's) body. This time it is in his stomach. He hasn't had any solid food for quite a while now, and was only given the go-ahead for broth today. Needless to say, he is pretty weak right now. I guess that lets me off the hook for cooking a Christmas dinner, anyway. Good thing Luby's has a drive-thru!

Anyway, we probably won't get the test results for a few more days, due to the holidays, but they have begun treatment, suspecting that the GVHD is the culprit. Good news: he is feeling a little better. Bad news: it is treated with steroids, which cause his blood sugar to soar, and his muscles to weaken. But they are on top of all of that, too.

The doctor says that he will be allowed to leave the floor and find a quiet place to visit with Chelsea and Jordan when they come. I confess that we are both a little down over this turn of events. But all of the days just run together around here, so maybe the actual day of Christmas won't seem so lonely. We are trying hard to remember the focus of the Day as what it really means anyway. Maybe next year we will be able to be with all of our family again. It just seems so long since we have been able to have that special time with all of them.

OK, I need to quit complaining and thank you all for the many, many letters, cards, and gifts of love that you have sent our way. I spent the evening catching up on opening cards and enjoying reading them. We are surrounded by some awesome Christian friends! I wish I could write a separate thank-you to each of you, but that would not be possible. So know that you are all loved by the Bennett family, and appreciated more than words can say. It's great to be a part of a vast family who is kept

In His Grip!
Debbie

December 26, 2006
Blessings

Merry (belated) Christmas!

I hope you all had a wonderful day celebrating the greatest gift of all in that Baby Boy who came to give us love and life. Although it was a different kind of day for us, we had a wonderful time. Our day started off feeling a bit "off-kilter" - not the hustle and bustle we usually expect out of Christmas morning. Roger's doctor came by and said that, in his "best estimate," he feels Roger will be in the hospital for another seven to ten days anyway. Then, after much discussion between the two of them, the doctor finally agreed to allow Roger to eat some mashed potatoes - his first solid food in over a week. Roger said they tasted wonderful! (And, by the way, as I was informed of this decision on my way to the hospital, I began a fruitless search for somewhere to buy mashed potatoes on Christmas Day - no way!) Luckily, the hospital cafeteria was able to accommodate.

We passed the rest of the day waiting for the moment when Chelsea and Jordan would arrive. Their plane landed about 7:15 p.m., then I rushed them back to the apartment where we packed up all of the Christmas gifts and raced over to the hospital with them. So, at about 9:30, all four of us were sitting in the hospital lobby, near a beautiful Christmas tree, enjoying each other as we opened gifts. We told the kids that it didn't feel like Christmas until they were there. Then, it didn't matter where we were: we were together and having a great time. It was really wonderful. The bonus about us starting so late is that there weren't many people around, so we had privacy, as well.

Tomorrow, I am driving up to my great-aunt's in Linden, TX, about 5 hours north of here, to meet up with my parents and one brother. I am looking forward to seeing them. Chelsea and Jordan will stay behind and take care of their Dad. I plan to make the trip up and back in one day, so I won't be away too long.

Please continue to pray for Roger's healing, as I know you do. This stomach thing is pretty serious, but luckily they caught it early and know how to treat it. It just takes some time. One of the main things that bothers him is the weakness that comes from not eating. It may be a few more days before they allow him any more solid food. Meanwhile, broth and ice cream – and insulin -- are the ticket, but we aren't too concerned with the sugars he eats, because he needs the calories. Such a round-and-round cycle.

So, from sunny Houston, to all of you, Merry Christmas and Happy New Year! May we all use this time to reflect on the blessings of being

In His Grip!
Debbie

January 01, 2007
...And a Happy New Year!

Hopefully your 2007 started out with nothing but good health and happiness. As for us, we are hanging in there, and looking for a good year ahead. Roger is still in the hospital, and things are back to the same routine around here, but he is feeling a little better.

We so enjoyed having Chelsea and Jordan here, if only for a few days. Roger was disappointed that he was not able to be out and about with them, but they visited him at the hospital, and I took them out to some of their favorite spots when we could manage the time. They really brightened up the holidays for us, and it seemed a little "flat" when they left. But, they have their own lives to attend to, and that is as it should be. School will be starting up soon for both of them.

Roger is still dealing with many issues but the doctors are beginning to see some progress. Bless his heart, he is so hungry. He is still only allowed broth, a plain baked potato or rice, and the occasional Jell-O. Well, I do make him some mashed potatoes in fat free chicken broth and take them up sometimes. I can tell by the fact that he keeps mentioning "real" food that he is feeling better. I can't wait for the day when he will be able to eat something he really wants.

Tonight, he got his room switched, since someone needed the "special" room he was in more than he did. So, even little things like a change of scenery out the window, or the new room layout, are things to be appreciated. He is now on the side of the hospital where he can watch the sunset. (He could have watched the sun*rise* from the other side, but, well...)

So another year has passed and a new one has begun. I have given up making resolutions, because something always gets in the way of them; but I am working on being the best person I can be. I was talking with a friend tonight about how it takes so little time just to be *thoughtful* of others. It seems to be a hard thing for so many, but I want it to be second nature for me. I fall way short of the mark most of the time, but it's a goal I am willing to strive toward. It sure makes a difference in my day when someone is considerate of me. I'd like to pass that feeling along anytime I can.

So while I am working on that one goal (added to all of my others), I remain today and forever

In His Grip!
Debbie

January 05, 2007
A Beautiful Day

It's a beautiful day in Houston: sunny after a lot of rain, 74 degrees, and Roger is OUT of the hospital as of this afternoon! We came home with a lot of equipment, medicine, and appointments to return daily for a while, but it feels like a vacation!

Just wanted to post a quick update. There is a lot to be done at the moment, getting everything set up and in order, but know that the Bennetts are having a great evening in the apartment tonight.

If I might ask for a little more prayer for a family here... a very dear friend of mine, one I have made since being here again this time, is going through a very rough time right now. Her daughter, after a myriad of complications, is now in the ICU, and in need of a miracle. A lot of family has arrived from Louisiana, and they would love to know that they are being prayed for. Just ask God to bless the Hills, and I know they will feel the peace of being

In His Grip,
Debbie

January 13, 2007
Better Each Day

We have just completed a week with Roger out of the hospital again, and so far things are going alright. That first night he was home was pretty challenging in that neither one of us had the strength to get him up off of the sofa, but we finally managed; and from that point on, he is gaining strength each day. This week, he began physical therapy, and that is helping. His muscles have been seriously weakened by the steroid regimen he has been on to treat the Graft vs. Host disease. It's not unexpected, but it is a new side effect to deal with.

The good news is that the GVHD seems to be under control and, as of yesterday, Roger was released to eat "whatever he can tolerate." So, I guess my days of not cooking are over for a while! Actually, I am glad to have that little "problem." He is still having to go for treatments on a daily basis, but that is better than being in-patient.

We had hoped that he would feel well enough to be in Tomball, TX, tomorrow with the group, but that will still have to wait a while yet. Disappointing, but we can deal with that. It won't be long until he is back in full swing, so we will concentrate on getting him stronger until then!

Reality has crowded in on us here once again this week, with the death of another friend. Unfortunately, we are in a place where we are surrounded with the possibility of death. We just cling to the hope that comes with the assurance of God's promises and to the knowledge that there are many, many friends and strangers here who will walk through those doors on their way home after being cured. We've said it before, and we still agree that this is a wonderful place to be if you have to be somewhere for this reason. We've had the privilege and honor to meet so many dear people here whom we would not have met except under these circumstances, and I hope that their paths were brightened by having met us, as much as ours have been by having met all of them.

As I said, we lost a friend this week, and she was one that you have been praying for. Please remember the Hills again, as they adjust to a life without their precious 23-year old Shareeka, who leaves behind a 2-year old son, as well as her parents and the rest of her family. Shareeka put up one of the bravest fights a young person ever has, and her family will miss her dearly. I feel a deep grief for my friend Sherry, her mom, as I came to know her well. They will need many prayers in the days ahead to remind them that their dear loved one is now in the best place of all: face to face and for eternity

In His Grip,
Debbie

January 27, 2007
Another Update

OK, OK, I know it has been two weeks since we posted last. You know what they say: "Time flies when you are having fun" (!!!). Seriously, we have just been going through all of the processes, and the ups and downs, and haven't taken the time to post after we get back to the apartment.

Last weekend, we actually had two days "off" (the first since October!) - which means that we were able to bring the medicines home and do them ourselves, rather than having to go into the clinic. It was great to sleep in and not have to be anywhere - it felt like a mini-vacation!

Not so this weekend, but it's okay. They have started Roger on a new type of chemo, which is part of the protocol he is on for this transplant. It's a mild form that is supposed to seek out any residual cancer cells that might not even be showing up at this point. According to all tests so far, he is again in remission, which is definitely what we want to hear. The reason for this follow-up chemo regimen is to make sure that he stays in remission this time. So, we are praying that this particular protocol is the one that will finally chase this disease away for good.

Lately, we have been feeling like we are stuck in a "cancer warp," where everything in our daily lives is about cancer and that's all it is about. It will be so nice to be able to focus on something else for a change. (Of course, I am not talking about relationships, or spiritual well-being; it's just the physical day-to-day that I am referring to.) Physically and mentally, it is very easy to get worn out, but this too shall pass.

Roger is feeling stronger, and that is a great thing. He still has "issues" that we deal with, but the doctor saw him yesterday, and was all smiles about his progress. That's always encouraging!

We had hoped to be able to make a Legacy Five concert in a couple of TX cities the past two Sundays, but Roger was not up to it. He was a little down about that, but the guys did surprise us one Sunday and drove down here on the bus. They parked on the Target parking lot, we drove to meet them, and got some wonderful visiting time in on the bus! It was great to see some familiar "home" faces. They are truly special friends, and it meant a lot to us that they would take that extra effort to come see us. I told Roger to just concentrate on getting stronger, and he will be back before we know it.

In ways, the time has passed quickly here (41 days in the hospital may have contributed to that); but in other ways, it seems we have been here a VERY long time. However, we are so blessed with all of the friendships we have here, and some new ones we have made, as well. God always provides a "silver lining" to those clouds! Hmm, I could get really deep here, but I will save that for another time. Right now, I have to get ready to go to the clinic.

Thank you for your continuing prayers and support. We are safe, warm, and dry; well-fed, well-cared for, and

In His Grip!
Debbie

February 01, 2007
Hospitalized Again

Yesterday found us admitting Roger back into the hospital. For the past few days, we have been watching some levels rise that have had the doctors a bit concerned. They indicate that his kidneys are not functioning well at the time. As a result, he has not been able to receive all of the treatments he was scheduled to have. So, yesterday, the levels had risen to a very high level, and the decision was made to admit him where he can be monitored and receive consults from more doctors... Putting heads together, so to speak.

The good news is that Roger was admitted in better shape than he was the last time, so perhaps it won't be a long stay. It will all depend on his response, of course, but we are glad to have the doctors and nurses in place to take care of him. Left unchecked, the problem could turn serious but, fortunately, nothing here is left unchecked!

It proved to be a long day yesterday, as we started it off by receiving a phone call from a friend here telling us she lost her husband yesterday morning. It was quite a shock, since we had just seen them on Friday, but he made a rapid decline after that and lost his battle.

When you are not feeling well anyway, news like that tends to creep in and take a seat in the front of your mind. It becomes necessary to really focus then and remember that God's plan has been in motion since the world was formed (even before that), and that He is still working it all out for His good. It is comforting to know that the outcome is not dependent on our feelings. What a mess we would all be in if that were the truth! So, we just have to wait, and listen, and remember that we are ALWAYS

In His Grip!
Debbie

February 05, 2007
[Note: This is the last post ever written by Roger.]
Seasons

Hello again,

Sorry it's been a while since I've written, but as usual, thanks to Debbie for holding me up. As you probably know, this transplant has been a particularly hard one to close the book on.

The good news: the doctors say that, on the cancer front, I'm in remission (thank God). But on the side effects side, I've not done real well. Many more little things that can grow into big things have happened. The latest is the question of my kidney damage. Scary thought... But starting Monday, I'll start seeing another specialist to try and get to the bottom of this new challenge.

I was talking with a friend the other night and the conversation turned to the difficulty Christians have after they or a loved one are pronounced all clear of cancer. I've been there, and I know the joy you feel when you see the Cancer Center getting smaller in your rearview mirror. Thankful does not seem to even touch the emotions that I've felt every time that's happened. Likewise, crushing doesn't describe the feeling I've experienced when another "R" word was used... Relapse. A desolate word.

Here's where the trouble starts. Christians sometimes are the worst prepared people for setbacks. That's the opposite of what God wants for us. I'm not telling you something I've heard; I'm telling you something I've lived. I was in remission for three and a half years and began to think that I would never have to deal with cancer again. But just around the corner, the relapse was waiting to ambush my body and spirit. The storm was fierce. I was weak and full of fear. But, through some great wisdom shared with me, I found an eternal truth. One word: Seasons.

323

Ecclesiastes tells us one of the greatest truths of all time: to everything in life, there is a season. A time to laugh, cry, celebrate, and mourn, etc.. The wisdom my friend shared was this: Rejoice in this season of remission, rejoice in the humor of life... Laugh as much as you can, even if it's at yourself. Rejoice in seasons of rejoicing, but keep in mind the other truth, that there will be seasons of mourning, seasons of tears, seasons when you feel that you are failing at everything, or that nobody cares. Death might make an unannounced appearance in your family, or maybe even an unannounced appointment with sickness that cannot be cured except by a miracle (which I believe happens every day). A miracle is typing this post. I've lived with a changing, aggressive disease now for over eleven years. Many times during this season it's been difficult. A perfect time to mourn. I've done my share. Separated from my family and friends for months at a time. Feeling sidelined from the most fulfilling job in the world. Sitting in a 10x10 hospital room, trying to relax, when I've just been told that I had a 30% chance of making it. Yet I've made it this far, laughing a lot, crying some. I've been at peace with the sickness and I've raged against it. But in each season I've lived, I've lived with the assurance that I was never solo. I had a protector every step of the way, and He has not abandoned me during any season. The God who sees the beginning of seasons since the beginning of time and will see each one until Death dies and time stops and we are gathered into His presence.

Can you imagine? A season with no end! No sickness, no hurting words, no broken promises or even medical appointments. No night, because in this season, night never falls. No tears -- they've been dried and wiped away by gentle, nail-scarred hands. I guess, to put it in my hometown (Strawberry, AR) language, it's a never ending open season of Glory!

Here's a closing thought for you. This could be just for you. Through great circulation of the *Singing News*, this little note will reach thousands. My blog is at http://rogerbennett.typepad.com (check it out), and I'm told by the internet gurus that its readership is growing every day. I tell you this because I'm humbled by your concern and prayers. I tell you this because the possibilities are that many, many people who thumb through the pages of the *Singing News* or click on the internet are living in a season of heartache and pain. You may be the one who needs to know that "this too shall pass."

Seasons, some good, some not so much. But all observed by an unseen Father who went through a very dark season when His Son died on a cross for a world that didn't even know they were lost. When God the Father turned His back on the scene, that had to be a terrible season. But, as nature shows, seasons change. Three days after Calvary, from the door of an empty tomb, that season of mourning changed with unimaginable power. Death had died once and for all and the season of eternal life began; and that season will never pass.

If it's you who needs this, surrender your will and your confusion and turn your seasons over to our Savior Jesus Christ. He'll be the only real peace you'll find.

In His Grip!
Roger

February 08, 2007
Health Update

I guess Roger likes to experience many new "seasons" (see previous post). He was released from the hospital last Friday, only to be re-admitted today. He has now developed shingles, along with a temperature from an infection or two. Because of the elevated kidney function levels that they've been monitoring, he needed to be inpatient to receive the medicines he needs to combat the new problems. The doctor told him today that, had his levels been more normal, these meds could be administered outpatient -- but Roger hasn't been "normal" for quite some time!

Hopefully, this hospital stay will be no more than over the weekend, but as we well know, things are never predictable around here.

I must run, as I have packing to do for him, and I am trying to time my arrival around shift changes... It's hard to get a parking space during that window of staff coming and going!

Please pray for us. Roger is in some pain with his shingles, and I confess, I am about as worn out as I can remember being in a long time. These days would be hard to navigate if not for the assurance that we are

In His Grip,
Debbie

February 17, 2007
A Weekend Off - Finally!

Yea! No need to get up and go into the clinic today or tomorrow! They finally gave us a couple of days off and sent us home with the meds. We are delighted. As long as no new symptoms crop up, we are able to stay home for two days -- and it couldn't come at a better time, since Chelsea is down visiting us this weekend. Last time she was here, her dad was in the hospital.

Roger was released from the hospital on Monday afternoon. We have, of course, had to go in for treatments every day this week, and he is still experiencing pain with his shingles. Friday, new tests were ordered to determine what might be causing his extreme fatigue - more than expected, as he is having a hard time staying awake for much of the day. That could be something as simple as medications that are not exiting his body in a timely fashion, but it does need to be checked out. We don't have a date for those tests yet.

However, he did have a 90 days post-transplant bone marrow biopsy this week. All results are not in, but the preliminary ones show he is still without disease in his marrow - absolutely great news!

Well, Chelsea and I are off to check out this bakery I saw the other day that advertises "eggless cakes" -- exciting possibilities for a vegetarian like our daughter.

By the way, she got the news this week that she has been hired for a job in Alaska this summer -- for five months, actually. There should be some fantastic photographic opportunities up there. She has also been asked, along with her best friend, to do a two-person photo show (display of her work) at the college she attends before she graduates this spring. Just an aside to brag on our little girl, who grew up way too fast!

It's a gorgeous day in Houston to be
In His Grip,
Debbie

February 21, 2007
Yet Another Admission

We are beginning to feel like a rubber ball, bouncing back and forth, in and out. Yesterday (I guess, technically it was Monday night late), Roger was re-admitted to the hospital.

After having the weekend off from going in to the clinic, when we got back in on Monday morning, we were sent down to the ER after he received his infusion (and that was a lovely 15 hours!). He had not felt well over the weekend, and didn't get out of the apartment to enjoy the mild weather. By Monday morning, his oxygen levels were very low, among other problems. Long story short, he seems to have an infection in his left lung that is probably either bacterial pneumonia or a fungus on his lung. We are hoping it is pneumonia, as that is easier to treat. Meanwhile, his shingles have spread some, so more aggressive treatment is needed for that; but the meds they give him tend to aggravate the kidneys, so that will have to be monitored as well. However, since he has been on oxygen, he seems to be feeling much better.

I am on my way out to the hospital, but just wanted to update you all. Thanks for keeping us in your prayers.

In His Grip,
Debbie

February 28, 2007
Waiting...

It has been a LONG few days. Roger is not doing well at the moment, and has a variety of complications. We knew when he was admitted that he was a bit confused, and that his oxygen levels were low, in addition to having shingles and the accompanying pain. After having many tests performed while inpatient, we have now determined that he has pneumonia (growing 3 different types of bacteria), meningitis (swelling of the lining of the brain), encephalitis (swelling of the brain itself), and an occurrence of leukemia cells in a spot on his head. Whew! I am hoping it sounds worse than it is...

We are still awaiting test results from the latest lumbar puncture (spinal tap) to determine whether the memory problems, weakness, and balance issues are due solely to the virus in the spinal/brain areas, or whether the leukemia disease is involved. It has been so difficult to watch his condition the past few days. He is definitely not the Roger we all know and love. I am praying for the best-case scenario: that the problems are caused by the virus alone, and treatments will bring him back to his "normal" self. He began radiation treatments today on the spot that showed the leukemia cells (he now has an interesting "tattoo" on his head). The best-case scenario there is that those were residual cells that did not get killed off during the chemo/transplant. If that is the case, and it is an isolated spot, then the radiation will take care of that. Again, tests are pending.

Some of this news I only learned yesterday, the rest I learned last Friday. I have spent a fearful weekend, learning to rely more fully on God. I know that His plan was set in motion before we were ever on this earth. I also know that I trust Him. Therefore, I need to be still and let God calm my fears.

I really debated about how much of this I wanted to share. I am not sure how Roger would feel about my letting all of this be known, but I can't ask him about it right now. The kids are coming down this weekend for a few days, and that will be a great boost. Maybe by then, he will be more alert and ready to visit. Until then, I ask for extra prayers, and rest in the promise that He will never leave us. He keeps us safely

In His Grip,
Debbie

March 06, 2007
Urgent Prayer Needed

As of about 5 a.m. this morning, Roger has been in the ICU here at M.D. Anderson. This will be a short update, just asking for prayer. We are not sure of what is causing the problems, but he is in respiratory distress, along with several other life-threatening issues. He is not conscious right now because of heavy sedation, and he will be intubated later today, so we can't talk with him. We do talk to him and tell him how much we love him, though.

Needless to say, it is a very hard day for us. Doug, his dad, is on his way down as well. Just pray for comfort for Roger, and grace for the rest of us. We know that God has everything under His control and

In His Grip,
Debbie

March 08, 2007
No Change Yet

Well, I hardly know what to write. It has surely been a long few days, weeks, etc. I spoke to the teams of doctors this morning, and they have no new news since yesterday, really. I know there are other tests scheduled for today, and yesterday, they inserted a line and began dialysis. I hope this will help pull some toxins out of his body, and maybe that will jumpstart things. The doctors still do not understand what is happening in his body. Besides the obvious infections, which I have described previously, there is still something unidentified that is not allowing him to heal. I have not been able to speak with him since Monday, and I never knew how many things I would want to ask him or talk to him about.

We are all holding up pretty well. Doug came down Tuesday night, and although it is terribly painful for him to see his only child in this state, he is bearing up. Chelsea and Jordan were able to be here on Sunday, so they had a couple of days where they could visit with him. Jordan had to fly back yesterday, and that was so hard. I didn't want to put him on that plane alone, and it was heartbreaking watching him say bye to his dad, not knowing what the future holds. I told him not to feel bad about leaving, since he was here when it really counted, and he is only a plane ride away, should he be needed again. Chelsea was able to extend her visit, and can be here a few more days.

My mom and dad are in Linden, TX, right now to be with her Aunt Ora (who is the whole family's favorite) as she is dying. They asked if I needed them here, but I told them to stay with Aunt Ora, as there is little to be done here right now.

If the tests that are run in the next few days do not give us more direction, there may be little that can be done for

Roger. I do not discount a miracle, but that is what it seems it will take at this point.

I know there are prayers coming our way continuously. We feel them, and we find much comfort in them. There is a peace in knowing that God is in control, and is working a perfect plan. It may not always feel good, but we continue to trust. I am glad I don't have to orchestrate it all.

Please just continue to pray. So many have asked what they can do to help, but that is what we need more than anything.

I'd love to see that miracle come our way, but whatever happens, we know we win. There is no downside for Roger.

I love you all, and appreciate your support.

We remain always, and securely,
IN HIS GRIP,
Debbie

March 12, 2007
Still Waiting

There is still no significant change in Roger's condition. We are still waiting and praying. He remains in a medically induced sedated state, unresponsive, and still on a respirator, dialysis. etc.

Thank you so much for your continuing prayers and support. They mean so much to our family.

Doug was here from last Tuesday until he went home yesterday to tend to some business there. Chelsea was able to stay a few extra days, but will fly home this evening. Please remember her as she makes a difficult journey home. Jordan is safely back in Michigan now.

On the way in early this morning, I heard a song that boosted my spirit. I hope I don't offend the writer by using his words on this post, but I wanted to share a few of them with you.

> *I will lift my eyes to the Maker of the mountains I can't climb, I will lift my eyes to the Calmer of the oceans raging wild, I will lift my eyes to the Healer of the hurts I hold inside, I will lift my eyes, lift my eyes to You.*

I give thanks to the Father, that although we are confused and hurting, we have peace in knowing we are safely

In His Grip,
Debbie

March 17, 2007
The Ultimate Healing

"Home Free, Oh I've got a feeling, At the ultimate healing, we will be home free!"
One of Roger's favorite songs to sing, and now he knows the whole truth about it. This morning, at about 8:30 a.m., he left his battle here on earth to rejoice in Heaven for eternity.

It has, naturally, been a very hard couple of days for those of us left behind. However, I am overwhelmed by the grace God has poured out on me. I feel a multitude of emotions simultaneously: grief, heartache, and sadness, surely; but also an immeasurable portion of comfort and peace which I can't explain any other way but God's grace.

It became evident a few days ago that the only earthly way out of this situation for Roger was going to be a miracle. By yesterday evening, it was evident that the way out for him was going to be a Heavenly miracle. I can only imagine what lies in store for him there! How must it feel to hear those words spoken by the Father: "Well done, My good and faithful servant!"

In the following days and weeks, I plan to share with you all some of the "God things" that have happened these last few days.

The comments I read on this web site have been of such comfort and encouragement to me. So many of you have said that you felt that Roger's work isn't done here yet. I agree! The legacy he has left behind will go on forever, and there are several projects that he has begun that I feel called to carry out - including keeping this web site up so that I can continue to share his message with many.

Arrangements are pending at this point, but will be made public as soon as they are finalized. Preliminary plans are to have a celebration service and burial in

Tennessee, and a later memorial service in his hometown of Strawberry, Arkansas.

Thank you, thank you, thank you for the prayers and love you show. The next few days will be difficult for us all, but we will make it through God's strength.

As for Roger, he has finally realized his ultimate goal, to be forever

IN HIS GRIP!
Debbie

March 19, 2007
The Celebration

I am home in TN, and will be making all of the final arrangements today. Please be in prayer for our family, as the realization is setting in more and more each day.

We will have a celebration of Roger's life and his homegoing on Wednesday, March 21, at 2 p.m. It will be held at Brentwood Baptist Church in Brentwood, TN. Visitation will also be held at the church on Tuesday evening from six to nine p.m., and one hour prior to the service on Wednesday.

There will also be a memorial service held on Saturday, March 24 at 2 p.m. at the high school gymnasium in Strawberry, AR. This will be a replay of the Wednesday service.

Arrangements are being handled by Williamson Memorial Funeral Home in Franklin, TN. Burial will be at Williamson Memorial Gardens, at the same location.

In lieu of flowers, donations may be made in Roger's name to the Southern Gospel Music Trust Fund. (Details to follow on that; I don't have all of the info right now.) This is a fund to help those who are in the Southern Gospel industry who may need to have expenses covered above what they are able to manage. They made a contribution to the Roger Bennett Benefit/Medical Fund in the past.

More posts will follow in the next few days. Until then, know that God is holding us in His arms, and keeping us

In His Grip,
Debbie

March 30, 2007
Beginning a New Chapter

It is so hard to believe it has been thirteen days since Roger left this earth for his Heavenly home. In ways, it seems like yesterday, but most of the time it feels like a lifetime has passed already. My heart aches with missing him so much. Most of the day, I am so busy, I don't have time to dwell on the loss; but suddenly, my heart will begin pounding, and I panic at the thought of being without him. So, I cry, and think of the good memories, and God comforts me with the knowledge that Roger is so happy where he is - free from pain and sorrow, and glorying in the very presence of Jesus. Although I wish he hadn't had to leave so soon, I would not wish him back here to this life for anything. I am truly happy for him and all that he has gained! And, I am also reminded that I am not grieving as one who has no hope. I WILL be with Roger again one day, and that makes Heaven even sweeter for me now. I did tell Roger, before he left, that he had better keep the mansion clean, because I didn't want to have to do housekeeping first thing when I get there!

The celebration services of his life were beautiful. I do think he would have been honored, and I know he would have been humbled. For such an outgoing person, he was really uncomfortable when he was being put in the center spotlight. I could just picture him ducking his head at a few comments. Our family appreciates so much the kind words everyone has had to say. It seems like everyone I have spoken to has had a "Roger story" of their own. How he encouraged them, gave them a kind word to keep them going, laughed with them, prayed with them, listened to them... The list goes on and on. And I am not surprised. Roger was a truly caring individual, and he wasn't afraid to show it. That's just who he was, and it makes us miss him all the more. For those of you who tried to log onto the website during the actual live stream and could not get it, we are sorry. That could have been a last practical joke on Roger's part -- crashing several servers at once! However, Legacy Five has hosted a link from their site where you may now view the service at your leisure. It was such a wonderful tribute to a wonderful man, that I wanted to be able to share it with many. I believe there is also information there about the Southern Gospel Music Trust Fund, where donations are being made in Roger's name. Thank you for that. Again, he would be honored, as is our family.

We are all getting along with God's tremendous grace. Chelsea and Jordan are busy finishing up the school year. Doug is getting back into his daily routine. I am swamped with papers, meetings, and planning. My parents are trying to get back into a routine after being in Texas for two weeks, burying my aunt on March 19, and getting back to Tennessee for visitation on the 20th, etc.

I am also trying to get thank-you notes out, but please be patient with me. I believe I still have a few to write from Houston, as well as all of the new ones. Please forgive me if I miss any. I am doing my best, but I am not well-organized at the moment. I still have to travel back to Houston to close up our apartment there before April 16, then Chelsea has to move out of her apartment in Nashville by April 30, and then she leaves for Alaska on May 4 for five months. I think I feel a HUGE garage sale coming on!

Yes, our lives have changed drastically, but we have the assurance that we are not left alone. We have a Savior who has promised to be all that we need. What more can we ask than to know that we are being held tightly

In His Grip,
Debbie

April 07, 2007
Assurances

As I begin composing this post, it is three weeks, almost to the very minute, that Roger left this earth to begin his Heavenly life. I think it's a fitting anniversary to be able to finally write about some of those "God things" that happened toward the end. I have to rely heavily on those these days, since the reality has sunk in all the way, and I miss him so incredibly.

About the 1st of March, as Roger was still in the hospital, and we knew we were dealing with a more serious situation each day, I had gone back to the apartment for a while. I was walking our dog (we had decided to have one member of our menagerie brought to us after Christmas, since we figured petting a puppy would bring some stress relief. Well, Boomer is 11½ years old, but he is still our "puppy") and enjoying a beautiful day of sunshine outside when I became overwhelmingly sad and weepy. I was thinking of all of the things that Roger would love to do, and how he would so enjoy just being in the sunshine, outside of that confining hospital, maybe just riding in the car. And, yes, I was feeling a bit rebellious, asking God, "Why? Why can't you just make it all better this time, like before? Don't You know what all Roger is missing? Don't You realize what all Roger wants to do?" So, I had my moment of a mass of emotions crashing around me, feeling like there was just too much at stake for the Lord NOT to heal Roger. Then, at the very second when I just thought I couldn't bear thinking about it anymore, God spoke to me - not audibly, of course, although it certainly felt as real as if He had - and He said, "Debbie, there is nothing here on this earth that even compares to what I have waiting on Roger in Heaven." That thought literally stopped me in my tracks, and a wave of peace came over me, knowing that that Promise

339

was true. And as I began to think about it in more depth, I thought of all of the things that I wanted to do with Roger here on earth, about all of the things Roger wanted to do here on this earth, and God was right (imagine that!): they couldn't possibly compare to the riches waiting for all of God's children when we finally complete our journey!

I cannot begin to count the hundreds of times I have taken myself back to that moment. I have times when panic begins to overtake me, thinking about the time I won't have Roger here with me; how much I miss him; how much the kids miss him, and all of our family misses him. Yet, in a moment, that peace that passes all understanding can come back to me, to let me know that ROGER is not missing ANYTHING! The time we live here without him won't even show up on the Heavenly calendar. It will seem like a moment to Roger, until the time comes when we show up at the pearly gates and get to experience that same Homecoming and welcome that he has already realized. As the song says, "What a Day that will be!"

I wish I could be some spiritual giant, who never has moments of doubt or fear, but God knows who I am, and He loves me anyway. And, in the words of another of Roger's songs, "It's Good to Know!"

There will be much, much more to come. Thank you for your love, prayers and support. Your kind words about Roger and your promises to pray for our family mean more than we can say. Believe it or not, I read EVERY post and card that comes our way. They are a huge part of my life, which at the moment, stands on the threshold of becoming something totally different from what I have known and loved for the past 25 years plus.

Scary, but there again, I have no choice but to trust.

Meanwhile, I cling to the assurance that I remain on this earth, but

In His Grip,
Debbie

April 09, 2007
A Difficult Week Ahead

Just a quick post to ask for your prayers this week. I am headed to Houston today to pack up and close up the apartment there. I know that it will be a difficult week, as I leave the last place I made a home for Roger and me. I also plan to go back to M.D. Anderson and visit with some special people who ministered to us over the years.

I hope you all had a blessed Easter. As I sat in church yesterday, I imagined what a celebration must be going on in Heaven - not just on Easter but every day!

God's grace is sufficient to supply all of our needs, and I covet your prayers this week, as I go about a myriad of tasks, all the while knowing I am

In His Grip,
Debbie

April 17, 2007
My Gift

One month ago today, right at this time, I was watching Roger take his last breath on earth. I still have times when I just don't comprehend the reality of it, as if he is only away on a long trip, and will come home soon. Then, other times, I am so overwhelmed by the enormity of the fact, I literally have trouble breathing. I miss him so much. I find it odd that almost 100% of the things I do and say on a daily basis can be so intricately intertwined with memories of how we did or said those same things together. I suppose you don't go around thinking of yourselves as "soul mates" while you are together, but when one is away, the other one feels like half of them is missing.

Yet, I have the assurance that he is not "missing," just absent from the flesh for a while. And the even bigger assurance is that I will see him again one day, and when I do, there will be no more separation. Again, I am comforted by the words of Phil Hoskins at Roger's service: "We will be WITH Roger a lot longer than we will be WITHOUT him!" So, I can wait, and even if I can't figure out how to make the TV work, or the internet come back up, I will survive.

I wanted to share the miracle gift that God gave to Roger and me the last few hours of his life. On Thursday, before he passed away on Saturday morning, I had taken Roger's Bible into the ICU room with me. Earlier, I had written down several scripture references that people had left me on the web posts. I didn't write down the verses, just the references, so I didn't know what a few of them might be saying to us. But, I was reading them all anyway, and had read several before I came upon Psalm 118:17, which said: "I shall not die, but live, and tell what the Lord has done."

342

Now, Roger had been in a coma-like state, induced by heavy drugs, since arriving in the ICU, but at that very second, when I read that verse, he opened his eyes and looked at me! Then he shut them again, and I asked him, "Roger, did you open your eyes? Can you do it again?" And he did. Then I asked him if he could hear me talking to him, and he nodded his head yes. I asked him if he could hear the scriptures I had been reading to him, and he nodded yes again. I asked him to squeeze my hand, and he did. (Interjection here: I had been reading him stories, etc., before, with no response.) So, while he was with me, I explained a lot of what was going on, and told him not to be afraid of the ventilator and tubes, and told him how much I had been missing him, and how much I loved him, and read him some more scriptures, before he went back to sleep. Well, needless to say, I was on top of the world, just having that moment with him. There was no more response that evening, but the next morning, I ran into Glenda, the chaplain (who spoke at his service), and told her about my miracle. I told her that I knew this could either mean he was getting better, or that I had just been given the best gift I will ever receive, and either way I was just so grateful for that special time. She and I went into his room, where he responded to her, made a nurse laugh (always), responded to the medical team making rounds, and even mouthed "I love you" to me, around all of those tubes. I was told that he was on such heavy doses of medicines that he should not have been able to even wake up, much less answer questions and respond that way. But, that was Roger, always being different, and giving everyone around him comfort, while he was in pain. But I will tell you that I heard the word "miracle" bandied around a few times, and so he was leaving another part of his legacy.

Later that morning, we learned that his tests, X-rays, etc., had come back showing system failures in all areas, so

343

we knew that our miracle was coming from Heaven for Roger. But I believe that God knew how much that interlude would comfort me and sustain me, even now, so He gave me one last gift from Roger to hold in my heart. I always told Roger he was the best gift-giver ever. He put so much thought into each gift he gave me, and then he was so excited to give it to me, he could hardly wait for the actual occasion. So, I guess he thought about what I would like to have from him, and he was right. Just to see my sweetie's pretty eyes, and have him hold my hand, then be able to say "I love you" again, and talk about the kids... That is my special gift.

And as far as that scripture from Psalm 118:17 goes? I believe it was significant that that is the one Roger woke up for. Maybe he was telling us all that he will be living on, on this earth, as long as we don't forget the message that he traveled so many years to spread: JESUS SAVES and we need to tell what the Lord has done!

I have several projects in the works right now that will keep Roger alive in our hearts, and continue the work which he had begun. Pray for me as I strive to complete these tasks, and do them in a manner worthy of both our Lord, and of Roger. I am still

In His Grip,
Debbie

April 23, 2007
Keeping On

It has been a very busy past week or so, with so many decisions to make, and so much work to accomplish. I sometimes find myself walking in circles, not having the "want-to" to get things done, but I know I face schedules and deadlines that must be met. Last week, I had to go to Chancery court to have Roger's will probated, and I also had to go back to the funeral home and order his marker. That was hard, trying to pick out something that would be appropriate, but I think it will be very nice. Because we were able to choose gravesites near the edge of the garden where he is buried (appropriately called the "Garden of Faith"), we were able to also place a bench near the site. It should all be in place in a couple of months.

Tonight, I went to see Chelsea's photography show that she was asked to do at her college. It was wonderful. She is so talented, and I was so proud. I did have some tearful moments, wishing her dad could see... Photography was something they shared together, and she dedicated her show to him, with some beautiful words and images. Maybe he can see from his place on high, or at least we can find comfort in thinking he might.

I have been feverishly working on some projects that have their own deadlines, and some have been almost too challenging for me. I am so grateful to have the work to complete, in Roger's memory; but I was always "behind the scenes," and left the production work to him. Now, I am being forced to learn the hard and fast way, and some days I feel like I just can't do it. That's when I really have to lean on God's promise that *"I can do all things through Christ, who gives me strength."* And, God has put some wonderful people in my path, who are more than capable of helping, as well as very willing. I have this little picture in my house that says, *"I do my best, and leave the rest to*

God." While I know it should read the opposite way, I am trying to do my best, knowing God is already in control. It can just be a little overwhelming at times.

I have had some good days lately, too, though. The hard part about the good days, is that there are things that I want to share with Roger. Since I can't do that, it kind of brings down the happiness level. I am waiting for the day when the good times just bring joy, and not sorrow. I know they will come in time. I am just missing him so much lately, and I also know that is natural. I still have joy in knowing he is HOME, pain-free, and eternally blissful. It is just that human part of me that grieves for myself and my family.

Meanwhile, as I said, I am working on projects, and they bring such happy memories. First up is the DVD project of the 2006 *Parade of Pianos*, recorded at NQC, with special guest Dino Kartsonakis. That was Roger's last professionally-recorded performance, and I want it to be done well. It is probably my biggest challenge, in that I am left to do a lot of the technical production of it myself, and anyone who knows me knows that I am NOT gifted in that area. So, that is a specific prayer need of mine. Side note: Chelsea will be doing the artwork for that project, as she was the photographer that day!

Second project, and one I am so excited about, is a second *Midnight* Meditations video and CD, which we will be filming in Scotland and Northern Ireland in June. Blessedly, Roger had a few songs recorded in the studio that he had not had a chance to finish as an album, so they will be the basis of a tribute to his life. This DVD and CD will be titled *Whispers in the Night*. This will be particularly bittersweet, as these places and people were so special to Roger, and I will be going back there alone, with many memories of him being with me there. I leave May 30, and then Jordan and his girlfriend Jessica will be flying over on June 9 to visit and have Jordan do some filming. We will all return home together on June 18. Chelsea will do some recording here in TN before she leaves for Alaska, then we plan to travel back in November for an official "release" concert. We hope to have both of these projects out by September. We are also re-releasing the first *Midnight Meditations* project as a DVD and CD set together, since it has not been out on DVD before, and hope to have this out by the end of May or first of June.

Then, there is the book… YES, I am going to write one, and put this journal in book form. I need LOTS of prayer on this one. Roger and I had begun to edit it last year, and it, along with a lot of other information, is locked in his computer, and I have not been able to access it. I know there is someone who can extract all of this for me, but I have not had the time to pursue that yet.

There are several other upcoming projects that I will be working on as well. Many people commented, while Roger was still with us, that they didn't think God would take him - there was too much work for him to do here. Well, he will be doing work here on earth for a long time, not just in what we already have of his projects, but he left so much that we can continue for a while with new things. I am so proud of his legacy. He was truly a remarkable man, and I am honored that I had the privilege of being his helpmate for 25 years. I only hope I can do justice to what he began.

I have rambled on a lot in this post, but you ask what you can do to help, and I have these specific needs that I would be humbled for you to lift to the Father on my behalf. Your love and support help keep me focused, and securely

In His Grip,
Debbie

April 28, 2007
Another Move

I woke up this morning, as I do each Saturday morning, counting the weeks since I lost Roger -- 6 weeks today -- and in some ways it still doesn't seem real. The first few days and weeks, I thought he might just reappear after a long road trip, but I know that his final road trip to Heaven is one he just would not want to book as a return journey.

I have kept myself so busy (some things by choice, others forced on me) that I only have time to grieve in segments. Then something just hits me full-on, and I am grounded by the reality. I understand that that will happen for quite some time, and I can deal with it, but boy, is it strong when it comes. I am only now getting around to listening to the newest L5 CD again, but there is a neat story in that.

During the last few days of Roger's life, when Chelsea and Jordan had to leave to go back to school, and Doug had to leave to go back to Arkansas, one of my oldest friends (not in age, I am quick to add; just in longevity - 35 years this summer!) came to Houston to be with me. She is a Registered Nurse, and besides being my friend, and loving and supporting me, she was able to answer a lot of questions as to what was happening with Roger. I do much better with facts. What a blessing Kathy was to me that week! So, the morning he died, as we entered the apartment after leaving the hospital, I told her I wanted her to hear a song Roger sang on the newest L5 CD, "Lord, Stay Close to Me." I told her it was a really personal song for HIM, and it gave HIM a lot of comfort (we even played it while he was receiving his transplant this time, and it made a fan of his APN). Anyway, I turned on the CD, and as he started to sing, I just fell to the floor and wept. It felt like he was in the room, singing just to

ME, telling ME that even though this day had come, and life is scary, the Lord will stay close to ME. I just felt him hugging me again, telling me that God will be with me through it all. It felt like all those months ago, he had recorded this song, just so I would have it on March 17, 2007 as a reminder. Romans 8:28 says "All things work together for good to those who love God," so I am claiming this as one of those "things."

Anyway, I was driving home from Chelsea's apartment the other day, after helping her pack, and as I put this song on for the first time since that day, I was reminded once again that all we have to do is ask, and the Lord is with us in a very real and present way. For me, right now, it is to comfort me and give me peace in this trial. For you, it may be a totally different situation, but always remember that He is as close as the mention of His name.

Today, we are moving Chelsea's apartment back home. I am still tripping over everything I brought back from Houston. Jordan moves back in on Monday the 7th. Oh, and Chelsea leaves for Alaska for at least 5 months on Friday, May 4th. Sometimes I have to wonder how much stress God thinks I can handle, but so far I haven't lost my mind - completely! I have a video crew coming in on Tuesday morning to tape segments of Chelsea and Scott Fowler to incorporate into the new video I will be doing next month in Northern Ireland and Scotland - and I don't even have the piano room cleared out yet! (Oh well, there's always Monday.) Then, on Wednesday, I will be in the video editing studio beginning to finalize what will be the last recorded performance of Roger - his 2006 *Parade of Pianos*. Please pray particularly for this project. Besides my being a novice at this type of thing (plenty of observations, but never in charge), there are some very exhausting negotiations going on between parties over this project. I wish all of my endeavors would be as simple as the new project I am working on with my Northern Ireland buddy, Ian. Just pray that God's glory will shine, and that I will be allowed to make this *Parade of Pianos* project a product that would honor Roger, and pay tribute to all of the other fine talent that was on stage with him that day.

OK, enough typing. I have to go pack at Chelsea's some more before the movers get there this afternoon. If you don't hear from me for a while, it will be because either the computer, or myself, may be buried under tons of furniture and clutter from all of the moves. I counted the other day, and in the past three years, this will be my seventh move... That alone is enough stress to put me away for a while. I believe that the last six are still in boxes here and there. On the flip side, should there be another natural disaster, I believe the Bennetts could single-handedly replenish a small village. Wish us luck, safety, the ability to get through this weekend without losing our cool, and mostly, the ability to remember that, no matter how stressful life gets, we are always

In His Grip,
Debbie

May 05, 2007
Philippians 4:13

> "I can do all things through Christ, which strengtheneth me."

Daily, this verse is becoming more real in my life. Each new daunting task or situation I face makes me know I cannot do this on my own. I simply do not possess the knowledge, the resources, or the physical strength to do what is required of me some days. Roger sang a song on

Legacy Five's last *Live* album: "But God sees it so clear from the start... I have a Father who's watching over... I need no other But God!" In our most troubled moments, He will guard our hearts and our minds. He gives us the assurance that one day - in His own timing - He will work things out. He is what He says He is; He will do what He says He will do! Our peace in God comes with confidence, certainty and assurance that things are working out. I doubt many of us have ever spent a night in a lion's den, or in a fiery furnace, but we do have biblical examples of those who did. With God's presence in their lives, they had the firm conviction that things were going to be just fine... and they were! Through their experiences, and so many more others', we can see that God does not leave or forsake His own. Our own worry about things (preaching to myself here, too) stems from a lack of confidence or trust in God... Hmmm... don't want to go there, so I need to remember that HE IS IN CONTROL. He already knows the outcome, so why not just leave it in His hands? When I remember to do that, my life is so much easier... and blessed.

I have had to remind myself of that several times this week. This is not a lesson that we learn once, receive a good grade on, then move on to the next lesson. I guess God knew that we would have to learn it many times, but isn't it interesting to see what new lessons we learn from our trials each time?

This week has been a particularly stressful one for me, Chelsea and Jordan, and in new ways for Doug and my family, too. It was one of those weeks when I wondered just how much stress God thought I could handle before losing it, but it all worked out. It took several days to get Chelsea moved back home from her apartment, between my schedule and her last week of classes. We put lots of miles on our vehicles, going back and forth (in addition to the moving truck) and went up and down the stairs more times than I thought a woman my age should have been able to do! We got it all back over to the house, but where we will put it all is still a mystery to me. I can't set up the room she will be in, because she is taking over Jordan's room, and he still has all of his things in there. He arrives home as a "Certified Practicing Luthier" on Monday evening. He called me this week to let me know that he and his buddies have found a house to rent, and he will be moving out the first of June. After the last two moves I have made lately, I had already decided I just could not do another one; but fortunately, he has lots of big strong friends with trucks, and I am going to be in Scotland anyway, so problem solved (well, for me anyway)! I took Chelsea to the airport yesterday morning so she could fly to Alaska for five months, and we were literally throwing stuff into her bags as we were leaving the house. I just told her to leave a big pile of what she couldn't fit, and I will ship it to her. It's going to be very quiet around here... although I do have the menagerie to tend, and my brother has graciously agreed to stay with me at least until Chelsea comes back home. Both of my brothers who live here in TN, as well as my mom and dad, are so good to check on me and see what needs to be done. Oh, and as I was in my barn looking for my own boxes, which are stacked behind everyone else's, the doorknob decided to break... and I discovered that there are termites eating up the office. OK, Lord, Roger would have been all over this, so what do I do now? But I know I can always call the exterminator, get the problem stopped, and then deal with the damages later.

One of the projects I am working on was causing me no end of stress and anxiety, and it looks like it has resolved itself this week. YEA! As far as the projects I am currently working on, it looks like we are getting close to being ready to manufacture the *Midnight Meditations* re-release, with the DVD and CD in one package. I also went into the studio this week and edited the 2006 *Parade of Pianos* project, which I was dreading because I knew nothing about doing that, but it was surprisingly easy. God has sent me patient, gifted people to help me along with all of this. I don't have a timetable for release, but look for it in early summer, hopefully. It was quite emotional doing this particular task, because I had not seen footage of the showcase until I went into the studio. This was Roger's last professionally recorded performance. The project was amazing, there were some powerful moments, and although my eyes could see how much he was struggling physically, he gave it his all, because that was what he did. He brought a spectacular performance together. At one point, the camera zoomed in on his hands, playing the piano, and it was one of those moments that just hit me hard. Those hands have been so much a part of my life for so many years, and I just thought about how he would always reach for my hand if we were walking together, or how he would always reach for my hand when we prayed, or he would just grab my hand and kiss it... and it broke my heart to know that I won't ever have those beautiful hands to hold again. I remember exactly how our hands fit together. Yes, it hurts, seven weeks after he left us, but I can't wait to hold his hand again and walk together on the streets of gold! And here is another way God works: Chelsea knew she wouldn't be here for Mother's Day or my birthday, so she gave me a gift before she left. She does such beautiful photography work, and she made me an enlargement of a picture of ROGER'S HANDS playing the piano, and even cut a mat for it and everything. The camera angle came in in such a way that the hand facing the camera shows his wedding ring. You can't tell me that God doesn't care about the "little things" that matter to us.

Doug seems to be doing well, although he had a tough week, too. He was on his way home from the funeral home, receiving his settlement from a policy he had there on Roger, when someone turned in front of him and hit him. No one was hurt, but there was some car damage.

Also, please pray for my Mom, Dad, and me as I leave Wed. to take them to the Washington, DC, area for a week. Daddy's last brother lives in that area, and I feel the need for the two of them to be able to visit, as age and health issues keep creeping in. Daddy lost his last sister the week I was in Houston packing up our apartment.

I appreciate your continuing prayers and remembrances of our family. As Chelsea and Jordan are traveling, and setting out on new ventures, please keep them in your thoughts. I will update you on their progress.

As for today, it's another Saturday, so my thoughts are flashing back to the last moments of Roger's life. However, I need to get going and shift my focus to what I am going to prepare for Mom's Mother's Day dinner tomorrow (yes, I am aware that we are a week early, but we won't be home next week). I am positive this will involve getting dressed so that I can go to the grocery store (they do appreciate that). But while I am running around, and while we are scattered here and there, we can be assured that we are always

In His Grip,
Debbie

May 13, 2007
Happy Mother's Day

Happy Mother's Day to all of the moms out there, and to all of those who made their own Mom's day special. My two children made my day special, but they always do, just by being themselves. Chelsea called from Alaska, where she is doing great. In the first week of her being there, she was made manager of the gift shop where she works, got a raise, photographed a wedding, and took a picture of the governor of Alaska at a reception, which has made the front page of the local paper! Talk about hitting the ground running... I am so proud of her.

Jordan got home on Monday evening, and is in the process of packing his things to move out into a house with 5 (!) of his buddies in June. Meanwhile, it sure is good to have him home. He is a thoughtful son, who must have paid a lot of attention to the way his dad treated me... he still opens doors for me, and kisses me, and tells me he loves me, no matter who is around.

I just returned home this afternoon from a two-day getaway to visit a friend. It was a much-needed break. The past week was particularly stressful for me, and the change of scenery did me a world of good. My trip to Washington, DC, was postponed, so I will now leave this coming Wednesday to take my Mom and Dad there to visit Daddy's brother and his family.

I still do not know for sure whether I will be able to attend the Legacy Five Celebration in May or not. I am going to try to go on Saturday night only, but I am reserving the right to change my mind if I don't feel emotionally ready. My mind is having a hard time processing the fact that it is all changed now. I don't think that there is much of anything in my life that is the same as it was before March 17. The life that I lived for 25 years with Roger, including all of the places I went with him, and the enjoyment I felt just being by his side in all of those places is gone. My kids are both leaving the house, whether temporarily or not, I am not sure. My role in Southern Gospel Music is very much in question, in my mind. I just don't know where I fit in anywhere right now. The projects I am working on are my way of feeling connected to all that was my life before.

I am not saying any of this to have a "pity party" or make anyone feel sorry for me. It just is what it is. And it gives me a new awareness of all of those people who have experienced the same feelings before me, and all of those who will in the future. There may be some kind of leading of the Holy Spirit in these feelings, and I will explore that aspect further.

So, all of that to say, I MAY see some of you over Memorial Day weekend, but if not, please understand why. I am trying to push through things that are hard for me, but that is a BIG hurdle for me to cross yet. I promise that I WILL be at National Quartet Convention, though.

My trip to Scotland and Northern Ireland is approaching fast. I leave May 30 and return home June 18. I feel like I will have a lot of the most stressful things behind me by that time, so I am looking forward to relaxing a bit. I am so looking forward to spending time with people who Roger and I felt so connected with there. Jordan and his girlfriend Jessica will also be with me then.

In His Grip,
Debbie

May 19, 2007
Observations on Grief

Nine weeks. Two months and two days. Time is always there to remind me how long it has been since Roger left us. I have recently thought a lot about the grief process (obviously), but in a more analytical way.

Grief is a universal emotion. If you have not experienced it, chances are you will. Grief comes in a variety of ways: over the loss of a job; the loss of a friendship; loss of material possessions; monetary losses; the loss of a pet... it comes in many shapes and sizes, and the biggest one is the loss of a loved one. So, at any given time, you may walk down the street and pass people who are grieving.

Grief is also a very personal emotion. No matter how many people have gone through your situation, grief has the ability to make you feel all alone in your experience. No two people will weather the storms in exactly the same way. In our own household, my grief is different from Chelsea's or Jordan's, and yet we all feel the power of the emotion. Different things will remind us; different "triggers" will set off the feelings.

So, in these observations, I realize that there are many people everywhere who are hurting. Some days it *feels* like no one could possibly understand the way I hurt. Then, I stop to think about all of the dear people who have undergone the exact loss that I have, or who have lost a child, or someone else precious to them. It is the same, but different. I have read every email and every card that has come to me, and I cannot tell you what comfort I get from them. My heart clutches with every single "Roger story." My heart aches with your stories about your own losses. I feel humbled that so many of you choose to remember us in your prayers, while going through your own pain and loss. The family of God is truly amazing.

My new task for the Kingdom of God is to be more aware of others who are going through their own grief process. I believe that God gave us these feelings so that we may better share with others, and thus help each other through this world below. Any burden is made lighter when someone else is helping to carry it. I am so grateful for all of the "Ropeholders" who help me to anchor myself. Let's not forget that there are many others out there who also need that anchor. In that way, we can all feel the safety of being

In His Grip!
Debbie

May 28, 2007
Memorial Day

Happy Memorial Day, and a very special "thank you" to those who have served and continue to serve our country so that we may experience freedom and safety. That is a calling that is so worthy, yet often goes without the proper recognition. I was able to take my father to visit the WWII Memorial in Washington, DC, last week, and it was a very moving experience. I was so glad to be able to show him how much his country appreciates his service, and I know he was really touched. It's beautiful, and I highly recommend seeing it if you have the opportunity.

This has been a hard weekend for me in many ways. I made the decision not to attend Legacy Five's Celebration. It was always a very special weekend to Roger, and I just did not feel ready to go yet. I figured anything that made my stomach upset to think about, didn't warrant being put into action, if it wasn't totally necessary. So, I will continue to deal with my feelings and be ready for the

Labor Day Celebration, as well as NQC. I had a dear friend from Houston come to visit me over the weekend, and it was such a blessing. She is one of the God-sent people in my life who "gets it," because she lives with seeing what we went through on a daily basis. Lisa began by being one of Roger's nurses, and God developed a relationship there that turned into a sisterhood. Oh, yes, and she likes to shop, which we did our fair share of this weekend, trying to get ready for this trip!

My thoughts and heart were never far from the Celebration, though, and I longed to be there in a sense, visiting with friends and drawing comfort; but in the greater sense, it was just still too raw to undertake such a huge task. I am leaving for Scotland and Northern Ireland in two days, and that will take a lot of my energy. I am very much looking forward to it, though, for rest and relaxation, and wonderful friendships to nurture.

Chelsea is doing well in Alaska, getting into a routine, and making friends. Jordan is busy getting ready for his move June 1, and then will be leaving here on June 9 to join me in Northern Ireland. I would say we are all settling into a routine, but it is still utter chaos around the Bennett household, with all of the moves, boxes, packing, and repacking.

Well, I must be off and do some packing, cleaning, and whatever else needs tending to. Thank you for continuing to keep us in your prayers. I will try to update from the UK, as I am able. Rest assured that I read EVERY comment, every card, every letter. I draw much comfort from these, and realize more every day that I am securely

In His Grip,
Debbie

June 04, 2007
A Safe Arrival and a Warm Welcome

After almost missing my connecting flight to Belfast on Wednesday (long, breathless story, but God's favor was with me, and I made it just in time), I arrived on Thursday morning to open arms and a nice cup of tea. Ah, it felt like home.

Roger and I always considered this our second home (Houston being our third - you would think we were some kind of jet-setters, if you didn't know the real story!), and it was so lovely being with friends we haven't seen in a while.

The memories and the fellowship can be bittersweet at times, but what a beautiful place to relive them. I have already had one opportunity to go out of my "comfort zone" by speaking a few words in church yesterday morning. I have always enjoyed the "behind the scenes" status, and much prefer writing to speaking. I could not tell you now what I did say, but apparently the Holy Spirit was with me, because several people told me they were encouraged by "my" words. That was my prayer: to say what the Lord would have me say, and have Him use me in some way. Then, last night, there were two pastors who had flown in from Wales to give testimonies of miracles, and it was a great day. The church has a new pastor from Wales himself, and one of the visiting pastors was originally from Scotland; so I had a "Roger moment" and thought that, with all of the countries we represented, maybe we should just all join hands and sing "We are the World." Yes, he still influences my daily life!

We leave tomorrow for Scotland, where we begin the filming for the new video. It's exciting, but I do have butterflies in my stomach. Please pray especially for good weather as we are outside on the locations. And pray for my strength, as I will be doing a lot of the narration, and I want to do a pleasing job for the Lord, and for Roger.

Jordan leaves on Saturday to arrive here Sunday morning. We had quite a panic the day before I left, when we discovered that his passport had expired the week before, and since 9/11, there is no expedited way to just go to a national center and get another one. I was six hours on the phone in the middle of the night just trying to get him an appointment. I would have flown him anywhere, but it was not to be. So, I finally found a company that would help me out. Please pray that he receives his new passport in time. I feel confident that he will, but I am sure some extra prayers would not hurt! (By the way, it was not really his fault: all of our passports are still good for five more years, except his, which was issued only for five years, since he was 15 at the time. We just didn't realize this.)

Meanwhile, I am enjoying my rest and am absolutely being pampered. I may have to take staff home with me from here to keep up the lifestyle! Until the next post, I remain, as always,

In His Grip,
Debbie

June 11, 2007
Continuing the Journey

How quickly my time here in Northern Ireland and Scotland is passing. The days have been full, the fellowship sweet, and now Jordan and Jessica have arrived safely. Yesterday in Northern Ireland was sunny and warm, and we went up to Scrabo Tower. If you have seen the first *Midnight Meditations* video, it is the place we took a grand piano up on top of a hill which overlooks the Mountains of Mourne, the Strangford Loch, and patchworks of green fields all around. It was one of the highlights of Roger's career, sitting there overlooking such beauty and playing "This is My Father's World." Needless to say, while it brought back many happy memories, it was a bit overwhelming standing there reliving them.

That's pretty much how all of last week in Scotland was for me. I found myself on plenty of highs, and then would come crashing down at moments, wishing for Roger to be here to share all of this with me. But, as I remind myself often, he will always be with me in my heart and in my memories, and what I am seeing and experiencing here on God's beautiful earth is not even in comparison with what Roger is experiencing in Heaven. So, in that respect, I don't wish him to be with me here. It's just the human element that creeps in when you least expect it. I am not naive enough to believe that it won't keep happening for a long time to come, but I am blessed enough to realize that at those moments, I have a Father Who wants to comfort me, and Who will always be with me to give me the strength to carry on. Not easy, no; but how would I bear it at all without God's promises to sustain me? That's a message worth sharing with those in need of comfort of any kind. God is only a breath away... a hand reaching out to Him... a heart yearning for peace. Anywhere. Anytime. Anyone.

I will share more about the actual experiences we have had during this project later, but until then, know that I am loving being in my "second home," and grateful to God for friends who knew Roger well and are so in tune with what is appropriate as far as content, etc. No matter where I go, and no matter the circumstances, God always keeps me

In His Grip!
Debbie

June 20, 2007
Back in the US

Well, I am back in the US again. I actually got home Monday night, but spent most of yesterday doing nothing but trying to stay awake and get rid of a headache that the rain brought. But, we are in such need of rain, that I decided it was worth it! (Like I could have changed it anyway?)

We (Jordan, Jessica, and I) had an uneventful trip home, which is always good. Not like the one on the way up, where I almost missed my connection to Belfast. Whew!

I will write in another entry about the neat things that we did and some really special moments. Right now, I still don't have my head all together.

I promise to write more soon. Right now, I have a LOT of laundry waiting for me! Thank you so much for your prayers during this trip. It was pretty emotional at times, but I made it through with the help of those prayers, some wonderful friends, and an extra measure of God's grace. Just wait until you hear some of the stories! Until then, may we all rest comfortably

In His Grip,
Debbie

July 01, 2007
Getting Back into the Swing of Things

Yes, I know it has been a while since I posted, but I have honestly not had a good week, and thought it better to wait until I was feeling better. I think it was the reality of coming back home after escaping for a while. Overall, I do pretty well, I think, but some days it just hits me harder than others.

We had too many "firsts" close together the past little while. My first birthday without Roger; the first Father's Day, which also happened to be the three-month anniversary of his departure; my first vacation without him, which was also the last family vacation we ever took together; etc., etc.

But, God is good, and I am feeling stronger again. I try hard not to stay in a down mood, but admittedly I do struggle from time to time.

I am leaving for a few days to go visit friends in Arkansas, and spend some time with my father-in-law. I have a lot of travel scheduled this summer, but it was planned, as I have a harder time being at home right now. Running away? Maybe, but it does help me cope. And with cell phones and computers, I can take care of things long-distance. Plus, it is so wonderful to visit with people I have not had the time to visit with in a while.

I wanted to share a "God thing" from a day in Northern Ireland. We had finished our videotaping in Scotland, and returned to the Belfast area to do one last site there. It was Inch Abbey, Roger's favorite place. Jordan had come in, and we waited to film there, so he could be there. It was beautiful. Jordan played his guitar, and did some interviews. Anyway, that morning, which was the only day we had to do this, they were predicting some heavy rains. As we were going to the site, it was raining lightly, and the clouds were looking pretty dark. However, we had faith that we would be able to get some footage, at least.

As we approached Inch Abbey, the rains stopped, even though we could hear thunder in the distance, but not too distant! I thought that was what was causing the exodus of tourists as we arrived, a blessing since we would love the privacy to film, and the freedom to do what we wanted to do. So, we set up the cameras, got the layout of things, and began shooting. We took our time, getting lots of great shots.

Now, during the time that we were there, we received about four different phone calls from four different areas of the surrounding towns, one of which came from less than seven miles from where we were. They were concerned about us, since it was literally pouring rain, as if the heavens had opened up, where they all were. As it turned out, the Belfast area that day received the worst rains and flooding they had had in several decades. The evening news showed cars submerged in water, flooded residences, and closed streets everywhere. And I mean EVERYWHERE. It seemed that no area in the county had escaped the torrential downpours.

Meanwhile, we were enjoying sunny weather, without a drop of rain. Not ONE DROP. In fact, we got so warm in the sunshine, we were questioning our choice of attire. It was supposed to be chilly. We filmed longer than we thought we would need, and got some really great footage. We could still hear the thunder in the distance, and as we finished our shoot, we knew it was getting nearer, as the clouds seemed to darken, and the wind picked up. But, again, not until we were completely finished. As we packed up the cars, and drove out of the Abbey, we were not three minutes down the country lane before we were hit with rain so hard that it was pouring mud off the hillsides onto the road. We just looked at each other in disbelief.

Now, when I told you earlier that there was not a place that had not gotten hit with the rains, I mean that. But, as we had prayed for God's Hand on us that day, it seemed as if angels had stood on the perimeter of where we were, and literally blocked the rain from reaching us. I will never forget the feeling when I realized what had happened. There really is no other explanation for it at all.

The rains continued through the night, with more flooding, but we had remained safe and dry.

As if we needed it, there was proof right there that God really does care about the day-to-day things in our lives. This was very important to me, and in the grand scheme of things, it would not have been the worst thing to happen if the shooting had had to be cancelled. But God knew how special this place was to Roger and our family, and He knew that it would be a fitting place to film part of the tribute to Roger's life. God is good, all the time. How comforting to be

In His Grip!
Debbie

July 11, 2007
Just Musing

Yesterday was a rainy, gloomy day, and I spent a lot of it in thought. I was not having a great day, so some thoughts were as dark as the weather, but they also led me to some more positive ones. I am so blessed that God reminds me of the good things in my life, even when Satan wants me to dwell only on the "bad" things. It is wonderful to have those blessings come to mind when you really need them!

But, I was thinking about a little story we have told in our family over the years, and it seemed appropriate to share it with you. When Jordan was about three years old, we were living in our home, then in Stow, Ohio. Chelsea was at school this particular day, and Roger was not at home, so it was just Jordan and me. I was in the kitchen doing whatever I was doing, and Jordan remembered a toy that he wanted, but which happened to be in the basement.

Now, we had set up a playroom down there, and when we bought the house, this room had been an in-law suite of sorts, so it wasn't a dark, cold place, but to a 3-year old, it was still a bit intimidating to approach alone. So, he asked me to go down with him to get this toy, but I was up to my elbows in whatever I was doing, and I told him it was okay, to just go down and get it, and come right back. He was not convinced, and told me that he was scared to go down there. So, I took the opportunity to talk to him about Jesus, and how He is always with us, wherever we go, watching over us, and keeping us safe. He thought about it for a minute, and turned to me, his little lip trembling, and said, "But, who will go with me and Jesus? I want someone with some skin on!" Needless to say, I laughed, hugged him, and dried off my hands and went to the basement with him.

But, this story reminded me yesterday of the fact that, even as adults, sometimes we all need "someone with some skin on." There are a lot of lonely people around, and the only way they will recognize Jesus at times, is through flesh and blood. I confess to wanting a "touchable" person when I am feeling sad, alone, or afraid. I am aware of Jesus' presence, even at these times, but I am also glad to know He provides us with other people to be His hands and feet. And even though I am human and desire visible hands and feet, it also feels good to BE those hands and feet to others.

Let's try to remember to be "someone with some skin on" to those who need it today!

In His Grip,
Debbie

July 21, 2007
Feeling Better

Sorry it has been a few days since I last posted. I confess to having a pretty bad week or so there. I seemed to be in a place where I just could NOT do anything productive, and that included making a post...

This past week was a full one, for sure. On Monday, the 16th, it was both my father's and Roger's grandfather's 85th birthday. We have always been fascinated with the fact that the two were born on the exact same day! (Side bar: Roger's grandfather has been recently placed in a nursing home, and besides the fact that it is hard on him, it brings a host of other complications among the family, that we would very much appreciate prayer for.) Of course, I remembered Roger being with us last year on Daddy's birthday, when we took him out to eat, and Roger was hobbling around on his crutches. Then, the next day, the 17th, was the four-month anniversary of Roger's departure here, so it was a pretty "down" day for us. Wednesday, the 18th, was Chelsea's 23rd birthday, and I felt bad for not being with her (but her friends gave her a party, and baked her a cake, and everything, so I am sure she had a great day).

Wednesday night, Scott and Taryn invited me over for dinner, and by Thursday, I was feeling much better again. It's funny how those cycles come and go, ebb and wane. You just never know when they will hit, either. But the grace of God is good to help us through those difficult days.

I have had a lot of people with "skin on" this week, and I appreciate them all so much. It makes such a difference to know we are not going through this life alone!

On a different note, I wanted to let you know that Roger's marker and the memorial bench I ordered have been set now. They are quite beautiful, and a nice tribute to him. If you are ever in the Franklin, TN, area, be sure to go by and "visit." I joke that my side is empty, because I don't know what to put on the marker, but I think I will just put "And Debbie, too" and be done with it!

Well, it's getting late, and I am proud to have survived another Saturday (18 weeks today), but with a much better attitude than last week, even. I am looking forward to getting some things accomplished this week! Please keep me in your prayers, as I journey on, while always

In His Grip!
Debbie

August 05, 2007
A Different Perspective

Yes, I know it has been a few days again since I posted, but I was actually away from home for a week or so, visiting with friends, and having a refreshing time. Yesterday, as I was traveling home, I thought a lot about Roger (of course), and the fact that yesterday was 20 weeks that he has been gone. In some ways, it has flown by, and in many other ways, it has been a lifetime. Yet, I am finding that God is still faithful, and life can go on, although in a much different way. I am thankful for the many ways He has helped me fill my time during these past weeks, providing opportunities for renewing friendships and relationships that have helped me get through some very difficult days. And the days are less difficult after 20 weeks than they were at six weeks, etc., so we keep going and trusting, and believing.

I received an email from a friend recently that really spoke to me, and after consulting with her, I thought it would be nice to share some of her thoughts with you. This email touched me and spoke to me, and I thought her words would mean a lot to some of you who may be going through difficult times. Although, of course, it is directed at my circumstances, there is a lot of "meat" in it that can apply to other situations, as well. I hope you enjoy this little "guest" perspective! Until next time, I remain very securely

In His Grip,
Debbie

I am sorry you have been having some really hard days, but I am not surprised, and I know you're not either. Marriage is about "oneness." That's why, when it's a right kind of marriage, it's so wonderful and why Jesus chose it as the perfect illustration of the relationship between Himself and His followers. When half of yourself is relocated to an "out of reach" place for a period of time, it is bound to be painful. After all part of yourself has been cut away, and even the all knowing Physician of all Comfort will use time and circumstances to realign and rebalance you for the next steps He has planned. He knows our "grief clocks" are all different, but as we trust He works. Trusting may very well be your most difficult task.

He doesn't care which grief emotion is struggling for supremacy--sadness, loneliness, emptiness, frustration, even anger will raise its ugly head. If you haven't already, you will one day (usually a day when lots of stuff is going wrong), probably, find yourself *really* mad at Roger for taking off for Heaven and leaving you behind. Even though you know he fought with all his strength, and wanted to stay with all his heart, that emotional surge of nonsense will still come flashing through your mental control center. It will even seem like a sensible feeling right then. Emotions are not logical, but they are powerful. We can't ignore them, but we also can't live by them. As you know, we have to live in "Truth."

I think the key to dealing with grief is to remember that "we do not grieve as those who have no hope." To be totally honest, when I lost some of the most significant people in my life, I was forced to realize that some parts of my own grieving times were *at least* partially self-serving. I mourned their loss, but also my own discomfiture. Life wouldn't be as comfortable and familiar anymore. The things that they did that were meaningful in my life were over. I had empty places where I had never had empty places before. It seemed strange (wrong even) that the rest of the world could just continue on without missing a beat when my world was so upended. I felt a strong sense of anger and even abandonment at times. I grieved for them, but I grieved for me, too.

When I finally got to the Dr. of all Comfort I found He prescribed for me a most powerful medicine: "Truth." Then He flavored it with "Love" and stirred in a little "Hope" (remember "Hope" in the Bible is a sure thing, not merely a possibility), so it went down a little easier. It produced two wonderful by-products: "Wisdom" and "Understanding." A review of truth reminded me there was actually nothing to be concerned with about my loved ones. They were securely in the place they had chosen to spend eternity, doing whatever a perfect God intended them to do and rejoicing in it (even without me being there – amazing -- just kidding).

I felt more than a tinge of envy I must say. I certainly couldn't say that about myself; but, of course, the "Truth" is I *could say* most of that about myself.... I just wasn't saying it. I had, after all, the personal attention of the "God of all comfort" whenever I wanted Him. He understood me and my situation perfectly, He wanted to be my "security," and He had definite "intentions" for me -- there was a plan. I just had to move outside of my familiar comfort zone one step at a time. (Trusting, again... sigh... do you ever wonder why we have to keep learning the same lessons over and over? It's like trying to get a kid to pick up his clothes or clean his room.) When I began to do that, the clouds started to lift. The "Sonshine" began to burn off the emotional fog, and "Wisdom and Understanding" started to emerge.

Our "grief clocks" may be different, but the Great Timekeeper keeps those that are His functioning perfectly. There's a lot of "ticking and tocking" going on, but "Wisdom" reminds us it's all working out in perfect precision. Even though you don't see it all now, aren't you glad you know the Timekeeper?

There were three things in Roger's funeral service that stood out to me. The first was the comment about coming to a fork in the road, and going on without Roger. I just could visualize that so easily. His path going steadily upward, while the rest of us continued on a winding pathway filled with curves, hills, and valleys, but always progressing horizontally. It seemed natural somehow, like when you're on a trip and you split off the road the last time to reach your final destination.

Another standout phrase was the wonderful reminder about being with Roger a lot longer than being without him that everyone seems to have grabbed a hold of. I think that has really been a life preserver for Scott Fowler and the other guys. I believe I have heard each one of them use that comment or some variation of it. A good dosage of "Truth," I would say.

The last idea was the reminder that real love has a price tag. If you love, you will suffer at the loss of that loved person or thing; but, all in all, that suffering is a good deal less than the joys of loving. Memories are God's proof of that. I am sure you will have 10,000 good memories, for every bad one that you can recall in five years. You are coming along Mrs. Debbie Bennett, don't ever doubt it for a minute. God's got a plan just for you and He's working it out.

August 13, 2007
Off Again!

I have so enjoyed reading the comments from the last entry. It is good to know that so many were touched by what my friend wrote. It seems that, no matter what our circumstances, the basics are the same. God's comfort is universal, and that is proof positive that He cares about all of us! As I read of all that other people are going through, it reminds me daily that there is a lot of suffering in this world. So, while we are here, we need to encourage each other, hold each other up, and wait for the day when all of our suffering will be no more. Heaven looks better every day!

I have been frantically working on a couple of projects that need to be done by the time NQC gets here. (And I will be at NQC this year from Wednesday through Saturday. Look for me at the Legacy Five booth, and at Pianorama.) So far, we are thinking we may J-U-S-T squeak into the last deadline, so if you think about it, could you pray that all goes well? I am trying to get the *Whispers in the Night* DVD that was done in Scotland out, as well as a companion CD, which features five songs that Roger had never released before.

All those details need to be more or less wrapped up today, if at all possible, as I leave tomorrow for eight days. I am going to Alaska to see my little girl, and can't wait! I miss her so much, and she is ready to come home, but will be staying on there until the first of October. So this little visit will serve to hold us both over until the fall. She has about three days off while I am there, so we will be doing some sightseeing, and I imagine I will be playing the "caddy" role again, as I help to carry an assortment of cameras and equipment. I don't mind, I actually have learned a lot about photography by following along behind her. She has such a good eye, and great creativity!

My trip to Skagway, Alaska, will take two days, even by plane. I make four stops before I finally arrive. It's not exactly right on the beaten path. So, if you don't hear from me for the next week, you will know all is well, and I am having a great time, escaping the triple-digit heat wave here in Tennessee. This trip has been booked for a while, but it surely is great timing. Those high-60's temperatures sound blissful!

By the way, Jordan has accepted an apprenticeship with a luthier (guitar-building) company in Murfreesboro, TN, where he is currently living. After 30 days, he is hoping to be hired on full-time, so please keep him in your prayers. We are very excited that he has found a place where he can put his schooling to good use.

A lot of information, but I just wanted to let you know we are all doing well. Some days are good, some not so good, but it is getting easier. I still have a few hurdles to mount, and some are coming up faster than I would like, but God is faithful, He is good all the time, and He holds me firmly

In His Grip!
Debbie

August 18, 2007
Alaska Update

God has really blessed this week in Alaska. I have NEVER seen such gorgeous weather up here (and I think I counted up that this is my 14th trip to this state!). Everyone here has been in utter awe at the temperatures and sunshine. Today, it is more like "normal" - that is, a little chilly, and drizzly, but still nothing to complain about. Chelsea and I have had a wonderful time together, and still have more time to go. She has been working, but I walk the approximately one and a half miles to see her each day, then walk back. It has done me a lot of good to get some exercise, especially with all the food we have been eating. I fell in love with Jewell Gardens, where she works. The flowers are beautiful, the tea is excellent, and the goodies and dinner are delicious. Last night after dinner there, we got to go to the glassworks on-site, and make our own ornamental balls. Chelsea took photos of me blowing into the pipe to make mine, and I hope they don't surface anywhere! Today, we walked down to the stream to watch the salmon run. What an amazing sight to see. All of those little fish following one single calling, just the way the Father planned. And doing it without complaining, although it is a hard struggle that doesn't end too well for them. But, they do it anyway, with an instinct that guides them onward, so that future generations will live. Hmm, there just might be a lesson in there somewhere, you think?

Tomorrow (she will be off work for three days now), we are going to ride the train that takes us up the very trail the gold miners carved into the mountains so many years ago. It has been a long time since we did that, so I am looking forward to it. Monday, we will go by ferry to Haines, Alaska, where we have a trip booked to float along the river in a bald eagle preserve. We used to do this as a family years ago, but the ship hasn't docked there in several years. There is a possibility of either a helicopter ride, or sightseeing flight on Tuesday, before I leave that evening, but we aren't sure. I flew from Juneau to Skagway on a 12-seater plane over mountains and glacial fields that looked close enough to touch. It was awesome!

It has been good to have all of these distractions this week, as yesterday was the 5 month anniversary of our losing Roger, and, of course, today is Saturday, and I still wake up reliving that last day every Saturday. This is actually the first "month anniversary" of Roger's death that I have been with Chelsea. Either she or I have been gone from home every other one. So, we have talked a bit, and shed a few tears, but have had a few funny remembrances, as well. Memories are funny things; sometimes, they seem too painful to bear, but other times, they are like your favorite soft blanket, enfolding you with warmth and comfort. I am not sure when the juggling act stops, if ever, but I am so grateful to have the memories I do have. Roger Bennett was a special man, no doubt, and I certainly feel less sure of myself without him. However, he left me a godly example to follow, and I am trying to figure out what path I will take as the days go by. It is still not clear, but it is less stressful for me to think about these days, anyway. So, I guess that is progress of a sort.

Chelsea is coming to a crossroads in her own life, where she will have big decisions to make, as well. When she finally comes home this fall, she will have to decide what her career path will be. It seems like the whole Bennett family is at one decision-making spot or another. But, we do have the assurance that if we seek God, He will guide and direct us, and keep us

In His Grip!
Debbie

September 01, 2007
Just One of "Those" Days

Happy Labor Day weekend to everyone. I have been having some pretty good days lately, but today was not one of them. Again, I woke up realizing it is Saturday, and reliving the last one I spent with Roger. I know there will come a Saturday when it does not consume me, but so far, most of them have been "down" days. Today seemed worse than usual, but I think it's because I am wrapping it up with the thought of what tomorrow holds, and it seems a bit large. This weekend is the Legacy Five Celebration at Opryland in Nashville, and I have committed to being there on Sunday evening, and also to meet with people for a couple of hours before the concert begins.

I know it will be a bittersweet time. I have shed many tears today, thinking about the last Labor Day Celebration. Roger was running people down on his scooter, as his leg was broken, and having a ball, despite the fact that his temperature kept rising, and he was so tired. But that was Roger. He never let anything get him down. I "visited" him today at the cemetery, and thought about all of the concerts and events to come that just won't be the same without him here. That was what we did: we went to these things TOGETHER. I don't know how to do it without him. But I know that I want to try, and I trust God to be there with me.

I confess that even as I write this post, I am crying. Please pray for me tomorrow. I don't want to be an embarrassment to anyone; I need strength. I am glad to do this, as NQC is just days away, and this will be a small hurdle to jump compared to that week. This will be a good start for me.

Sorry, I didn't mean to write such a crybaby post. But, I know that when I need prayer, you are all faithful to lift me up, and so I turn to this outlet. Thank you for your consistency and love. I would love to someday be able to meet each reader of this journal face to face and give you a hug and a smile. You are great!

I learned this week that the new *Whispers in the Night* DVD and CD *WILL* be out in time for NQC! I am so thrilled that it all came together at the last minute. I have such a great network of people to help me get all of this done. I hope you all have a safe and happy weekend, and stay safely, as I am,

In His Grip!
Debbie

P.S. Just writing to you has already made me feel better!

September 05, 2007
One Hurdle Jumped

It took me a couple of days to get to write this post, but I wanted to say thank you for all of the prayers you sent my way. I truly felt them, especially on Sunday, as I attended Legacy Five's Celebration event. I am so glad I went. It was good to visit with several friends, and meet new ones, too. I enjoyed getting to talk with the L5 families, as well, and was watched continually to make sure I didn't lose it!

I went a couple of hours before the Sunday evening concert began, and was available in the lobby to visit and hear some great testimonies of Roger's influence in some lives. I LOVE to hear how he touched others with his ministry and walk. Then, Legacy Five opened the evening with a video of Roger singing "Joy." This video was filmed one year ago at the Labor Day Celebration, 2006. Roger sang the verses, and then the guys stepped out on stage to sing along with him on the choruses. I was standing backstage watching this on a monitor, and even though I knew what was going to happen, it still hit me hard. The whole weekend, I was flashing back to last year's event, remembering Roger being there, and it was difficult knowing that that was all in the past, never to be experienced again. Immediately after the song was over, Scott introduced me and I walked out on stage to an outpouring of love, both from the group, and from the audience. It was overwhelming, and I failed to maintain my composure! Legacy Five presented me with two dozen red roses, and also had a white candle and a single white rose lying on the piano. I spoke a few words (I don't really know what I said, other than thank you) and left the stage. I stayed to hear some of the singing from the various groups, and intended to stay to hear Legacy Five sing, but found I was just not able to. I was on my way in to listen to them, when they began their program with "Strike up the Band," and once again, I had that flashback from last year, and knew there was a big piano solo in that song, and I just could not do it. So, I still have that hurdle to jump of actually watching them perform with a new piano player, but I feel I am on my way. I am very glad the group has Tim Parton as their new member. It's just at this point, ANYONE else on that piano bench will take me a while to get used to.

I have spent the past couple of days making some very last-minute preparations for National Quartet Convention next week, but I am so happy to say that they are all falling into place. I have very qualified help for the week, and some exciting things in store, as well. The new DVD and CD are going to be there, and as soon as we get back from NQC, they will be available for mail orders, as well (the office will be closed next week). Rick Goodman has worked diligently to make a dream of Roger's happen: we will have a Baby Grand piano with Roger's signature on it, and it will also be able to play itself - as if Roger were playing it! It is going to be amazing, and I can't wait to see it! I will have more information about that later, as well.

I will write more soon. I need to go now and plan some signs for the booth, as well as make a table cover for the product table. I will be located in the Legacy Five booth, and will be there from Tuesday until the end of convention. Busy, busy, but

In His Grip!
Debbie

September 13, 2007
At NQC

Well, I have made it through two days here at National Quartet Convention, and am getting ready for day three. So far, so good. The hardest days are ahead, what with awards and Parade of Pianos still to go, but I am glad I am here. Driving up on Tuesday was a bit disconcerting, and when I got to the convention center, I had a great big knot in my stomach, thinking about walking in those doors. But, as I got over the threshold, it started getting better. I had a couple of "moments" early on, but it has done me a lot of good to be here, and talk to so many old friends, and new ones, too. There is a whole lot of love around here! And it is amazing to hear about the difference Roger has made in so many lives. People thank me for sharing him all of those years, but my reply is always the same: It was truly my pleasure, because he was doing what he was called to do, and he loved it. I could no more have asked him to stop traveling, playing, and sharing, than I could have asked him to stop loving. He was an amazing person, and it makes me proud to know that so many people miss and love him.

I am still finding myself drawn out of my comfort zone in many areas. I did an interview with Paul Heil of the "Gospel Greats" radio program this week. I have had much planning to do for this week, in getting the booth and product ready. (I had NO idea how much is involved with that! And, thanks to Scott Fowler for sharing his booth with me. He is the greatest!) I even purchased a 5x8 enclosed trailer, loaded it myself, pulled it to Louisville behind my Explorer (in the rain), backed it into a parking space when I arrived, and unhitched it from my vehicle! I told my dad that it was that truck-driving blood coming out in me (he was a trucker for almost 45 years). You just never know what God can help you accomplish, until you try. Fortunately, I am blessed with a spirit of either not being afraid to try, or ignorance that I can't, I am not sure which! Roger used to just shake his head at some of the things that I did try, but I won't embarrass myself here by letting you know what some of those things were...

Thank you for the prayers - this week, especially. I can feel them coming my way! I will post more after I go home from this week, but meanwhile, rest assured that I am comfortable in the knowledge that I am

In His Grip,
Debbie

September 17, 2007
Home from NQC/Another Anniversary

It's been a rather non-productive day for me today, but I figure I am entitled. In addition to being very tired from a long, emotional week at NQC, today is the six-month anniversary of Roger's death. I can't believe it has been that long, and I can't believe it has ONLY been that long. Depends on the day you ask.

Last week was a remarkable week for me, in many ways. I found a lot of healing taking place, being showered with love, and memories of my sweet Roger. I heard many stories of how he has touched so many lives, and I cannot hear enough of those. He was truly a special, special person, and it's good to know that I wasn't the only one (or, rather, our family members were not the only ones) who thought so. I always really knew that, but, again, I can't hear it enough...

There were some wonderful tributes made to Roger last week, and it was an emotional roller coaster for me. I did pretty well most of the time, but there were a couple of times when it got to be too much for me to contain. I suppose that's okay, too, and if it's not, then too bad! It was strange not to see him there. It felt like he should be coming around the corner at any moment.

We were blessed to have all of the new product available, and humbled by the many who were anxious to have it.

I realize that I may be rambling in this post, so I won't continue too much longer. It's been a day of reflection and rest, mixed in with some sadness, and also gratefulness for God's many blessings.

The first six months without Roger have been "difficult, but do-able," strictly because I am

In His Grip,
Debbie

September 29, 2007
Taking a Break

I have been up to my ears in papers, trying to get my (2006!) taxes done this week before the IRS comes to take me away... It has been hard, in more ways than one. Several years ago, Roger decided to take over the tax situation solely, and I was content to let him. However, that did present a major challenge for me, since I don't know where to get some of the information that I need, and I don't know where he put some other info. But, again, I am slowly being able to recreate what I need, and hope that it's enough. Just in case, though, I will list my prison address when I go!

Seriously, though, I will be so glad to get it behind me. Just the "doing" of it makes for a lot of memories that are painful. I seem to see him surrounded by all the papers, and it has been very hard on me emotionally to get it done. There seems to be a mental block there. I have an appointment Monday afternoon with my accountant, and as a reward for making it through, I am getting a haircut, and picking Chelsea up at the airport at midnight Monday! (Assuming the weather is OK, and her small plane can leave Alaska.) I am so excited about her coming home. The two of us will go to Murfreesboro on Tuesday night after Jordan gets off from work, and have dinner with him. Chelsea and Jordan haven't seen each other since their Dad's funeral.

Meanwhile, we are in the midst of yet another move. My parents, and one brother, are moving back to Arkansas, so we will probably journey down this week, if all goes well, to close on the house they are moving to. I will surely miss them, but I am very excited that they have the opportunity to move back. Daddy is Arkansas born and bred, and this is the most excitement I have seen out of him in some time. They will be closer to my other brother and his family, which includes a six-month old great-grandchild. And, as a bonus, they are moving to an area that will put them about 12 miles from Roger's dad, Doug, and the majority of his family. So, when we go to visit, it will be easy to see everyone! Roger's grandpa is in a nursing home now, and knows us sometimes, and sometimes doesn't. I should be able to schedule more frequent visits now.

That trailer I bought and learned how to pull will certainly come in handy!

Today is my brother Tony's birthday, so I need to go shower and get to the store, as I am in charge of making him a diabetic birthday dessert (reference the cake I made for Roger once that was more like concrete - I am going in a different direction this time!). We are having a fish fry tonight to celebrate.

Thank you for all of your kind comments on NQC. It really was a special week, in many ways. For those who have asked, yes, I do have more projects to accomplish. I will be working on more of Roger's products, and I AM going to get this journal into book form. I have a few more ideas germinating, that I am pretty excited about. I will keep you updated on the progress, but I am taking a few weeks off to get some other things done, and travel again. We are going back to Northern Ireland and Scotland in November for the release of the new *Whispers in the Night* DVD and CD (the new product is now on the store at www.rogerbennettdirect.com). While you are there, check out the new tote bag with Roger's signature on it!

OK, break time is over, and that shower is calling. I hope you all have a blessed weekend, and keep safely

In His Grip!
Debbie

October 03, 2007
Together Again

I finally have my little family together again, for the first time in over six months. Last night, Chelsea and I went to Jordan's house after he got off from work, and had dinner out and spent some time catching up. I admit, it was bittersweet. I sat looking at the two of them, and my heart was filled with the blessings of being in that moment, yet it recognized the empty place where Roger would have been. His favorite thing in life was being a daddy. I know he would be proud of the way they are growing up, as I am. He instilled some very strong values in each of them, and that will remain with them as they face life's challenges. It surely was good to have that time with each other last night.

I made it through the tax thing, finally faxed the last numbers (I hope) last night, and don't want to do that again. I had to basically reconstruct the entire year, which was difficult on its own, and terribly emotional, as each entry created a memory... The "last" this, and the "last" that. Heart-wrenching, at times. I just have to keep reminding myself of that almost-audible voice from God last February, where He told me that there is nothing on this earth that can compare with what Roger is experiencing now. That is comforting to think about.

My mom, dad, two brothers, and I are headed to Arkansas today to close on the house they will be living in there, and start on all of the business of getting it ready to move into. Now that Chelsea is home, she will be managing the zoo around here, but she doesn't mind, since a bigger animal-lover would be hard to find. I told her last week that I was ready for her to get home so she could "wear" her cat, instead of me having to. Leia has been in the middle of all of the papers and forms I have had strewn about me for the past week, and wanting to be in my lap while I am typing. She is happy to see her "mommy" now, though!

Gotta run and pack, and ship product off before we head out. Please remember us in your prayers as we travel. That trailer is coming into play again!

In His Grip,
Debbie

October 13, 2007
Another Hurdle Jumped

Well, it's the 30th Saturday since Roger passed away, and again, I sit and reflect on the day itself. Seems that is the pattern with Saturdays, but it is not as hard as it once was. This one is full of thinking and memories, though, due to the event that we just attended. Thursday was Roger's induction into the Southern Gospel Music Hall of Fame, and Chelsea, Jordan, and I were honored to be in Pigeon Forge, TN, to accept his appointment. It was a beautiful ceremony. As it happens, this weekend is the one year anniversary of the last time Roger was ever able to be on stage. And, it happened that his last performance was in Pigeon Forge, so the emotions ran high for me. On this weekend, one year ago, Chelsea and I were in Houston, setting up the apartment so it would be ready when Roger came down, getting ready for that third transplant. S o many thoughts swirl around all of these events... They go from happy to sad in instants, then swing back again.

When I was getting ready for the induction ceremony, I jotted down my thoughts on paper, trying to organize them into some sort of coherence. There is a lot to be said about a person's life, and it is terribly hard to boil it down

387

to two minutes. I wrote it out in speech form, tried to remember what all I wanted to say, and still missed some of it as I stood, accepting his award. Chelsea and Jordan were standing with me on stage, and once again, I didn't maintain my composure. I was okay until I stepped onto the stage. However, they told me I did remember most of it. Just in case, though, I decided to print the written version of my speech here, just to share it with you. So, here goes:

It is such an honor for Chelsea, Jordan, and me to be here accepting this appointment to the Hall of Fame for Roger. When he learned he was to be inducted - last February, only a few days before he went into the hospital for the last time - he was pretty much in disbelief. If you knew Roger personally, you knew that he was uncomfortable being in the spotlight for self-recognition. For all of his stage antics and joking ways, he was truly a humble man. I myself made it a point to tell anyone who would listen about his upcoming induction, and I always saw a smile in his eyes when I did. I know it meant a lot to him, and I will always be grateful that he had the happiness of knowing about it.

Roger was a special man in so many ways. For over 27 years, he *lived* and *loved* the Gospel music ministry to which he was called. And, if there ever were a person called to this ministry, Roger was one. Whether he was young and strong, or too sick to make it off the bus during the day, when it came time for him to be on stage, the Lord gave him the strength, and Roger gave 110%. But more than just a performance, he made a promise to never leave the stage without sharing the Gospel and telling an audience that Jesus is the answer to all of life's problems, no matter what they may be. In that way, he left a legacy for us all to follow. He also left a legacy of love and caring. He was a wonderful husband, father, son, and friend. If he loved you, he wasn't afraid to tell you. Chelsea, Jordan, and I were blessed to hear those words on a daily basis. His compassion and generosity were extended to friends and strangers alike. I could stand here all night and never begin to tell the stories about Roger, both on-stage and off, but I did want to share one highlight in his career.

In 1998, our family was privileged to travel to Northern Ireland where we filmed a video called *Midnight Meditations*. This video was probably his most-used ministry tool, as his testimony of God's faithfulness in our lives through his battle with cancer gave hope to so many. It also contained his piano playing, set to beautiful scenery, and in one scene, we actually carted a grand piano up a steep hill, set it in front of a monument, and Roger played hymns, while looking over mountains, lakes, and patchwork fields. Roger said that that was one of the most spiritually inspiring things he was ever blessed to be able to do. This monument, Scrabo Tower, stands as a tribute to a Marquis in Northern Ireland. One of the things that stood out to me, though, was an inscription over the tower door that said, "Fame belongs to History, Remembrance to Us." This summer, I went back to that tower, re-read that inscription, and realized why, over so many years, that had always stuck in my mind. Roger's induction into the Southern Gospel Music Hall of Fame will mean that, down through history, people will be able to see, hear, and read about his contributions to the field. But, for those of us who really knew and loved Roger, we have the blessing of real memories. Some make us cry, but most make us laugh, because that's the kind of person he was.

"Fame belongs to History.....Remembrance, to Us."   Thank you, friends, and SGMA, for honoring Roger today, with this induction, and with your presence.   But more than that, thank you for remembering him in your hearts, forever.

So, reflecting once again on these special memories, I will continue my day, firmly

In His Grip,
Debbie

October 31, 2007
Back Again

It has been a very tiring few weeks, but I think a lot of that has to do with my emotional state. Seems like this time of year is made of many memories. I can't help but remember that this time last year, we were starting on another journey in Houston, which we prayed would be the cure this time. Well, it was, but just not in the way we had hoped. Still, I am grateful that Roger is healed and happy, I just miss him terribly.

Grief is funny. (Yeah, real funny...) The farther out we get from Roger's Homegoing, the better able we are to handle the fact that he is no longer here with us. However, lately it seems like the farther out I get, the lonelier I get, and the more I miss him. It would be great to be able to talk about things with him, get his opinions and feedback, share life's ups and downs with him. My head knows that is not possible, but my heart won't stop wishing. I have learned that what people say is so true: NEVER take for granted what you have. It's easy to do, but try to be aware of the blessings of the "little" things in life, and appreciate them while you can.

Onto the more mundane, we got the folks moved to Arkansas, and though they will have to make one more trip back for things that wouldn't fit on the truck, they are settling in. There are some things that must be done to the new (30-year old) house, but those seem to be coming along okay. I have decided that if I ever have to move, I may just set fire to most of it, and start over. I can't even fathom having to pack up and move all of the "stuff" we have accumulated around here!

Chelsea is now in Northern Ireland, a few days ahead of my arrival, so that she can visit with friends a while longer. I leave on November 7 and return on November 19, just in time to drive to Arkansas for Thanksgiving. We will be in three concerts with Allison Durham Speer in Scotland and Northern Ireland, debuting the new *Whispers in the Night* DVD that was filmed there this past summer. I am looking forward to some good cups of tea and great visits with friends.

I had a great dinner with Jordan last night, and we had a good talk, as well. Then, I cut his hair a little before he went home, in anticipation of his shaving his beard off. (Yea!) He was growing it out for something particular, and is now ready to let us see that handsome face again.

Well, I guess I am off to my folks' old house here in TN, trying to corral all of the stuff to be taken back. I have to list it on the market this week, so if anyone needs a five-year old house in Spring Hill, TN, let me know! It's one of the few left that won't take three incomes to own.

Until next time, I am
In His Grip,
Debbie

November 07, 2007
Off to the UK!

I am leaving this morning for the airport, where I make my way over to the Belfast, Northern Ireland area for a few days, with a quick trip over to Scotland thrown in there, too. I am looking forward to seeing dear friends again. We are going to be in three concerts with Allison Durham Speer, where we will be promoting the DVD I filmed there this past summer. It should be a great time. Chelsea has been over there a few days already, visiting with friends. Jordan is staying behind this time, as his work schedule won't allow him time off.

Jordan turns 21 on the 11th of this month, so, since I won't be here, we got together last night for dinner. I can't believe my baby is grown up. I had a hard time picking out his birthday card this year. It didn't hit me until I was actually standing in the store that this is the first card I have bought him that's from "Me" and not "We." Deal with that in the middle of the Wal-Mart aisle... But we had a nice time, and his buddies have a get-together planned for him on the day. One of his buddies who is in the Marines will be able to be home for it, so that makes it more special, and his girlfriend Jessica is coming home from school in Chicago. I am sure he won't even miss his old mom!

My mom, dad, and one brother (whose birthday is today) just pulled out of my drive with the last load - everything that didn't fit on the truck a couple of weeks ago. Their house here is empty and a little sad, but they are quickly settling into their new home in Arkansas. They have seen Roger's dad off and on since they have been there, and I think they all enjoy knowing they are close enough to do so. When I return to TN from this trip, we will be going down to AR for Thanksgiving. Between the jet lag and the turkey, I may be in some serious sleep mode then!

Thanks for the prayers for a safe trip. I am sure the Lord will bless it. I am carrying some product with me, so my suitcases are full. Hope I weighed them correctly. They are all so close to the limit, that if I didn't, there will be some surprised people in the Nashville airport getting free DVDs today!

I am listening to my heating unit make some very bad noises, and thinking that I had better sign a check to leave with my other brother for some repairs or a replacement, I am afraid. It's always something... BUT, it's never too much when you are

In His Grip!
Debbie

November 21, 2007
Home Again/Happy Thanksgiving!

I decided to combine the two subjects, since I am off again to Arkansas this morning to spend Thanksgiving with family there. We arrived home from the UK late Monday night, and I spent yesterday in a fog, tired from the busy weekend of concerts in Scotland and in Northern

Ireland. What a great weekend it was, though! There are quite a few stories to tell about the trip, so they may be interspersed in a few posts.

Let's see... In no particular order: Jordan celebrated his 21st birthday here in TN while Chelsea and I were abroad. We did call him, though, on the day, and he had a good one. Chelsea's friend, Hannah, went over with me, and as it was her first time there, we got to do some sightseeing through "fresh" eyes. It was great! Hannah is also a photographer, so she and Chelsea had a great time taking pictures. That is always fun for me to watch, as I learn a lot about what to look for, and it really makes you take in the scenery in a different way, concentrating on the beauty more. It was very beautiful, too, if a little chillier than when I was there in June! It's always amazing to see all that green, especially after the drought conditions we have had here this year.

It was great to visit with friends again, old and new. If you are ever in doubt of what true Christian fellowship is like, just head to Northern Ireland! It is abundant there.

One of the highlights of our trip was being invited to the Parliament in Belfast for a tour and lunch with MLA Mervyn Storey. He was a delightful host, and we had a splendid time. We were also in concert with MP Rev. William McCrea, and what we really noticed was that both of these men, although in the political arena, are NOT afraid to stand up for their beliefs. In fact, they are very outspoken about their faith, and are eager to share with anyone who would listen. That was so refreshing, and it made me wonder what would happen if some of our politicians would do the same, without being afraid of "political correctness"... Sad to say, we probably won't find out.

Over the weekend, we were at concerts in Glasgow (Motherwell) Scotland; Bangor, Northern Ireland; and Dundonald, Northern Ireland. Allison Durham Speer and her husband Brian flew in for these concerts and it was a precious time. Allison is truly gifted in her talent and ability to share with her audience. I really enjoyed spending time with Brian and Allison, and hope to be able to visit more soon! In introducing the DVD that I made there this summer, they played a couple of clips from it, and I was able to speak about the significance of doing the video. People were so gracious to listen, and speak to me later about Roger's influence in their lives. It was an emotional weekend, not only for doing the concerts, but because of two significant dates that fell on the weekend. On the 16th, I was taken back one year to Roger's actual last transplant date. We were so full of hope that he would be cured. Ultimately, we know he had the best cure, but it made me sad to think of it. And then, on the 17th, it was the eight-month anniversary of his Homegoing. Needless to say, there was a lot on my mind. I guess it was good to have the concerts fall on the weekend that they did, so that I could be reminded of the fact that although Roger is gone, his legacy truly does live on. In fact, the first song I heard in the first concert in Scotland, sung by a local group there was "Freedom," a song Roger wrote. It's quite an honor to think that his influence reaches many countries and continents.

One of the biggest surprises I had was a tremendous gift I received. I have spoken about the significance of Inch Abbey, an 11th century monastery ruins in Downpatrick, Northern Ireland. Roger was drawn to that place from the moment he first laid eyes on it so many years ago. It was like a pilgrimage for us each time we visited, and he always loved the peace he felt there. Jordan and I recorded part of the *Whispers in the Night* DVD there. Years ago, we had met and become friends with a local artist in the area named David Long. He had presented us with some of his paintings, and they have a place of honor in our home. On this trip, I was overwhelmed when my dear friend, Ian McDowell, who has been instrumental in helping me get this DVD into production, and who was also instrumental in the *Midnight Meditations* video, took me to David Long's home and presented me with an original painting of Inch Abbey, which he had commissioned for me. It was one of the most thoughtful gifts I have ever received, not to mention one of the most beautiful! As an added bonus, David Long has had prints made, and we have them for sale. They are signed and numbered, and I will have them on the web site soon. What an honor!

I must be off now, to pack for the next leg of the journey. I wish you all a wonderful, safe, happy, and well-fed Thanksgiving. I will be spending mine with parents, brothers and their families, my father-in-law, and of course, my children. There will be a seat unfilled this year, and that will be hard for us all, but I know in my heart that this will be Roger's best Thanksgiving ever, for he is eternally

In His Grip!
Debbie

December 10, 2007
Trekking Through the Season

It has been a strange holiday season, to say the least. My feelings are pretty mixed on this one. Frankly, I would just as soon wake up and find that it's January already, but I know that won't happen. I still can appreciate the wonder of the REASON for the season, but the timing of it is lost on me this year. It took me a while to even be able to listen to Christmas music without tearing up, or to go into a store and not feel sorrow at seeing the decorations.

If you know me at all, you would know that Christmas has always been a very big deal at the Bennett house. To use a phrase of Roger's (as only he could put it), it always "looked like Christmas threw up at our house" (I told you, only he would put it that way!). There were multiple trees up, and decorations of all sorts everywhere. Even in Houston, I always decorated and had a tree. This year, though, I just could not bring myself to do it. No decorations, not even a tree. I asked Chelsea and Jordan if they could handle that, and they were of the same mind. It's not that I think Christmas left because Roger did, it's just too close yet to be able to celebrate in the same way. So, this year, we are heading to Arkansas the weekend before Christmas to be with extended families there, and coming back to Tennessee on Christmas Eve to spend a quiet time here.

Before I get to Christmas, though, I will have another big day to get through. December 17, besides being the nine-month anniversary of Roger's death, would have been our 26th wedding anniversary. I have wonderful memories of our 25th, even though Roger was so sick. It was a very special day. He was distressed that he couldn't go shopping (rest assured that he did eventually, and did it in style!), so I suggested that we each sit down and write a letter to the other. We did, and I will treasure that letter for the rest of my life. His handwriting was so shaky, but he labored on, and filled pages with his love for me. How blessed I am to have had him in my life...

After the first of the year, I will be back to working on new projects. The book is the first one I will pursue, along with a few other new things to add to the web store. (By the way, if you haven't checked out the store lately, you really should see the new painting that has been added. It's pretty awesome!)

The *Singing News* magazine has generously invited me to be a part of the February issue. Editor and family friend

Danny Jones will be interviewing me in an article in the magazine, as well as extra features in his online journal. It is quite an honor for me to be able to share what is going on in our lives.

I hope you all are having a special holiday season, and remembering that there would be no Christmas, if not for the little Christ child, born in a manger, Who came to save us all. If you, like me, have lost a loved one this year, let's remember that they are having their best Christmas ever - every day they celebrate WITH the One Who brought them safely home, and keeps them

In His Grip!
Debbie

December 31, 2007
The End of a Year

...And what a year it was. Probably the foggiest, busiest, certainly the saddest year of my life. In ways, I am glad to see 2007 behind me. In other ways, I would love to cling to parts of it, and never let them go. But, time does go on, and as they say, waits for no man (or woman).

Our holiday season this year was as good as it could be, and being with family was wonderful. I think everyone just kind of "stepped around" the hole that was there, with Roger's absence. It was the first time in five years that I have been home for Christmas, so it was good to spend it with all of the extended family. And, since my folks now live just down the road from Roger's dad, it was easy to make the rounds. We ended up seeing almost everyone, although a few cousins got missed. Roger's grandpa is still in the nursing home, and I don't believe he really knew us this time. My dad has been having some health problems, as well, and will be seeing the doctors this week. And as if that weren't enough, I spent the first minutes of Christmas Eve going into the ER in Arkansas, with a kidney stone. Chelsea drove us home later in the day. I also will be seeing a doctor this week. One good thing about that, though, is that it sort of took my mind off of other things (and the drugs they gave me weren't too bad, either!).

So, over all, we are hoping for a better 2008. I ask myself how it can get better, when so much is gone, but I know that life goes on, and we have to make the best of what we have. I just miss my friend, my partner, my other half. I still feel so incomplete. I have decided that most of it is Roger's fault for spoiling me so. When you are made to feel like a princess on a pedestal, it's hard to go back to being a commoner again!

Seriously, though, as this year comes to a close, it's a time for reflections on the moments we have lived. Did we make a difference in someone's life? Did we show Jesus to ones who were seeking? Did we really love to the best of our ability? And then, there are the perpetual resolutions that come every January 1: I will eat better, exercise more, lose weight, become more organized, spend more time in prayer and Bible study... That list goes on and on. One thing I am trying to do is to make each encounter I have with others meaningful. I realize more now how precious life is, and how we just don't know how much of it we have left. So, with each word I say, each instance needing patience, each opportunity to tell someone I love them, I want to make it count.

That's what I will try to do this year, thankful all the while that God keeps me safely

In His Grip!
Debbie

January 15, 2008
New Year, New Beginnings

Okay, I am duly chastised for taking so long to update. I took a little time "off" to get in touch with some feelings, and to get to feeling better, so now it's time to get up and start again. And, for those of you who thought I was complaining about being a "nobody" in the last post, I really did mean it in jest...

I am beginning 2008 with a new determination to get some projects completed that I have been putting off. I know I have said it many times, but the book will be one of the first. Never having done a book before, it's taking me a little longer to get my game plan together, but I am looking forward to having a copy in my hands by spring. I also have several home projects that are in the beginning stages, which means things are in turmoil around here, but I think I am seeing a little light at the end of the tunnel there, as well.

Each task I complete, I think about how proud Roger would be of me. Not that I am boasting, because I have nothing to boast about on my own; but it makes me feel warm to think of him smiling at me and appreciating my efforts. The 17th of this month brings another anniversary - 10 months since he left us. It is amazing to me how it can feel like an eternity on one hand, and only a short time, on the other. I suppose it will always be a struggle of some kind, but one that becomes more manageable as time passes...

One thing I have noticed about myself, is that I no longer keep track of how many weeks it has been since Roger passed away. I used to wake up every single Saturday morning, thinking about the exact amount of time it had been. At some point, though, it became less about the weeks, and now I look at it in months. I know that is strange, but it feels like an accomplishment to me.

It's kind of like being able to take a slightly bigger step forward than the tiny baby steps I had been taking. Many of you will know exactly what I mean by that.

Then, there are still those days when I feel like I am carrying around a stone in my chest, the literal embodiment of a "heavy heart." Unfortunately, there are many of you who know what that feels like, too. At those times, "lonely" can't even begin to describe the ache deep inside, the sense of loss, of being separate from all that mattered most, the sense that happiness will never be yours again. But, we are so blessed that at those very darkest times, God still hears our cries and comforts us. I was reading Psalm 13 today and it blessed me. David was crying to God, asking how long he would be forgotten, and have to struggle with an anguished soul. But it's like a light came on when he asked those questions, and he ended up trusting, rejoicing, and singing to God, praising Him for being so good.

It's like that for all of us at times. No matter what our grief or burden, no matter how gut-wrenching our sorrows seem, when we stop and praise God, our outlook is so much brighter. In the midst of our most powerful struggles in this life, God is always there. He is our Comfort; our Protector; our Source of Strength. He really does care.

Roger often related a story on stage about feeling so depressed while in the hospital that he couldn't even pray . Then, he remembered Paul and Silas in prison, and how their chains were loosened when they sang praises. So, he began to sing, and he said he felt the chains fall away with each verse, each phrase. By the time he was into the second song, the nurse came into the room and asked him if he was okay, and he was able to say, with a solid certainty, that he really was! I learned a lot of lessons from the special man that Roger was. I don't want to forget them.

Thank you, dear Roger, for reminding us all, even in your earthly absence, that we are still safely

In His Grip!
Debbie

January 30, 2008
New Opportunities

2008 is already almost a month old. Time really flies. I have had the blessing of visiting with several friends this month. It seems like I have to travel to visit with most of my friends. That is one of the "perks" to the lifestyle we lived. We found friends all over the country, and all over the world. I just wish more of them lived closer. It gets lonely at home.

Please pray with me as a new opportunity is presenting itself in my life. For years now, I have known that when my kids were older, and things were more settled in my life (?!?), I would love to do volunteer work in some capacity. I just wasn't sure where it would be. As I was visiting with my "family" in Houston recently, I learned of a program that immediately spoke to my heart. To make a long story short, I have an opportunity to possibly become a courier for the National Bone Marrow Donor Program, being one of their volunteers who actually travel to collect the bone marrow/stem cell donations and bring it quickly back to the recipient... a huge gift of life, and one which means a great deal to me. I will find out more as time goes on, and the program is highly selective, but again, I have been blessed with friends who have put me in contact with the proper people. I am scheduled to attend a training session in March in Minneapolis. I am very excited. I can envision a real fulfillment, in being able to carry a gift of life, and pray for the people involved, whether I ever see them or not. Most of my life has been "behind the scenes," and I am quite comfortable with that!

Thank you for all of the kind comments about the article in this month's *Singing News Magazine*. I was very honored and humbled that they wanted to do an article on me and my family, and I thank Danny Jones, the editor (and family friend!) for being so kind. If you don't subscribe to this magazine, you really should. Contact Legacy Five's office for more information, or go to their website, www.legacyfive.com.

Well, I am off to a walk-in clinic. Seems like, after not having time to be sick for over four years, that's all I can do lately. I get over one thing, and move to another. This time, I am afraid I may have either bronchitis, or the beginnings of pneumonia. That's a new one for me. Oh well, not complaining, just getting tired of being "down" with something or another.

Life goes on, and thankfully, we have the assurance that we move forward, safely

In His Grip!
Debbie

February 14, 2008
A Day for Love

Happy Valentine's Day to everyone. This is a hard one for me, my first without a Valentine in many, many years. Of course, it never was about the day itself, so it's not really any different from most days.

I confess to having had a lot of "down" days recently. I guess it's just the time of year.. .thinking about all of the last "lasts." It's almost the day marking the last time Roger went into the hospital, and of course, his birthday and one-year anniversary of his death are just around the corner. I think a big part of it, too, is that it feels like once the 1-year mark has passed, it's just too far gone... Do the memories now start to fade? Will I be able to remember them as clearly? Just some panicky feelings in the middle of the night (or day) that leave me feeling confused. I know it probably sounds a little crazy to anyone who hasn't been there, but I am guessing that there are many of you who can relate exactly to what I am trying to put into words.

I was blessed to have a great love in my life. Roger treated me like someone very special, and I hope he felt that I treated him that way, too. We weren't perfect, by any means. We had our share of disagreements, but we were lucky to learn what was important in life. We may have had a more abrupt awakening to life's priorities than we would have liked, but we wouldn't have traded the journey and what we learned along the way for anything more comfortable. Even on the days when I don't feel like making an effort, I still can cling to those life lessons.

Yesterday was probably an all-time low for me on this, my new journey. Between things going wrong at the house, feeling more lonely than ever, and feeling like I just didn't care about it all anymore, I spent most of the day having a pity-party. In my head, I know that it's normal to have days where grief hits you harder than others. I just don't like them! I told Chelsea that I just miss talking to Roger. Even if all of the same things were going on, he could always make me feel better about it all, just by talking to me. I miss that companionship. I miss that friendship. I just miss him.

Anyway, I know that things will begin to look up again, and that I will find my motivation to continue moving forward. I have two very special gifts in Chelsea and Jordan, and especially on Valentine's Day, I want them to know they are loved. So, go and tell those whom you love how much they mean to you. Appreciate having them in your life.

Most importantly, though, remember the ultimate love of our Savior. His unequalled sacrifice keeps us loved, and

In His Grip!
Debbie

February 29, 2008
Time Marches On....

....No pun intended. Try as I might, I can not make March stay away any longer. I have tried hard to mentally push it back, but it is here, nonetheless. So many days in March will be marked with a huge dose of reality. March 6 is the last day I heard Roger's voice speak to me. March 7, he went into ICU. March 10 was his birthday. March 17 will be the anniversary of his Homegoing. March 21 and 24 were the dates of his memorial services (one in TN, one in AR). I can't believe, in some ways, that it has already been a year. In other ways, it feels like a lifetime. But, as sad as it makes me to be without him, I can't help but be joyful that he is where he is now, at peace, and healthy, and living with the One he sang, played and lived for!

There have been a few things happen lately that have made me feel like I am helpless without Roger: things around the house; mortgage "glitches;" having no sounding board or help with the "big" things. Yet, I know that God is faithful. He has never failed me, and I know He won't in the future. I suppose it's more the time of year than anything that has me feeling more vulnerable. And, yes, I know it's natural. I don't beat myself up over feeling this way anymore. I just take it in stride, then pull myself back up and move on.

I have, in recent days of Bible study, found several passages in the book of Psalms that have ministered to me in my weakness. The psalmist David really had a way with words! So, I thought I might share a few of these passages, in the hope that someone else may get an equal blessing.

Psalm 33:20-22 (KJV) Our soul waiteth for the Lord; He is our help and our shield. For our heart shall rejoice in Him, because we have trusted in His Holy name. Let thy mercy, O Lord, be upon us, according as we hope in Thee.

Psalm 34:17-19 (KJV) The righteous cry, and the Lord heareth, and delivereth them out of all of their troubles. The Lord is nigh unto them that are of a broken heart; and saveth such as be of a contrite spirit. Many are the afflictions of the righteous; but the Lord delivereth him out of them all.

Psalm 37:23-24 (KJV) The steps of a good man are ordered by the Lord, and He delighteth in his way. Though he fall, he shall not be utterly cast down; for the Lord upholdeth him with His hand.

Psalm 42:5 (KJV) Why are thou cast down, O my soul? And why art thou disquieted in me? Hope thou in God; for I shall yet praise Him for the help of His countenance.

Be blessed, enjoy God's fellowship, and remain
In His Grip!
Debbie

March 07, 2008
Roger's Legacy Lives On

How interesting life can be. On the days of the month when I knew Roger would consume my thoughts, I find that others are thinking of him, too. I knew they would, but I find it is happening in new and unexpected ways.

I received a phone call from the National Marrow Donor Program's volunteer coordinator this week. As I have mentioned before, I am going to be in Minneapolis next weekend for my training to become a courier for the program (and I am still very excited!). I was asked to write a letter of "introduction" - to try to let people know who Roger was. Wow! How do you sum up a life in a few words? Answer: it can't be done, but I gave it a good try. It seems that his message and music are going to be used to inspire the workers and coordinators there at the national center... A rally, of sorts, before the new volunteers come in for training. I am so honored to be able to share him and his gift of encouragement with a whole new group of people. His gift of love to us all just keeps going and going.

Pray for me as I go to Minnesota next Thursday through Saturday, but pray also that God will be honored through Roger's testimony, and my efforts to make a difference in others' lives.

God is so faithful. I am having some "weepy" times these days, but He is always there to comfort me and keep me going. I am looking forward to new opportunities, as He keeps me firmly

In His Grip!
Debbie

March 10, 2008
A Birthday Remembered

Happy First Birthday in Heaven, Roger! I got a note from Danny Jones (editor, Singing News Magazine) this morning, and he told me he was out last night, and when the clock turned to midnight, his first thought was, "Today is Roger's birthday. I wonder what kind of party God throws in Heaven!" I think we all can imagine that every day is a "party" there. No more growing older, with all that entails. There's something to long for!!

I am keeping very busy the next few days. Chelsea and I both have gotten roped into working Easter Bunny sets again this year, each at different malls. She is working hers full-time, I am just filling in a few days here and there. I have a photo on our mantel of our last Easter together, 2006, when I was working the set. (Don't ask -- I have a great friend who can talk me into anything!) This photo is a family photo - we are all in it - but you wouldn't know I was there. Actually, it is one of my more photogenic shots... all smiles and BIG EARS and all! Thankfully, this year, I am more visible on the set, with no fur involved. I also have a photo that Chelsea took that same year that is one of my favorites. It's a shot that, if someone said, "Take a picture that will capture Roger's personality," would be the one. He was sitting beside me on the chair (remember, I am "invisible"), and told Chelsea to count to three and then snap. She counted, "One, Two, Three;" and on "three," Roger leaned over and gave the Easter Bunny a full kiss on the mouth. It's priceless! (One day, I am going to figure out how to put more photos on this site, and it will be one of them.) Luckily, there was no one else in line at the time, but I can imagine what any onlookers or store merchants must have thought!

Just a good memory on this day. I am going to go by the cemetery on the way to work and put out new flowers that Chelsea and I picked out. We thought he would like tulips and daffodils, as Spring is hopefully on its way after the snow over the weekend.

Wherever you are today, be blessed, and happy

In His Grip!
Debbie

March 17, 2008
Anniversary Day

Well, today was the day I had been dreading for a while. I don't really know why it should have been different from most days, but I guess it just brought everything into more of a sharp focus. One year without my Roger. I miss him terribly.

Anyway, I was so busy today with one "challenge" after another around here, that I hardly sat down -- which, I suppose, was a good thing. It didn't keep the memories and thoughts at bay, but it did keep me from dwelling too long on them.

I want to write a post that does justice to a wonderful person, but today is not the day for that. I am a little too heart-sore. So, I will save that for another day, when I feel more like it. Maybe tomorrow, maybe next week, but it will come.

I just wanted to thank you all for the cards, flowers, and mostly the prayers. They have surely been felt. What I thought would be a totally disabling day has been tolerated fairly well, and a peace that I didn't think possible was with me today. Again, thank you for your faithfulness. I am so glad I am a member of a family who knows the value of being

In His Grip.
Debbie

April 01, 2008
A Life Well Lived

I have one voice mail on my cell phone that I have saved since December, 2006. It is from Roger. While the entire message consists of only 13 syllables, I treasure it as if it were an entire speech. There are a myriad of reasons why it is so special, apart from the fact that it is from Roger. I will try to explain, and in doing so, show how significant it is to Roger's own life.

Roger had very few good days during his last transplant, either before or after. So, on Tuesday, December 12, 2006, when he felt like getting out and riding around in the sunshine, I was happy to oblige. We were passing by a church that had a sign out front with a scripture and reference, and I really liked it, so I asked Roger to call my cell phone and leave me a message, telling me the reference, so I could study it more later. So, here is my message from Roger:

"Debbie, remember Micah 6:8... Micah 6:8."

This is what that verse says:

He hath shown thee, O man, what is good;
and what doth the Lord require of thee, but
to do justly, and to love mercy, and to walk
humbly with thy God? (KJV)

Wow, talk about a verse to live by. What does the Lord require of us (me)? A real thought-provoker. Recently, one of our Adult Bible Study classes at church has centered around this very verse. Chuck Swindoll wrote a book entitled *A Life Well Lived* about this verse. (It's a great book, with lots of insight as to how Micah, a prophet in the Old Testament, dealt with the problems of his day, which were much the same as the problems of our day.) We are commanded to show fairness, compassion, and humility toward others.

411

When I think of our last stay in Houston, in particular, I remember the huge impact Roger made on so many lives. He was a man with a mission, and I saw him live it every day. No matter how he felt, which was never very good, he was a beacon of light to others. He was a bearer of good news, a source of inspiration, a calmer of fears. Behind the scenes, he was always thinking of others, and there were many acts of compassion that were carried out anonymously. And always, he was humble. Roger faced the great adversity in his life with dignity and grace. I think that's what the people in Houston will remember most about him, for they knew him as Roger the patient, who was battling cancer, who was living with hope, and who was sharing that hope with others. Many of you knew him in his capacity as a musician, writer, emcee, and also as a source of inspiration. You see, whatever role he was playing at the time, I can say he did it with the zeal of one who knew what he was doing, and what he was living for. Whether his platform was a stage in front of thousands, a living room sofa talking to his kids, or a hospital room, talking to one other individual, he had the same goal: sharing the love of God. He lived Micah 6:8 well.

Although God is our ultimate example, I am thankful for the earthly example I had in Roger. My days may not be filled with physical pain and suffering, but I have some rough emotional waters to cross. Sometimes they can be overwhelming, and I think that I just can't cope. But then, I remember that God is there. He hasn't left me. He wants to help me. And I can think of the way that Roger plowed on through in his difficult times, and it makes it easier to get through the stormy seas.

I want to be remembered someday as one who had a life well-lived. I can think of no better way to enter the gates of Heaven than to hear the Savior say, "Well done, My good and faithful servant."

412

I will follow this post later with details of my upcoming new journeys, but I just wanted to take the time right now to share a little of my heart with you. As we walk through the days we have here on earth, let's strive to make ours a life well-lived, following God's commands, and knowing that He will keep us forever

In His Grip,
Debbie

April 08, 2008
The New Journeys Begin

As most of you know, I completed training in Minnesota to become a volunteer courier with the National Marrow Donor Program. It was very exciting, and the people there could not have been more gracious to me. Because I had written a letter to be read to the staff there prior to my arrival, and because they shared Roger's music and a little bit of our story, many people already knew who I was, and they were so wonderful. I have to say, though, they were wonderful to everyone there. What a great group of people, giving of their time and energy for such a worthy purpose! I met some really special people, and I feel fortunate to be a part of such an incredible organization.

Now, to put it all into practice...

I have two "trips" scheduled this month. However, due to privacy laws and other issues, I will not be able to tell you where and when I am going. I may be able to share that I have an "opportunity" or something of that nature. So, in that same mysterious manner, I have an opportunity to make a difference tomorrow. Please pray that all involved will be blessed, whatever their situation (and that this novice will get all the particulars right!).

I think this opportunity is coming at a good time for me. I have had some very difficult days lately. I am not sure what the catalyst has been, but I have really been emotional, and it seems like nothing I do has turned out right. I am pretty sure that some of it has to do with passing the "one-year mark" since Roger passed away. It's like you go through that first year thinking about all that has to be done right away, getting things squared away, plotting new courses, and then after the anniversary passes, you have time to think, "Wow, nothing about this is temporary."

For me, I have come to the realization that my entire adult life revolved around Roger, and his ministry. I was always involved, although behind the scenes mostly. Roger was already a part of Southern Gospel Music before we married, so this life is all I have known for over a quarter of a century. Now, I am tethered to a past where I no longer have a place. By that, I mean, that my involvement is no longer hands-on. There are no more scenes to be "behind." Nothing in my life is the same as it was a little over a year ago. It's weird, it's sobering, it's sad, but it's real.

I will always be involved to the extent that I have more of Roger's life to share, and in doing so, I am also sharing myself. For that, I am grateful, and I have many ideas that I want to implement. It will just be a different platform now. I know countless others have walked this path before me, so I am confident that it can be done. I am just finding it hard to do it solo. You never fully appreciate the value of being a part of a team with a spouse, until you don't have it anymore. More than ever, it feels like a part of me has been cut away.

Now, lest it seems like I am whining without ceasing(!) -- I am fully aware that when God closes a door, there is

414

always a window open somewhere. I probably need to be praying for more patience while I wait to see what He has in store for me. I know the courier position will be a good start for me. I truly am excited to be able to be a part of a cause that is so near and dear to my heart. And, who knows where this, or any other adventure may lead? In addition to the Micah 6:8 verse I talked about previously, I am also willing to say to the Lord, as in Isaiah 6:8 - "Here am I, Lord, send me!"

Wherever my paths lead, and in whatever timing God has planned for me and my life, I can rest assured, even on those "bad" days, that I am always

In His Grip!
Debbie

April 13, 2008
Opportunities

I had a very fulfilling few days this week. My journey took me from Wednesday to Friday, and when I finally arrived back home, I was exhausted, both physically and mentally. I think, though, that it was mainly mentally, being my first trip out as a volunteer, and trying extra hard to get it all down right.

I did. And it was a very rewarding feeling to know that the efforts that had been made would somehow make a difference in many lives. What I thought could possibly be a stressful journey was made calm by the amount of prayers I prayed through it all. If nothing else, my prayer life will increase during these opportunities! I knew that many of you were praying as well. There were weather issues aplenty during this trip, airline disturbances, etc.;

yet everything went smoothly, and I am looking forward to my next opportunity this coming week.

Obviously, I won't be doing this every week, but the first two trips happened to fall this way. There are over 250 volunteers with the NMDP, in addition to staff nationwide who travel when they can, so trips are spread out among many people. However, there are over 300 bone marrow transplants performed every month! So, I hope to be able to help out many times over the course of a year.

I will close now with thanks and gratitude, both to faithful prayer warriors, and to a great big God Who is compassionate, faithful, and always willing to keep us

In His Grip!
Debbie

April 16, 2008
On My Way Again

I promise to write a post soon that updates everyone on how each person in our family is doing, but tonight will be a shorter update. I have another "opportunity to make a difference" tomorrow (Thursday), so I will be saying extra prayers for everyone involved. I will be back home Sunday night.

I had a great evening this past Sunday night. I went to my first Southern Gospel concert since Roger passed away. I had been to hear a song or two here and there, and didn't do too well, so I had really been putting off going to a concert. However, Rodney Griffin had e-mailed me a while back and told me that Greater Vision would be in town. I also talked to Gerald Wolfe last week, and he encouraged me to come out, so I did... and I had a really nice time. As it turned out, Legacy Five was off that night, and Scott Fowler came, too, so I had someone to sit with. It really did my soul a world of good to remember how much the music ministers to me. If you have a chance to hear the song "You Can," that GV sings (Rodney wrote it, surprise, surprise!), you will understand when I say that even though Rodney says he wrote it for Jason, it was for me that night. It has a powerful message that tells us that when we can't see what the plan is, "You [God] Can." I did very well during the whole concert, until the pastor called for an encore and Gerald called Scott down to sing "Champion of Love" with them. That one was my undoing, I have to admit. The last time I saw that song performed, Roger was singing on stage, standing there in his little boot cast, and I could see it in my mind's eye as clearly as I did that night.

In all of the storms and trials of life, that's something worth clinging to. That faith is what keeps us going. I have missed Roger terribly today. I think part of it has to do with it being a pretty Spring day, one I know he would have enjoyed. But, then I think back to that day when Roger was lying in the hospital, so gravely ill, and at my wit's end, God spoke to my heart and told me that there is nothing on this Earth that is better than what He has for Roger [us] in Heaven. That makes me long for Heaven so much more! And while I go about my business here below, no matter what life throws my way, I know that I remain

In His Grip!
Debbie

May 01, 2008
A Bennett Update

Home again from another trip. I was in seven states, including my own, in the month of April, but it was a very fulfilling month, and I look forward to even more opportunities to travel with the NMDP, helping others in need. (Having said that, though, I need a good night's sleep!)

I seem to be going through another round of sleepless nights lately. Some have to do with dreams. I have been dreaming of Roger a lot lately, but they are dreams that leave me sad when I wake up. In most of them, we are together, and it's good; but it usually ends up with my being unable to get to him, or his inability to join in - like at a concert, or a family outing, or a dinner, or whatever. Anyone who has had unsettling dreams about a lost loved one knows what I am talking about. You start your day in a fog, and it takes a good part of the day to get out of that "blue mood." Nevertheless, I always welcome a chance to "see" him again. It's just that it seems to emphasize how much I have lost with his death... and not only me, but all of us who loved him so much.

Our family is coping well, over all. I promised an update, so here it is:

Chelsea, my daughter, is at home with me. She helps me out by working at our mail-order business (www.rogerbennettdirect.com), and loves to travel with me when possible. She is finishing up this semester at school. She actually graduated with her photography degree last Spring, before heading to Alaska for five months, but she took a continuing education course this year. She and I will be heading to Arkansas for a couple of days next week, visiting with my parents and Roger's dad and grandfather. When my folks moved back to Arkansas last fall, they ended up 11 miles from Roger's dad. It's good to know that they are close enough to visit and keep an eye on each other! Roger's grandfather is still back and forth between the nursing home and hospital, and it's always a toss-up whether he will know us when we visit or not.

My parents are still getting settled in to their new home in Batesville, Arkansas, and are busy doing yard work now that Spring is here. Roger's dad, Doug, is still as lively as ever, and I enjoy our talks on the phone. He is the direct source of Roger's sense of humor, and is the story-teller from whom Roger learned his craft. His health remains good.

Jordan, my son, still lives about 45 minutes from me, and will soon be looking for another job, since his company is laying off. After he was laid off from his luthier job, he found a construction job to help pay bills, and now it seems that one is laying off, too. We all know it's a sign of these times, but it's still hard to take. His dream, of course, is to get his band going. I know I am his mom, but I also know that he, and his band-mates, are extremely talented, and it will just take being in the right place, at the right time. It will happen someday, I am confident. Both Chelsea and Jordan have a busy social life with friends.

My brother, Tony, still lives with us, and is a great help with the zoo and the yard work. He also fries some great fish!

As for me, while I travel a lot, and enjoy it very much, I find I have a harder time getting motivated around the house here in Tennessee. Please pray that I will be able to get this book done. I have had a mental block with it, I confess. When I look at the writings, it is difficult, reliving those times, and reading Roger's writings. I love having them, and I am blessed by them. I just have to jump over another hurdle and get it done. I am working my way up to that!

Chelsea and I manage to keep things going fairly well, and we are making progress daily in the areas where we are lacking. All of the animals (all four cats and three dogs!) are faring well, also, although the mobile rabies clinic last Saturday was not a highlight of their day. And I still have to round up one cat, who seemed to know what was going on, and hid out until after the clinic had gone... It's always an experience!

Oh yes, another new venture: Chelsea and I are tentatively planning to join a mission team from our church July 31 through August 10, if all goes well. We will be going to a city on the outskirts of Warsaw, Poland to help in the restoration of a Jewish cemetery. Our church has previously sent a team to help there. It is a mission that really speaks to my heart, since I am an avid student of World War II history (my dad served in the army in that war). Poland had the highest Jewish population pre-WWII, but lost most of its population due to either flight or death, because of the Holocaust. Because of that, there are few left to tend those resting places, which are very sacred to the Jewish people. Going in to do this physical labor provides opportunities to put into action the compassion we, as Christians, feel, and to share our reasons for doing so along the way. Please pray for us as we prepare for this journey.

Well, that's about it for now. I do plan to be at the Legacy Five Celebration over Memorial Day weekend, but don't know the exact time yet. I also have a booth reserved for National Quartet Convention in September (right across from Legacy Five's), so if you are there, please come by. I promise that book will be there! I always look forward to meeting many of you, whose names I know well from this journal. And it goes without saying, that I look forward to seeing old friends, as well... and HUGS!

So, until then, I hope you remain, as my family and I do,

In His Grip!
Debbie

May 15, 2008
Family Time

Chelsea, Jordan, and I just got back last night from a little family vacation. It was particularly great, since these times together are fewer and farther between with "grown" children. We had a wonderful time, visiting several major theme parks. However, I did find out that my 46-year-old body wears out a lot faster than a 21- or 23-year-old's body does! That didn't stop my getting on every roller coaster ride they did, and we trekked many miles over the three days we were there. These are great memories, and we talked a lot about Roger, since he would have loved being there, too. In fact, we did take this particular vacation as a family more than once. Bittersweet...

We found ourselves laughing one moment, then being close to tears another, remembering times we had together. It is priceless to have the memories, but painful to realize that those times are over. I sometimes wonder if the happy times will ever outweigh the sadness.

Overall, we still are doing fine. Life goes on, and we keep busy. Jordan is pursuing new employment, Chelsea is working, and we are both getting geared up for our upcoming mission trip to Poland, gathering funds, and juggling schedules. The summer is getting full already, and I am wondering how to get it all done.

Hope to see many of you at the Legacy Five Celebration. I am still unsure which day I will be there, but I am leaning toward Saturday afternoon and evening.

Until then, I remain

In His Grip,
Debbie

May 27, 2008
Whirlwinds

A whirlwind... Sometimes we all feel like that's what we are caught up in. Mostly they are busy times of our own choosing, our own not knowing how to say "no" or prioritize. I certainly am guilty of that at times. Right now, my whirlwind is of my own choosing, but I am enjoying every breeze that is in it!

I am sitting in an airport waiting for my next flight. I have already picked up the bone marrow I will be taking to someone whose life is dependent on it. It's such a sobering thing to think about, and yes, it does bring back many memories; but the feeling it gives me to be able to serve in this capacity is SO worth it. I absolutely thank God every day for the blessings He has given me through this opportunity. Besides this trip this week, I am scheduled for another next week, and one in the middle of the month so far. Again, my own choosing, but it's a delight.

When I get home, there will be whirlwinds of a different sort. Company is coming, the house is in need of cleaning, those taxes are still not done, and I have set myself a deadline to finish this book, so that it will be out before September. Some of those are winds that I wish would blow right on over! So, I would appreciate your prayers for my self-motivation, as it somehow seems to dwindle, the closer to home I get. I know, I know, I do know the reason why, in most likelihood. But lately, it seems like God is doing a work in my heart to help me in the process of moving forward again. I had been mired in clay for a while there.

I had a wonderful visit with so many people at the Legacy Five Celebration on Saturday. It was humbling to have so many dear ones "loving" on me, and letting me love them in return. I had the chance to visit with several friends, and signed a few of the new books about Roger (go to Legacy Five's website for the new tribute book and CD - they are a wonderful testament from his friends about his character). And I felt like another hurdle had been jumped, one which, again has softened my heart to the changes that are coming about in my life.

I think about Roger's last post - "Seasons" -- and realize that, yet again, he was a man who had a lot of wisdom (although he often chose to hide it in impish ways!). His mission: to encourage and show Jesus in his own life. Judging from the love that was poured out to me over the weekend, if from nothing else (and I have so much more to take that knowledge from), his mission was successful. Thanks, honey, for showing us the value of being held firmly

In His Grip!
Debbie

June 08, 2008
Another Year Older

I have been keeping very busy with volunteer trips lately. I keep "picking up" new ones, and have been averaging one every week. I am not sure what makes the summer so busy for bone marrow transplants, but there are a lot of people out there who need help and prayers. It is my great pleasure and privilege to be able to be one of the many who are used in this way. As a "bonus", I have now done enough domestic trips that I can be put on the international list. That should be very interesting!

I had a birthday on Friday, one which I was reluctant to see come (aren't they all, anymore?). I turned 47 (isn't a lady supposed to keep her age a secret?), and I confess this one was a mental hurdle for me. When I hear that number, all I can think of is that is the age my Roger was last... Well, technically, he had turned 48 one week before he died; but we never really "knew" him as 48. He will probably always be 47 in my mind. So, it makes me wonder if I will have this on my mind for an entire year. And then, what will 48 bring? I am sure that with God's help, I will get used to it, and be able to deal with it, just as He has brought me through so many other obstacles.

I have the last birthday card Roger gave me. When I ran across it earlier this year, it was like he had written it specifically for a time when I would read it after his departure. He always gave me a funny card, then a serious one. Just like him. He wrote in the serious one, though, among other things, that he wished for my happiness and contentment always. I am sure that God uses these little things to speak to us at the point of our need. There are days when I feel so all alone and helpless, and then I get a gift like that, when I know that Roger would want me to keep moving forward, to find the happiness that I know God wants for me as well. Even when things don't go exactly as WE had planned, GOD has not forgotten us, and His plan will work for our good, as He promised us in Romans 8:28. It's that "patience" thing I have to work on myself!

I hope this summer brings great joy to each of you, my dear friends. I will keep busy with volunteer work, visiting family and friends, my 30th (!!!!!) high school reunion, a mission trip to Poland, and, of course, all of those things that must be done around the house in Tennessee. Keep praying for that book!

Thank you for all of your cards, and comments on this site. I check often for a word from you, too! Until next time, I am snugly

In His Grip,
Debbie

June 19, 2008
Busy, Busy

I am sure, now that summer is here, that we are all much busier. I know I am, and I apologize for not writing more. (Besides that, my internet is acting up at home, among other technological issues that are driving me to distraction...) So, I am writing this entry from a hotel, while on one of the many courier trips I have been on this month. Lately, I have had one per week (five in a row, so far), and still have a couple more on the books. I am not sure what has made the summer so busy for transplants, but there is a network of blue tote bags and coolers keeping those airport security guards hopping!

I have had the opportunity to see a lot of the country, mostly from air or in a taxi, but there are still some awesome sights to see, while whizzing past! God's creation is awesome!

Tuesday, June 17, was the one-year, three-month anniversary of Roger's "promotion," and it was a day that hit me kind of hard. I am never sure why those quarter-year, half-year, etc., anniversaries seem more poignant; yet they do. I was thinking of where I was one year ago on that date, which happened to be Father's Day. I was in Northern Ireland, having completed filming of the *Whispers in the Night* DVD. Jordan was with me, and Chelsea was in Alaska. We have journeyed a lifetime since then.

This past weekend, on Father's Day, we were in Arkansas, having a family cookout, so I got to see my father and my father-in-law, and my mom, of course, along with brothers, sister-in-law, nieces, nephews, and their families, and the star of the show, my great-niece, who was born 11 days before Roger passed away. It was a fun time. I took a photo with my dad, and it was cute, so I was showing it to Chelsea, and she said, "Sure, rub it in." She meant it in a joking way, and we both smiled, but it made me feel so sad for her and Jordan. It was the first Father's Day we have all been together since Roger died, and that hit me, too. Then, on the seven hour drive home, I had WAY too much time to think (I tend to do deep thinking when I drive, which may not be the safest thing to do - I even used to write songs as I drove - that's where "He's Been There" materialized), so by the time Tuesday rolled around, I had myself worked into some real blues. Fortunately, though, they haven't lingered unnecessarily, and I have been able to deal with the emotions and keep moving forward.

Recently, I have come to the realization that the only way to keep my sanity, is to move forward. Roger and I had so many discussions during all of the time we were together 24/7. What a blessing. His desire was for his family to not stop living, should he go first. So, we are trying, though the "living" is not the same, naturally. We have some new directions, simply because the situation mandates it. But, it is also nice to know that we have his blessing, should we decide to test some unfamiliar waters eventually.

There is a huge difference between JOY and HAPPINESS. I hope you know the difference in your own life. Joy comes from God, in knowing the peace that passes all understanding, no matter the situation. Happiness is dependent on circumstances, and comes and goes. I can't say I have been happy in quite some time, but I am grateful beyond any measure that I have a deep, abiding joy. I am ready for that spark of happiness to show up again. And, I know, as long as I remain in God's will, I will find it, and rest peacefully

In His Grip!
Debbie

This entry is one of the ones found in a forgotten journal of Roger's after his death. It was written during his second transplant, but after reading it, I decided to make it the last page of this book. These are his own words, but I felt that they summed up his life, particularly his last few years...

One of my favorite things to do is to sit in a lobby full (or not full) of cancer patients and talk to them. My intent is to find those who are a few days behind me and be an encourager to them. <u>I love it!</u> To see them size me up to see if I am real, then to catch on, and finally take in the news that there is life beyond the diagnosis, gives me a real physical and spiritual rush.

Doctors tell us that chemicals called endorphins are released when we are exercising, and cause us to feel a burst of pleasure. I feel this way after a talk in the waiting room.

I guess I am one of those patients who can "pass" for a non-cancer patient on certain days. So, when people realize that I have been through the valley of the shadow of death, and yet I give God the glory for my weakness, they gather strength to hear that the only consistent element in this sickness is God's Presence; they often also find strength.

I thank God for the great blessing of sharing!

I am In His Grip,
Roger

Roger during his "Kojak" phase.

Roger and Debbie in Galveston, Texas

Roger with his mother, Mary Jean,
during the earlier part of his career

Jean and Doug Bennett, 1994

431

Roger and his father, Billy Doug, visit on the porch in Arkansas.

Doug made many trips to Houston during Roger's treatments.

On the porch, Father's Day 2005

Roger and the kids four-wheeling in Colorado, 2000

Roger with his best friend and business partner, Scott Fowler

The Bennetts in Alaska, July 2005

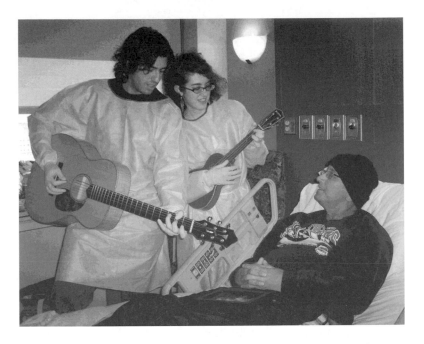

Jordan and Chelsea entertaining Roger in the hospital

The Bennetts during their last Christmas together, 2006

Roger and Scott visit with hero, mentor, and former boss,
bass legend George Younce

Roger with another close friend, Maurice Templeton

436

Chelsea and her dad enjoying an evening at the pond

Jordan and his dad engaging in an intellectual pursuit –
videogames

Chelsea's graduation, 2002

Jordan's graduation, 2005

One of Roger's greatest joys was performing
on stage with Legacy Five

Roger's surprise visit to L5's Celebration, 2004

439

Jordan toured with the group for a while, playing bass

Celebration 2005

Roger and Debbie with good friend,
former M.D. Anderson Chaplain Glenda McDonald

Roger's former nurse and family friend, Lisa Norman,
with the Bennetts' dog Boomer

Roger playing with special guest Dino Kartsonakis
at Roger Bennett's Parade of Pianos, 2006

Roger and Debbie Bennett, Easter 2006

Debbie and Roger enjoying an afternoon
at the beach in Galveston, TX

The Bennett family together on their front porch

Roger recording a keyboard part for the album
put out by son Jordan's first band

Chelsea and Roger horsing around
in Galveston, Texas

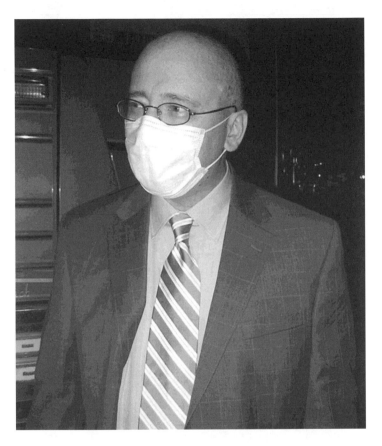

Roger closely followed all of his doctors' orders
so that he could continue to travel with Legacy Five

During Christmas of 2003, Roger was
privileged to appear on a Nashville news station,
sharing the miracles that happened
surrounding the first transplant

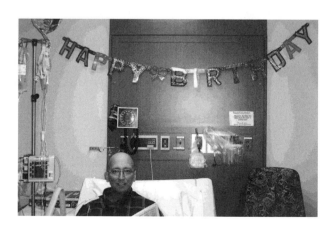

Roger's nurses and other staff members at M.D. Anderson
always did a great job of brightening up the hospital

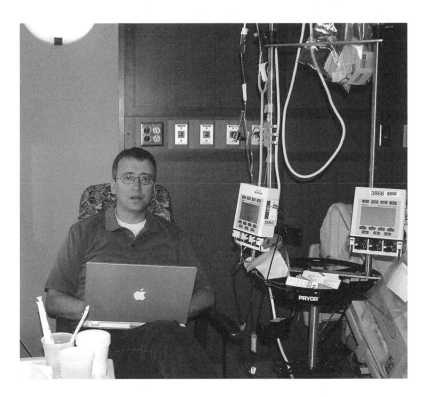

Who's a cancer patient?

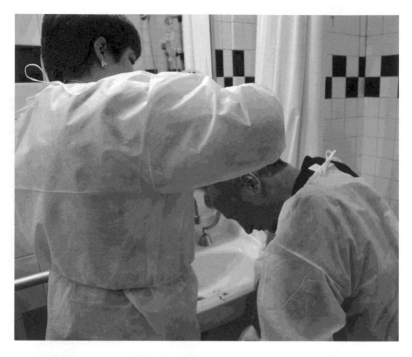

Debbie giving Roger a pre-chemo beauty treatment

Roger Douglas Bennett
March 10, 1959 – March 17, 2007
In His Grip!

If you would like to help other members of the Southern Gospel ministry, you may make a tax-deductible donation in Roger Bennett's name to the Gospel Music Trust Fund.

Send your contributions to:

The Gospel Music Trust Fund
PO Box 144
Goodlettsville, TN 37070

www.gospelmusictrustfund.org